Equitable and Inclusive IEPs for Students with Complex Support Needs

Equitable and Inclusive IEPs for Students with Complex Support Needs

A Roadmap

by

Andrea L. Ruppar, Ph.D.
University of Wisconsin–Madison

and

Jennifer A. Kurth, Ph.D.
University of Kansas

with invited contributors

·P·A·U·L·H·
BROOKES
PUBLISHING CO®

Baltimore • London • Sydney

Paul H. Brookes Publishing Co.
Post Office Box 10624
Baltimore, Maryland 21285-0624
USA

www.brookespublishing.com

Typeset by Progressive Publishing Services, York, Pennsylvania.
Manufactured in the United States of America by
Integrated Books International, Inc., Dulles, Virginia.

The individuals described in this book are composites or real people whose situations are masked and are based on the authors' experiences. In all instances, names and identifying details have been changed to protect confidentiality.

Library of Congress Cataloging-in-Publication Data

Names: Ruppar, Andrea, author. | Kurth, Jennifer A., author.
Title: Equitable and inclusive IEPs for students with complex support needs :
    a roadmap / by Andrea Ruppar, Ph.D., University of Wisconsin-Madison
    and Jennifer A. Kurth, Ph.D., University of Kansas, with invited contributors.
Description: Baltimore, Maryland : Paul H. Brookes Publishing Co., [2023] |
    Includes bibliographical references and index.
Identifiers: LCCN 2022051155 (print) | LCCN 2022051156 (ebook) | ISBN 9781681254630 (paperback) |
    ISBN 9781681254647 (epub) | ISBN 9781681254654 (pdf)
Subjects: LCSH: Children with disabilities--Education. | Individualized education programs. |
    Educational equalization. | Inclusive education. | BISAC: EDUCATION / Special Education / General |
    EDUCATION / Special Education / Developmental & Intellectual Disabilities
Classification: LCC LC4015 .R87 2023 (print) | LCC LC4015 (ebook) | DDC 371.9--dc23/eng/20221026
LC record available at https://lccn.loc.gov/2022051155

British Library Cataloguing in Publication data are available from the British Library.

2027   2026   2025   2024   2023

10   9   8   7   6   5   4   3   2   1

Contents

About the Downloads vii
About the Authors ix
About the Contributors xi
Preface xiii
Acknowledgments xxiii

I   Before the Meeting 1

1   Getting the Team Together 3
     With Samantha Gross Toews

     Appendix: Planning Worksheet—IEP Team Members 11

2   Organizing IEP Preparation and Communication 13
     With Samantha Gross Toews

     Appendix: IEP Team Data Collection Plan 23

3   Fostering Collaborative and Trusting Relationships with
     Families and Students 29
     With Samantha Gross Toews and Jessica A. McQueston

     Appendix: Resources for Communicating with Families 46

4   Discussing Data and Making Decisions 55

     Appendix: Skill Data Collection Plan 77

II   Developing the IEP 79

5   Describing Present Levels of Academic Achievement and
     Functional Performance 81

6   Planning for Special Factors, Extended School Year, and
     Alternate Assessment 95

     Appendix: Summer Activities Planning Tool 106

7   Determining What Gets Taught: Curriculum and Goals 109

     Appendix: Resources for Determining What Gets Taught 127

8   Identifying Supplementary Aids and Services.. 131

     Appendix: Ecological Assessment with Supplementary
             Aids and Services... 145

9   Determining the Least Restrictive Environment 147
     With Katie M. McCabe

     Appendix: Determining the Least Restrictive Environment (LRE)
             Decision Flowchart 163

III At the Meeting and Afterward...165

10   Setting an Agenda and Setting the Tone: Communication
     During the IEP Meeting...167
     With Lingyu Li, Sarah Bubash, and Yuewn-lann Radeen Yang

11   After the Meeting: Implementing the IEP 179

     Appendix: Resources for Implementing the IEP 186

References...191
Index...199

About the Downloads

Purchasers of this book may download, print, and/or photocopy the planning worksheets and forms in this book for educational and professional use.

To access the materials that come with this book:

1. Go to the Brookes Download Hub: http://downloads.brookespublishing.com

2. Register to create an account (or log in with an existing account)

3. Filter or search for the book title *Equitable and Inclusive IEPs for Students with Complex Support Needs: A Roadmap.*

About the Authors

Andrea L. Ruppar, Ph.D., Associate Professor, University of Wisconsin–Madison, 1000 Bascom Mall, Madison, WI 53706

Andrea L. Ruppar, Ph.D., is an associate professor of special education in the Department of Rehabilitation Psychology and Special Education at University of Wisconsin–Madison. Dr. Ruppar's research focuses on decision making among special education teachers and other professionals, especially related to students with extensive support needs. Prior to working in higher education, Dr. Ruppar was a special education teacher of students with complex disabilities from preschool to adulthood.

Jennifer A. Kurth, Ph.D., Associate Professor, University of Kansas, 1122 W. Campus Dr., JRP 541, Lawrence, KS 66045

Jennifer A. Kurth, Ph.D., is an associate professor in the Department of Special Education at the University of Kansas. Her research centers on efforts to promote inclusive education for students with complex support needs, and she prepares educators to deliver high-quality, inclusive education to learners with complex support needs. Prior to working in higher education, Dr. Kurth was an inclusion specialist for students with disabilities in both elementary and secondary schools.

About the Contributors

Sarah Bubash, M.Ed., Ph.D. Candidate, University of Wisconsin–Madison, 431 Education Building, 1000 Bascom Mall, Madison, WI 53706

Sarah Bubash taught as a special education teacher for 10 years before deciding to pursue her doctorate in special education. Her research interests focus on increasing inclusion for students with complex support needs within the general education curriculum and environment. Specifically, she trains preservice teachers to center disabled voices by using creativity and imaginative thinking to design effective and inclusive educational supports.

Lingyu Li, Ph.D., Assistant Professor, Lehman College, Carman Hall, 250 Bedford Park Boulevard West, Bronx, NY, 10468

Lingyu Li is an assistant professor in the Department of Counseling, Leadership, Literacy, and Special Education at CUNY–Lehman College. Her scholarly interests include inclusive education for emergent bilinguals with dis/abilities, inclusive education teacher education, critical disability study, and students with intellectual and developmental disabilities. Li's current research aims to capture the real dilemmas faced by classroom teachers as they implement recommended inclusive practices for students living at the intersection of language and ability differences.

Katie M. McCabe, Ph.D., Assistant Professor, University of Colorado–Colorado Springs, 1420 Austin Bluffs Pkwy, Department of Teaching and Learning, University Hall 224, Colorado Springs, CO 80918

Katie M. McCabe is an assistant professor in the Department of Teaching and Learning at the University of Colorado–Colorado Springs. She earned her Ph.D. in special education from the University of Wisconsin–Madison in 2021. Dr. McCabe's scholarship focuses on the implementation of inclusive practices for students with disabilities who require complex supports. She is specifically interested in building capacity to make inclusive education decisions in rural schools.

Jessica A. McQueston, Ph.D., Assistant Professor, Sam Houston State University, 1908 Bobby K Marks Dr, Box 2119, Huntsville, Texas 77341-2119

Jessica A. McQueston is an assistant professor in the special education program at Sam Houston State University. She is a disabled scholar and incorporates a disability studies approach to her work. Her research focuses on identifying and addressing barriers to inclusive education for students with disabilities, particularly those with extensive support needs. Previously, she was a K–6 special and general educator for six years in Albuquerque, New Mexico.

Samantha Gross Toews, Ph.D., Assistant Professor of Special Education, California State University, Northridge, Special Education Department ED 1204, 18111 Nordhoff Street, Northridge, CA 91330-8265

Samantha Gross Toews is an assistant professor in the special education department at California State University, Northridge. Her research focuses on instructional practices that support students with extensive support needs to access academic instruction in general education classrooms and professional development strategies that support teachers to implement inclusive practices. Before teaching at the university level, Dr. Toews was a special educator at a fully inclusive urban elementary school in California.

Yuewn-lann Radeen Yang, M.S., Ph.D. Candidate, University of Wisconsin–Madison, 431 Education Building, 1000 Bascom Mall, Madison, WI 53706

Yuewn-lann Radeen Yang is currently pursuing a doctoral degree in special education at the University of Wisconsin–Madison. Her experience supporting students with extensive support needs as a teacher contributed to her desire to continue learning how we can prepare teachers to best serve students receiving special education services. Her current research interests include understanding teacher identity development and preparing preservice teachers for inclusive education.

Preface

"I do not like the world as it is; so I am trying to make it a little more as I want it."

–Helen Keller, circa 1912

Special education, as a system, is designed to be flexible, providing educational teams and families options for arranging individualized supports and services for students with disabilities in school. But when special education became legally mandated in 1975, many students with complex support needs were not attending school at all. The lucky few students who were permitted to attend school were sent to separate buildings and classes, with age-inappropriate materials and activities. If instruction was occurring, students were learning skills normally taught to toddlers, even as they progressed through elementary and high school. Categories of "TMH" (i.e., trainable mentally handicapped), "SMH" (i.e., severely mentally handicapped), and "PMH" (i.e., profoundly mentally handicapped) were applied to students based on educators' perceptions about their functioning level. Although "TMH" students were considered capable of learning basic daily living skills, students in the "SMH" and "PMH" categories were considered "custodial" and therefore unable to benefit from education.

As the field of special education advanced throughout the 1980s, 1990s, and 2000s, outdated assumptions about the capabilities of students with complex support needs persisted. In 2004, I (Andrea) moved from Seattle with my teaching degree in hand and began working at a public special education school on the North Shore of Chicago. I was shocked to find that, still, assumptions about students' capabilities were driving educational decision making for students with complex support needs. Students who attended the school required extensive supports throughout the school day and were sorted into special classes based on their disabilities: "autism," "physically handicapped," and, yes, "PMH." One day, an 11-year-old child drove his electric wheelchair down a flight of stairs when nobody was looking. When the medics carried him out of the school on a backboard, I knew I needed to find a solution to segregation.

In my years as a special educator, I noticed that each district approached students with complex support needs in different ways. Some districts had special schools, like the one where I taught. Others had special districts, special classes, or simply special teachers. I eventually taught in a district that had no separate classes or spaces. Every space and experience was available for students with and without disabilities. Here, I supported students who had the same needs as the students I had taught in special schools and special classes. My students were not special, however; they were members of the school community. I had never worked in an environment like this. Suddenly, I was the only thing that was "special" about their "special education," and I realized that maybe I wasn't so important after all!

This led to an identity crisis for me as a professional. There were new things I needed to learn. When I was teaching in self-contained classrooms for students with autism, I knew exactly what to do. I organized my students' days, guided by picture schedules and Picture Exchange Communication System (PECS) training and systematic instruction (thanks in large part to my time working in the PEACE program at Thurgood Marshall Elementary). But after having worked in the most restrictive school settings, I realized that segregation negatively affects students as well as teachers. Perceptions about age appropriateness and dignity shift, imperceptibly, over time, until the students realize precious few of the joys of childhood and adolescence. And moreover, students leave schools with limited generalizable skills to apply in inclusive adult lives.

But translating my experience from self-contained classrooms and schools to an inclusive school was difficult. I noticed that I, too, had been affected by the segregation of students with disabilities. My focus as a teacher changed from being a "do it all" teacher to an accessibility specialist, focusing on how to make the content and activities of general education classes accessible to my students with complex support needs. And I found that my colleagues were unfamiliar with the individualized education program (IEP) process for students with complex support needs because students with complex support needs had never attended their school before. They needed practical resources to get started.

THE ROLE OF THE IEP

As teachers, we both recognized that IEPs presented an important opportunity to make possibilities for students with complex support needs real. The IEP document lends a certain amount of gravity and importance to a conversation. What starts as brainstorming must, by necessity, become a realistic and actionable written plan. However, the multiple individuals involved in a team for students with complex support needs can make the IEP challenging to coordinate and implement.

Coordinating with other professionals and families is an essential duty of a teacher for students with complex support needs. Because in any given district fewer than 1% of students will have complex support needs, school teams that serve students with complex support needs have unique decisions to make. In addition, team members might have varying levels of experience working with students with complex support needs because—due to the small size of the population—it's possible that they have never had the opportunity to learn these skills through practicum, student teaching, or prior professional roles. A team supporting a student with complex support needs must make ongoing decisions together, which often means learning new teaching skills and support strategies along the way.

WHO ARE STUDENTS WITH COMPLEX SUPPORT NEEDS?

Students with complex support needs require accommodations and modifications to access learning and school activities throughout most or all the day. Although no single label defines this category of students, they typically are identified with disabilities under the Individuals with Disabilities Education Improvement Act (IDEA) of 2004 (PL 108-446) categories of intellectual disability, multiple disabilities, autism, and other health impairment (Taub et al., 2017). According to IDEA 2004 regulations regarding participation in state assessments, approximately 1% of the school population is eligible to take the state alternate assessment due to "significant cognitive disability." This statistic—1% of the school population—is imperfect because data indicate that districts often over- or under-assign students to take the alternate assessment. Nevertheless, 1% is a handy metric when considering whether a student's support needs are complex enough that the extent to which the student requires supports must be planned for every minute of every school day.

HOW ARE IEPs FOR STUDENTS WITH COMPLEX SUPPORT NEEDS DIFFERENT FROM OTHER IEPs?

In many ways, an IEP for a student with complex support needs should look like IEPs for students with less extensive needs. All IEPs must follow IDEA guidelines and include the following components:

1. Present Levels of Academic Achievement and Functional Performance (PLAAFP)

2. Special factors

3. Challenging and measurable goals

4. Description of how and when student progress toward measurable goals will be monitored and reported

5. Description of supplementary aids and services that will support student access to and progress in the general education curriculum

6. Explanation of the extent the student will *not* be educated with nondisabled students in the general education setting

7. Statement of student's participation in state and district-wide assessments

8. The frequency, duration, and location of each service and when it will begin

However, for students with complex support needs, planning each of these areas is an intensive process, requiring deep and close collaboration with multiple related service providers, general education teachers, and family members. Students with complex support needs are at the most risk for being isolated from peers in separate classrooms, which hinders their academic, social, and emotional growth (Kleinert et al., 2015; Morningstar et al., 2017). Even more unfortunately, decision makers in special education often harbor low expectations for school outcomes and fail to understand what outcomes are possible.

This text aims to serve as a guide for teams navigating the IEP process for a student with complex support needs. Because this group is diverse in age, cultural background, and disability characteristics, we provide examples throughout the text of students and their IEP process. Overall, we hope that these examples demonstrate how similar decision-making processes can facilitate a variety of students' access to education. We hope that you find something helpful in these examples that will guide your own decision-making processes.

PRINCIPLES FOR TEACHING STUDENTS WITH COMPLEX SUPPORT NEEDS

This book reflects core principles guiding instruction for students with complex support needs, based on decades of research and our practice as educators and teacher educators. Three of these principles guide every decision:

1. *Dignifying:* Decisions are made that acknowledge and celebrate the inherent dignity of each student; these decisions value the intrinsic worth of each person, and educators avoid decisions that aim to "cure," "fix," or otherwise conform. Dignity acknowledges that disability is a natural form of human diversity, and labeling, negative attitudes, and practices that only target remediation diminish dignity by perpetuating a view that disability is somehow negative or shameful rather than a rich expression of human variation that drives creativity, innovation, and personal, and interpersonal growth.

2. *Inclusive:* Every decision is weighed against the likelihood that the consequences of the decision will result in inclusive lives and opportunities. Humans are complex social beings; we need to be together and learn together so that we may live together. We seek solutions that enhance inclusive opportunities in our schools, homes, and communities. Separation and segregation are avoided at every turn; we urge teams to look for solutions to facilitate robust inclusion in all aspects of life.

3. *Ambitious and enviable:* As noted earlier, for far too long, people with complex support needs have been the recipients of woefully low expectations, which has resulted in their segregation and poor economic, social, and health outcomes. Instead, we seek to make decisions that reflect ambitious and enviable outcomes for all students, including those with complex support needs. We envision a world in which people with complex support needs receive high quality academic instruction in schools, participate in healthy and robust friendships and relationships, direct their own lives and supports, relentlessly pursue their own interests and priorities, and have careers of their choice while living where and with whom they choose. To achieve an enviable life outcome such as this, students must be supported in schools to obtain the skills, relationships, memberships, and supports they need throughout life.

UNDERSTANDING STRENGTHS-BASED IEPs

An IEP document is a communication tool shared among teachers and other important people in a student's life. Although the IEP "form" might seem like an impersonal bureaucratic document, the information contained in the document has important implications for how a student's rights will be protected under IDEA 2004. For students with complex support needs, who are at extreme risk for isolation and poor school experiences, each IEP decision communicates to the team about expectations and school-based activities.

Unfortunately, there are many poor examples of IEPs for students with complex support needs. Unambitious goals, academic goals that do not align with grade-level standards, and goals that fail to consider a student's communication needs are common (Kurth et al., 2021). Students' present level of performance data often reflect a smattering of skills in a variety of poorly connected areas (Ruppar et al., 2019) and rely on data that are approximate and casual rather than specific and measurable. Supports and services are determined based on what is "available" rather than what would benefit the student. The document itself is premised on identifying deficits and provides no structure to support emphasizing strengths or competencies. Although IEPs with these characteristics are technically in compliance with the law, they do not effectively provide a clear roadmap for high expectations and inclusive practices. These are all common flaws. In this text, we hope to steer teams away from these potential problems and toward strengths-based, equitable IEPs for students with complex support needs.

A strengths-based IEP for a student with complex support needs will include contributions from many different school-based providers as well as the student and their family. An IEP case manager (typically a special education teacher or administrator) will coordinate the student's school-based services and ensure supports and specialized instruction are planned for every activity throughout the day so that the student's education is fully accessible. IEP goals will include academic goals that align with general education standards but differ in depth or breadth. Goals might also address other skill areas that are essential for the student to reach ambitious post-school outcomes and can be applied in a variety of known and unknown environments (Ruppar et al., 2022). Because general education content is more likely to be taught in general education settings, students with complex support needs must access general education settings where students with and without disabilities learn together (Jackson et al., 2008).

Families' input in the IEP process is especially important for students with complex support needs. Students' families are uniquely aware of their child's needs, strengths, abilities, and preferences, and they have particularly important knowledge about the supports that might work best. As IEP teams develop supports, families can decide to replicate those supports at home as well. The team works together to identify and provide the appropriate supports for the student. Sometimes students with complex support needs receive therapies or other services outside of school. These providers can also provide valuable insights about the student and their progress.

Almost always, students with complex support needs have complex communication needs and require augmentative communication, which is to supplement speech, and/or alternative communication, which is to replace speech. Together, these systems are known as augmentative and alternative communication (AAC). Even if a student can communicate some words using speech, supports are often helpful to increase students' ability to communicate in a variety of contexts and with a variety of people. As such, communication is a central component of any educational planning for students with complex support needs and should be a top priority when identifying supports and specially designed instruction.

TYPES OF IEPs

When thinking about an IEP, most people think of an annual IEP. However, there are several different kinds of IEPs, including triannual or re-evaluation IEPs, Individual Family Service Plans (IFSP), and transition IEPs. The following sections will outline key information about each type of IEP.

Annual IEP and Re-evaluation IEP

Held every year, the annual IEP is a collaborative process in which the team compiles and reviews data about student progress during the past year to design a plan to move forward during the next year. Every three years, each student has a re-evaluation IEP. The annual and re-evaluation IEPs have the same required components. The difference between the two is that the re-evaluation IEP requires formal assessments to be conducted in each service area of the IEP to determine if those services are still needed, or how they might need to be adapted.

Students whose challenging behavior impacts their access to and progress in their curriculum, goals, or social relationships will have a behavior support plan (BSP) added to their IEP. This plan will identify a goal in the area of behavior and outline the supports and services the student will need to achieve their goal. As part of the behavior support plan data collection process, a functional behavioral assessment (FBA) is often completed by the special education teacher or a behavior analyst to identify the function of the challenging behavior as well as functional replacement behaviors.

Individual Family Service Plan

An IFSP is a family-focused service plan for a young child with a disability or developmental delay. Children are eligible for this type of IEP from birth to 3 years old. Most students with complex support needs entered the special education system before age 3, which means most had an IFSP at one time. An IFSP focuses on supports for both the family members and the child because it is essential to consider family contexts when designing interventions for infants and toddlers (Movahedazarhouligh, 2021). For example, if a child is identified as eligible for physical therapy, the assigned therapist will likely work collaboratively with the family and child to identify strategies to support the child's physical development in the home. The goal of an IFSP is to identify and provide early intervention to infants and toddlers. A child who is referred for an IFSP will participate in a variety of formal and informal assessments that will result in a collaborative service plan. The IFSP is revisited each year in the same manner as an annual IEP.

Transition IEP

Students who are over 16 years of age are also required to have a transition plan added to their IEP. A transition IEP is a plan that is added to an existing IEP prior to or when a student with an IEP turns age 16. Although federal IDEA legislation requires a transition plan be created by the time a student is 16, many states require or suggest the IEP team develop the plan by age 14. It is never too early for the IEP team to begin discussing transition with the student and family. The transition plan outlines supports, services, and goal areas that will facilitate student transition from school to adult life. Areas of focus in transition plans include the following:

> Academic and functional achievement of the child with a disability to facilitate the child's movement from school to post-school activities, including postsecondary education, vocational education, integrated employment (including supported employment), continuing and adult education, adult services, independent living, or community participation. (IDEA 2004)

The transition plan team should be highly collaborative and center student interests and priorities. Student interviews, preference assessments, and access to opportunities to learn about post-school options before giving input on goals are key forms of data collection for a transition plan. Student participation in the design of their transition goals and overall plan have been linked to better post-school educational and employment outcomes (Mazzotti et al., 2016). Unfortunately, students with complex support needs are less likely than their peers with IEPs and less complex support needs to be given an opportunity to provide input on their transition goals (Lipscomb et al., 2017). IEP teams can support student and family participation in the planning process by using formal and informal, strengths-based transition assessments. As with all other areas, no single transition assessment will be sufficient in collecting robust data (Rowe et al., 2015). A mix of general person-centered planning activities and transition assessments should be utilized. Several common assessments and tools can be found in Table 2.1 in Chapter 2.

PURPOSE OF THIS BOOK

The purpose of this book is to provide useful and research-based information about developing person-centered, measurable, inclusive, and ambitious IEPs for students with complex support needs (i.e., significant cognitive disability, autism, or multiple disabilities) which support inclusive practices. Students with complex support needs have correspondingly complex IEPs, which typically include many academic, functional, and social-emotional goals. They invariably require assistive technology and communication supports and usually access services from a variety of related service providers. Communication with families of students with complex support needs is also very intensive, and the perspectives of families take on a different dimension for students with complex support needs, in comparison to those with less complex needs. Decisions about least restrictive environment (LRE) for students with complex support needs are challenging, and teams often base LRE decisions on inappropriate criteria (Kurth et al., 2019). Finally, IEP meetings for students with complex support needs can be contentious and lengthy, involving many different team members. The recent landmark *Endrew F. v. Douglas County* (2017) Supreme Court decision further highlights the importance of developing IEPs for students with complex support needs that are reasonably calculated to enable a student to make progress on appropriately ambitious goals and curriculum. We aim for this book to be a practitioner-focused guide to developing inclusive, legally and ethically defensible IEPs, reflecting the "more than de minimus" standard from *Endrew F.* for students with complex support needs, which would aid teams to make sound decisions in very difficult situations.

How to Use This Book

As the title suggests, we organized this book as a step-by-step guide for IEP teams working with students with complex support needs.

Section I: Before the Meeting   This section describes the initial work of organization and communication that an IEP team leader or case manager—often the special education teacher—must do to prepare for the IEP meeting and documentation. Chapters 1–4 address the steps described below:

Chapter 1: Getting the Team Together   Understanding who should be at the table during planning and IEP meetings can be challenging, especially when students interact with multiple professionals. Early and active engagement with families in a collegial manner is essential to setting the stage for establishing a collegial atmosphere among team members. This chapter provides practical advice for 1) identifying and communicating with team members; 2) involving the family in meaningful ways; and 3) working with outside service providers.

Chapter 2: Organizing IEP Preparation and Communication   In the pre-planning process, it is important to ensure that each team member has the opportunity to make a meaningful contribution to the educational plan. The IEP case manager needs to gather reports, data, and informal information from each team member as well as the family. This chapter identifies strategies for effective communication during the pre-planning process to integrate information and priorities to develop an IEP that is reasonably calculated to ensure student progress on the general education curriculum.

Chapter 3: Fostering Collaborative and Trusting Relationships with Families and Students   Effective communication with families is an essential skill for a special educator. Team members sometimes encounter difficulty contacting families, understanding their needs, and communicating cross-culturally. Beyond initial contact, however, all members of the IEP team should be collaborating with families in relation to goals, supplementary aids and services, and other IEP decisions. Many factors can affect how teams communicate with parents and engage with them in an ongoing manner. Special educators must be prepared to compassionately engage with parents (or equivalent adult caregivers) as partners under a range of circumstances. This chapter describes effective practices for meaningfully collaborating with families throughout the IEP development process and beyond. Just as importantly, IDEA 2004 requires student involvement in the IEP process. Strategies for enhancing student participation in the IEP process will be discussed.

Chapter 4: Discussing Data and Making Decisions

Understanding how to make data-based educational decisions is an essential skill for special educators. Many team members share data during the decision-making process. Different types of data might be considered with more or less weight, and the nature of conversations at IEP meetings around data can have consequences for students with complex support needs. The family's data are often discounted or given less consideration than data provided by professionals, even if those professionals have only interacted with the student for a short period of time and in limited contexts during the assessment process. Ways to lead outcomes-oriented discussions around data which value all team members in an equitable manner will be described.

Section II: Developing the IEP

This section explains the steps involved in drafting the IEP document section by section, as follows:

Chapter 5: Describing Present Levels of Academic Achievement and Functional Performance

The Present Levels of Academic Achievement and Functional Performance (PLAAFP) section of the IEP sets the groundwork for the remainder of the decisions during the IEP process. Creating a strengths-based narrative about the student is both an art and a science, as word choices can suggest a variety of solutions. A complete picture of the child provides a holistic view of their strengths and instructional needs. Only a comprehensive and cohesive narrative can set the stage for a robust educational plan.

Chapter 6: Planning for Special Factors, Extended School Year, and Alternate Assessments

Students with complex support needs may require a variety of special factors considerations, particularly related to communication and behavior. Strategies for considering these special factors are described. This chapter also describes the extended school year option for students with complex support needs to maintain and generalize skills. However, school districts vary in relation to the ways students with complex support needs are offered access to extended school year services. Key considerations for determining the need for extended school year, and ways to ensure ESY can be successful, will be offered. This chapter also discusses why, when, and how alternative assessments may be used.

Chapter 7: Determining What Gets Taught: Curriculum and Goals

A meaningful IEP is developed based on individual student needs, with a rich and personally relevant curriculum as the backdrop. The goals are the engine of the IEP and are uniquely calculated every year based on the student's current level of performance in areas of need. Student strengths should provide a jumping-off point for goals as well as instructional methods. While curriculum content can be individualized, it also needs to be grade-aligned and age-appropriate. In addition to academic skill areas (e.g., literacy, social studies, math, science) additional curriculum areas such as social-emotional skills, recreation, functional, and self-determination skills can be included in the IEP. This chapter will provide guidelines for determining curriculum areas and individual skills for IEP goals.

Chapter 8: Identifying Supplementary Aids and Services

If the goals are the engine of the IEP, supplementary aids and services are the linchpin which ensures students are being taught in general education settings for most or all of the day. Supplementary aids and services are not defined in IDEA 2004, but research suggests they cover physical accessibility, instructional supports, social-behavioral-communication supports, and supports for collaboration. Guidelines for choosing and writing supplementary aids and services into the IEP will be provided, including tips for ensuring they are implemented in a replicable and research-based manner.

Chapter 9: Determining the Least Restrictive Environment   Although a student's educational placement should not dictate IEP content (*L.H. vs. Hamilton County Department of Education,* 2018), research has demonstrated that teams often consider contextual factors when determining goals, supplementary aids and services, and curriculum content. It often seems that the student's educational placement is the elephant in the room during most conversations pertaining to the IEP for a student with complex support needs. The availability of a continuum of placements can be both an advantage and a disadvantage; while a variety of placement options can allow teams to make highly individualized decisions, the availability of segregated placements can also predispose teams to consider more restrictive placements than if no such option was available. Recommendations for determining that the most appropriate educational placement for students are based on student needs rather than preexisting programs will be provided.

Section III: At the Meeting and Afterward   This section discusses how to run the IEP meeting effectively and, afterward, follow through with implementing the IEP.

Chapter 10: Setting an Agenda and Setting the Tone: Communication During the IEP Meeting   The IEP meeting itself is a forum for team members to exchange information, develop and modify goals, and collaboratively plan IEP services. However, power differences among team members, standard operating procedures of schools and districts, and different communication styles among team members can create challenging contexts for decision making. Tips for setting agendas, defining roles and norms, guiding and participating in conversations, avoiding jargon and other alienating language, and having difficult conversations are provided.

Chapter 11: After the Meeting: Implementing the IEP   The IEP meeting is only the beginning of a child's education program for the year. Following the meeting, team members should follow up with each other, including the parents, to communicate progress or necessary changes to the IEP. In order to do this, team members need clear communication systems in place, as well as systems for collecting data. This chapter provides suggestions for keeping communication open throughout the year, ensuring ongoing collaboration among team members, and sample data collection and communication tools.

Throughout the book, chapters include activities to help educators get started on these steps in developing the IEP. Assorted reproducible planning worksheets and forms are provided in the chapter appendices; these are also available as downloadable resources. For details about how to access the downloads, see About the Downloads.

CONCLUDING THOUGHTS

This book is offered as a practical guide to IEP development that is reflective of a team approach to developing dignifying, inclusive, and ambitious special education services for students with complex support needs. As the quote from Helen Keller at the start of this preface reminds us, we—advocates, allies, and people with complex support needs—do not need to accept the world as it is. We can be part of a change that results in enviable lives for all people; making that change occur relies on us altering how we think about and provide supports and services to people with disabilities in schools. We hope the strategies and examples shared in this book provide you, the reader, with ideas to accomplish this ambitious yet attainable outcome.

REFERENCES

Endrew F. v. Douglas County School District RE-1. 580 U.S. __ (2017). https://www.supremecourt.gov/opinions/16pdf/15-827_0pm1.pdf

Individuals with Disabilities Education Improvement Act (IDEA) of 2004, PL 108-446, 20 U.S.C. §§ 1400 *et seq.*

Jackson, L. B., Ryndak, D. L., & Wehmeyer, M. L. (2008). The dynamic relationship between context, curriculum, and student learning: A case for inclusive education as a research-based practice. *Research and Practice for Persons with Severe Disabilities, 34*(1), 175–195. https://doi.org/10.2511/rpsd.33.4.175

Keller, H. (n.d.). [Transcription of speech written by Helen Keller circa 1912.] American Foundation for the Blind digital archives. https://www.afb.org/HelenKellerArchive?a=d&d=A-HK02-B212-F02-002.1.1&srpos =1&e=-------en-20-1-txt-%22I+do+not+like+the+world%22------3-7-6-5-3-------------0-1

Kleinert, H., Towles-Reeves, E., Quenemoen, R., Thurlow, M., Fluegge, L., Weseman, L., & Kerbel, A. (2015). Where students with the most significant cognitive disabilities are taught. *Exceptional Children, 81*(3), 312–328. https://doi.org/10.1177/0014402914563697

Kurth, J. A., Lockman Turner, E., Burke, K. M., & Ruppar, A. L. (2021). Curricular philosophies reflected in individualized education program goals for students with complex support needs. *Intellectual and Developmental Disabilities, 59*(4), 283–294. https://doi.org/10.1352/1934-9556-59.4.283

Kurth, J. A., Ruppar, A. L., Toews, S. G., McCabe, K. M., McQueston, J. A., & Johnston, R. (2019a). Considerations in placement decisions for students with complex support needs: An analysis of LRE statements. *Research and Practice for Persons with Severe Disabilities, 44*(1), 3–19. https://doi.org/10.1177/1540796918825479

L.H. et al. v. Hamilton City Department of Education (United States Court of Appeals for the 6th Circuit 2018).

Lipscomb, S., Haimson, J., Liu, A., Burghardt, J., Johnson, D., & Thurlow, M. (2017). *Preparing for life after high school: The characteristics and experiences of youth in special education. Findings from the National Longitudinal Transition Study 2012. Volume 1: Comparisons with other youth: Full report* (NCEE 2017-4017). National Center for Education Evaluation and Regional Assistance.

Mazzotti, V. L., Rowe, D. A., Sinclair, J., Poppen, M., Woods, W. E., & Shearer, M. L. (2016). Predictors of post-school success: A systematic review of NLTS2 secondary analyses. *Career Development and Transition for Exceptional Individuals, 39*(4), 196–215. https://doi.org/10.1177/2165143415588047

Morningstar, M. E., Kurth, J. A., & Johnson, P. J. (2017). Examining national trends in educational placements for students with significant disabilities. *Remedial and Special Education, 38*(1), 3–12. https://doi.org/ https://doi.org/10.1177/0741932516678

Movahedazarhouligh, S. (2021). Parent-implemented interventions and family-centered service delivery approaches in early intervention and early childhood special education. *Early Child Development and Care, 191*(1), 1–12. https://doi.org/10.1080/03004430.2019.1603148

Rowe, D. A., Mazzotti, V. L., Hirano, K., & Alverson, C. Y. (2015). Assessing transition skills in the 21st century. *TEACHING Exceptional Children, 47*(6), 301–309.

Ruppar, A. L., Kurth, J. A., McCabe, K. M., Toews, S. G., McQueston, J. A., & Johnston, R. (2022). Present levels of academic achievement and functional performance: Unravelling the narratives. *Journal of Disability Studies in Education*. Currently online first.

Ruppar, A. L., Kurth, J. A., Toews, S. G., McCabe, K. M., & McQueston, J. A. (2019, December). *Reporting present levels of performance: Narratives and their consequences for students with significant support needs*. Presentation at the TASH Annual Conference, Phoenix, AZ.

Taub, D. A., McCord, J. A., & Ryndak, D. L. (2017). Opportunities to learn for students with extensive support needs: A context of research-supported practices for all in general education classes. *The Journal of Special Education, 51*, 127–137. https://doi.org/10.1177/0022466917696263

Acknowledgments

We wish to thank the many students, families, and colleagues who have supported us in learning to develop strengths-based, inclusive IEPs. As former special educators, and now—as allies and advocates—we have had the opportunity to participate in many IEP teams. We hold in our hearts our former students and their families, who motivated us to push for change so that every child would have a place to flourish and learn in safe, welcoming, and inclusive schools.

We (Andrea and Jenny) almost never met, many times. We just missed meeting each other in our teacher education programs at the University of Washington in the late 1990s and early 2000s. Later, we read each other's work enthusiastically as we both entered academia in the 2010s. The 2015 TASH conference in Portland, Oregon finally brought us together. We are grateful to TASH and their excellent annual conferences which allowed us to meet, become colleagues, and become friends.

We thank our friends and families for supporting us during the writing process. We are also grateful for the food, fun, and health-care services in San Diego in Fall 2021, which allowed us to complete this book despite the sidewalk crack that conspired to take Andrea out.

Teachers Chloe Malmgren, Jessica Peacock, Heather Danser, and Megan Gross provided some of the stories that appear in examples and vignettes throughout the book. We are grateful to Joanne Juhnke and Miriam Oakleaf; Karan, Mike, and Gabe Penton; and Elizabeth Herman, whose IEP experiences helped us understand pitfalls that can be avoided through careful planning, empathy, creativity, and authentic collaboration.

We are grateful for the support of current and former doctoral students, who contributed to the research that led to this text. Sami Toews, Katie McCabe, Sarah Bubash, Radeen Yang, Lingyu Li, Elissa Lockman-Turner, Jessica McQueston, and Russell Johnston: We could not have written this book without your feedback, ideas, data collection and analysis, and insight.

Finally, we would like to acknowledge four of the most influential figures in the field of special education whom we have lost during the writing of this book and whose marks are indelible in this text: Lou Brown, Tom Skrtic, Pam Hunt, and Jim Thompson. Your trailblazing research and advocacy will continue to guide us as we try to carry on your legacies. Thank you for your relentless energy in pursuing educational equity for people with complex support needs. You have inspired us beyond measure.

To our students

Before the Meeting

The first section of this book discusses strategies and tasks individualized education program (IEP) teams use to plan for an IEP meeting. We start here because these strategies are foundational in establishing an equitable partnership among team members and are necessary for ensuring the IEP document the team develops reflects the priorities of the student, family, and other IEP team members.

If you are reading this book as a pre- or in-service educator, you are or will be involved in the IEP process for one or more students with complex support needs. Very likely you are responsible for managing the process and the IEP team. Doing this work well requires your commitment

- To being a strong leader and setting an example for your team

- To being an effective organizer and communicator

- To being a caring advocate who supports your students and their families

- To being a thoughtful decision maker who uses data wisely

Chapters 1–4 explore what these commitments look like in practice. You will learn what you need to know to manage the steps involved in preparing for the IEP meeting.

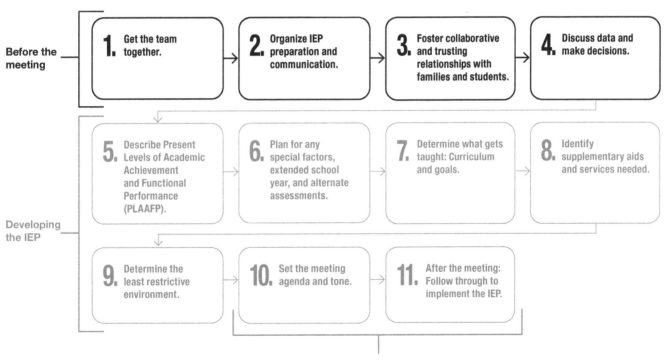

The skills and strategies discussed in this section are revisited and built upon during the rest of the book, emphasizing how foundational these are to creating an equitable, inclusive IEP.

Getting the Team Together

With Samantha Gross Toews

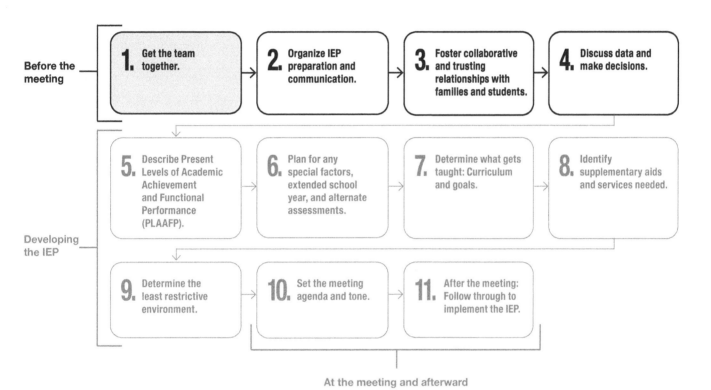

The development of an equitable, strengths-based IEP that promotes dignity, inclusion, and ambitious student outcomes starts with gathering required and invited team members who are committed to developing supports and services that will achieve these outcomes. Yet, understanding who should be at the table during planning and IEP meetings can be challenging, especially when students interact with multiple professionals. Furthermore, early and active engagement with families in a collegial manner is essential to setting the stage for establishing a positive atmosphere and productive team. (Throughout this book, we refer to "families" rather than "parents" to acknowledge that parenting roles are varied. Sometimes grandparents, stepparents, partners, biological parents, and others take on parenting roles. To be inclusive of these many forms of parenting, we use the term "families" throughout.)

In addition to partnering with families, meaningful engagement with general education teachers is essential for ensuring that inclusive education is successful. In this chapter, we also consider how procedural requirements, such as Prior Written Notice and IEP development timelines, serve purposes beyond mere legal compliance in creating an equitable, inclusive IEP. This chapter provides practical advice for 1) identifying and communicating with team members; 2) involving the family in meaningful ways; 3) working with outside service providers; and 4) effectively involving general education teachers, including those who might be resistant to inclusive education.

UNDERSTANDING THE COMMITMENT: *Leading Your Student's IEP Team*

If you are a special education teacher reading this book, you are most likely tasked not only with gathering an IEP team for your student(s) with complex support needs but also with leading that team. Your commitment to effective leadership will make a lasting difference in the quality of education your students receive and their outcomes throughout their school years and beyond.

1. Take a moment to jot down characteristics you associate with good educational leadership.

_____

_____

_____

_____

_____

2. Now, think of a student with complex support needs with whom you work. What are some particular questions or concerns you have about gathering a strong IEP team for that student?

_____

_____

_____

_____

_____

IDENTIFYING AND COMMUNICATING WITH TEAM MEMBERS

A team supporting a student with complex needs is typically large and diverse. This student population includes students who have multiple support needs, including those who experience communication, physical, sensory, social, and/or cognitive barriers in multiple settings and activities due to their disabilities. Even though students with complex disabilities might qualify for special education under any one of the 13 disability labels under the Individuals with Disabilities Education Improvement Act (IDEA) of 2004 (PL 108-446), one thing that connects these students is that they could be eligible under several—or even most—IDEA categories at the same time. Therefore, a primary disability category of intellectual disability, other health impairment, physical disability, or autism does little to describe the special education needs of students with complex disabilities.

Although every IEP team is composed of at least one special and general educator and a representative of a local education agency (LEA), such as a school district, teams supporting students with complex needs, will also include a variety of professionals, and often can include outside service providers as well. Prior to the beginning of the school year, the IEP case manager (usually a special education teacher) should identify the IEP team members for each student, looking carefully at the current or previous IEP to determine which team members have been involved historically and which will remain involved in planning for the year. Several important topics should be discussed prior to the school year with the IEP team, including the implementation of accommodations and modifications, access considerations, and the findings from person-centered planning, each of which are discussed next.

Ensuring Accommodations and Modifications Are in Place on Day 1

It is typical for teams supporting students with complex support needs to meet early in the school year to make a plan for supporting and teaching the student. However, meeting in the late summer—before school starts—allows teams to pre-plan accommodations and modifications to be ready for when the student comes to school. This is an important moment to recognize how ableism (a prejudice against people with disabilities) might affect the timing of these decisions. Imagine you have arrived at your first day of school and nothing is accessible for you. Your desk is too small or too big, you don't understand the words written on the wall or the directions the teacher is giving. Adults scramble when you arrive to find and create accessible materials on the fly, drawing even more attention to you and the stigma around your disability. Worse yet, the staff talks to each other while you are there, asking questions and sounding frustrated as they problem-solve. This potentially traumatizing experience can be avoided if teams ensure accommodations and modifications are in place at the outset of the school year.

Addressing Considerations for Access

Access is an ongoing process, not a single event (Piepzna-Smarasinha, 2018). Therefore, teams need to adjust supports as needed. Sometimes, a simple adjustment can make the difference between access and exclusion. For example, Carson, a kindergartener with multiple disabilities, was passively engaged in the music class drumming unit, sitting and listening to the other students play the floor drums. However, the floor drums were inaccessible to him because of his wheelchair. The physical therapist provided a standing positioner, which allowed Carson to reach the floor drums that were previously inaccessible from his wheelchair. This is one example of how ongoing problem-solving is essential for individual students' access to equitable education.

Taking a Person-Centered Approach

Finally, planning educational services for students with complex support needs requires a uniquely person-centered approach rather than a systems-centered approach. A systems-centered approach is one in which students are assigned placements and instruction based on the current available supports and services. In contrast, person-centered planning is a type of structured conversation in which people who are very familiar with the student come together to consider options, express a vision for the future, identify potential barriers, determine supports, and design an action plan to reach desired goals (Downing, 2010). Whereas a systems-centered approach benefits the system over the individual, a person-centered approach identifies individual strengths, needs, and wants, and builds supports and services around those priorities.

Common person-centered approaches, such as Making Action Plans (MAPS; Forest & Lusthaus, 1990), Planning Alternative Tomorrows with Hope (PATH; Pearpoint et al., 1993), and Circle of Friends (Perske & Perske, 1988), serve to "de-mystify the process of educational planning and create contexts through which shared understanding can be built" (Baglieri & Shapiro, 2017, p. 164). For a practical step-by-step guide to curriculum planning for students with complex support needs, *Choosing Outcomes and Accommodations for Children* (*COACH*; Giangreco et al., 2011) is a longstanding, highly recommended, research-based resource. Person-centered planning is discussed in greater depth in Chapter 4.

DETERMINING WHO SHOULD BE INVOLVED

This section will identify typical IEP team members for students with complex support needs. According to IDEA, every IEP team must minimally consist of the following members:

1. At least one special education teacher

2. At least one general educator

3. A representative from the LEA, often a school administrator

4. The parent or guardian of the student (i.e., family members)

5. A person who can interpret and discuss all educational data (often the special education teacher)

6. The student, to the greatest extent possible

7. Others with special knowledge or expertise about the student

In addition, an IEP team for a student with complex support needs is likely to include other members. Related services providers, such as occupational and physical therapists, speech-language pathologists (SLPs), and Board Certified Behavior Analysts (BCBAs) are all common members of IEP teams for students with complex needs. Each of these team members must actively contribute to the development and implementation of the IEP in an ongoing process. Together, they are a multidisciplinary collaborative team. What are the tasks and roles of each of these team members? We next describe the important roles each of these members play.

Special Education Teacher

The special education teacher most often leads the multidisciplinary collaborative IEP team for students with complex support needs. Special education teachers contribute their expertise in several areas to the team: specialized academic instruction, teaching adaptive skills, adapting and modifying curricula, and inclusive practices such as embedded instruction, collaborative planning, working with paraprofessionals, facilitating social relationships, and communication instruction (Kurth & Gross, 2014). As the IEP team leader, the special education teacher compiles information from all team members and translates the information into a cohesive plan for support and instruction across all school settings. In addition to acting as the IEP team leader and primary service delivery provider, the special education teacher should advocate for the student's right to access a quality education with their peers in general education settings.

General Education Teacher(s)

The IEP team must include at least one general education teacher, and possibly more than one, depending on the student's age, strengths, and preferences. General education teachers have in-depth knowledge of curriculum content, grade-level standards, the routines and activities of general education, instructional strategies, and the social environment of general education classes. General educators' input is essential for describing what occurs in all aspects of the general education setting, making their contributions valuable in assisting the team in determining what is taught and how a student with complex support needs might require supports and instruction to be successful in general education. Input from the general education teacher(s) is also needed because general education classes are the least restrictive environment (LRE) on the continuum of placements under IDEA and should be the first placement considered for every single student. The general educator(s) should be included in all levels of IEP development, including data collection, design of supports and goals, and implementation of the IEP.

Local Education Agency Representative

Because many decisions require allocation of funding, such as the purchase of materials or designated staff, the IEP team must also include a representative of the school system who has the authority to commit resources. This person must be qualified to provide specially designed instruction, have knowledge of the general education curriculum, and be able to commit to the resources needed so that student services can be provided as described in the IEP and ensure that those services are provided.

Family Members

The importance and roles of family members in the IEP team cannot be understated. Families typically know the student best and represent the long-term interests of the student. Because of their vital knowledge, family members can ensure teams focus on the big picture so that the lifelong interests and priorities of the student are centered in every decision.

Someone to Interpret Evaluation Results

An individual who can interpret the instructional implications of evaluation results is also a required IEP team member, per IDEA. This person, often a school psychologist, is especially important in initial and triennial review IEP meetings, but attendance at annual meetings is just as important. This person can interpret a variety of results, including district or state assessments, observations, direct assessments of student skills, classwork, and progress monitoring data. This individual must be able to discuss these results with the full team and help plan how to address the implications of evaluation results in IEP goals and services.

Student

The student should play an active role in the design of their own goals, supports, and services. Deliberate discussion of desired goals and the planning of steps to achieve them are an excellent way to increase student self-determination skills. In addition, providing a student with the opportunity to make choices about the ways to access content and work toward goals can increase the student's motivation and ultimate achievement of goals (Mazzotti et al., 2016).

Other Professionals With Expertise About the Student

In addition to the team members required by IDEA, the IEP team for a student with complex support needs often includes other professionals with expertise about the student. The sections that follow identify other professionals who are often included on the IEP team and describe the different types of support they provide to the student and the IEP team.

Speech-Language Pathologist   Communication is a frequent area of need for students with complex support needs. Speech-language pathologists (SLPs) bring expertise about language development, assessment, and intervention to the IEP team. It is particularly important that SLPs who work with students with complex support needs have training and experience with augmentative and alternative communication (AAC), as many students will benefit from targeted high- and low-tech AAC intervention (Beukelman & Light, 2020). AAC is defined by the American Speech-Language-Hearing Association (ASHA) as "an area of clinical practice that addresses the needs of individuals with significant and complex communication disabilities characterized by impairments in speech-language production and/or comprehension, including spoken and written modes of communication." The role of an SLP on the IEP team is to provide direct language support and collaborate with other members of the team to ensure language development opportunities are maximized throughout the school day. Push-in services in a natural setting (e.g., general education classroom, recess), rather than pull-out speech services in a therapy room, can increase student access to important speech interventions (Hernandez, 2012). An SLP who delivers direct speech intervention to a student in a general education classroom can model strategies and supports for those team members, which can be used when the SLP is not present.

Physical Therapist   For students with physical disabilities, a physical therapist (PT) can work on a wide range of physical skills that support access to the general curriculum, including strength, stability, postural control, balance, gross motor control, endurance, functional mobility, and accessibility in the educational environment. A PT should assess the school environment to identify barriers to accessibility and opportunities for a student to strengthen gross motor skills. PTs work with all members of the IEP team to ensure the student is supported to use adaptive equipment, such as wheelchairs, walkers, standers, gait trainers, and other seated and lying positions. Students who use wheelchairs should transfer among wheelchairs and other supportive standing, sitting, and lying devices throughout the school day, as appropriate for the activity. The PT should create a positioning schedule and train all IEP team members to facilitate transitions among equipment to maximize student independence and participation in general education activities.

Occupational Therapist   Like the PT, an occupational therapist (OT) supports and teaches students motor skills to increase their participation and independence in the general curriculum. The OT brings expertise in environmental design and adaptation to reduce barriers, assistive technologies that increase access to valued activities, strategies for integrating supports into natural settings, and design of incremental goals that will facilitate success in long-term outcomes such as successful transition to post–high school employment, independent living, and/or further education (American Occupational Therapy Association, 2016). It is very common for OTs to work closely with students with complex support needs on fine motor skills that will increase independence in everyday tasks, such as eating, using school tools (e.g., pencil, keyboard, scissors), and general hand coordination or strength. As with all other related services providers, OTs should provide direct services in general education settings, to support students in applying skills in different environments (i.e., generalization) and to model for other team members to support students' access to support when the OT is not present.

Addressing Sensory Needs

Autistic people and others report that their sensory needs must be met to successfully learn and participate in educational activities. However, research has also suggested that sensory therapies, at a minimum, do not result in any measurable outcomes on their own. This does not mean that students do not need sensory supports. However, be aware of how much time students are spending related to sensory needs in comparison with other educational activities. Students who spend large portions of their day in sensory rooms by themselves are not likely to be receiving equitable access to curriculum.

Paraprofessional   Paraprofessionals play an important role on the IEP team, as they often spend extensive time providing direct academic, behavioral, and social support to students. In fact, in one study by Toews and colleagues (2020), paraprofessionals were observed to be the most common adults to provide instruction to students with complex support needs who were included in general education classes. It is necessary for teachers to consider that their paraprofessional staff have, generally, not received any formal training in supporting and teaching students with complex support needs. For this reason, it is essential that IEP team members provide focused training and supervision to paraprofessionals in all responsibilities they are asked to take on (Brock et al., 2017). Some common activities for paraprofessionals include supervision of individuals and groups of students across school settings, creating and delivering instructional supports, assisting students in self-care (e.g., eating, using the restroom, dressing, positioning in adaptive equipment), collecting student performance data, implementing positive behavioral support plans, and maintaining student safety across the school day (Westling et al., 2021).

Nurse   A school nurse should participate on school teams for students with health care support needs who receive health interventions (e.g., breathing treatments, administration of medication, tube feeding). The nurse should work with the team to identify a schedule for medical support provisions and train team members on how to provide any necessary medical supports to the student.

Adaptive Physical Education Teacher   An adaptive physical education (PE) teacher supports students with disabilities to access physical education. It is important for adaptive PE to be provided in the least restrictive environment. This will require the adaptive PE teacher to collaborate with the general PE teacher(s) for the school to identify supports that will facilitate student participation in general education PE.

School Social Worker or Counselor

A school counselor or social worker might be needed when a student has mental health or social/emotional needs. This professional will collaborate with other members of the IEP team to promote academic achievement, social/emotional wellness, and college and career readiness.

Vision and Hearing Specialists

Vision and hearing specialists may also be IEP team members for students who are blind, D/deaf, or hard of hearing. These team members can assist in designing supports and services to meet the hearing and/or vision needs of the student in the general education environment.

Behavior Specialist

A behavior specialist, who may also be a BCBA, might join the IEP team to support the development and implementation of a behavioral support plan. Behavior specialists might assist in designing supports, monitoring those supports, and providing training to IEP team members.

CONCLUDING THOUGHTS: GATHERING THE TEAM

An old African proverb asserts that it takes a village to raise a child, and in the case of IEP development for students with complex support needs, a large team with varied expertise is essential to design an individual program that meets the needs of the student. Each team member brings a unique perspective and expertise to the IEP team, but by joining together and sharing these perspectives and expertise, the team can be positioned to create robust plans that improve educational and developmental outcomes for students.

REVIEWING THE COMMITMENT: *Leading Your Student's IEP Team*

This chapter provided guidance on how to assemble an IEP team for a student with complex support needs. If you are tasked with gathering and managing a student's IEP team, your commitment to effective leadership is crucial for that student's education.

Think back to the characteristics of effective leadership you identified at the start of the chapter. What leadership qualities will be most important for you to bring to your work in gathering and leading your student's IEP team?

_____

_____

_____

_____

_____

_____

Think back to the questions or concerns you identified at the start of the chapter. After reading through the chapter, what ideas do you have for addressing these questions and concerns?

_____

_____

_____

_____

_____

_____

ACTING ON THE COMMITMENT: *Start Identifying Team Members*

At this time, you may want to get started on identifying and getting in touch with IEP team members. Use the worksheet in the Chapter 1 appendix to begin putting this information together. Be sure to note any logistical or other challenges you will need to plan for in working with each person (for example, if a team member is an itinerant service provider who is not at the school every day, you will need to plan around this).

A reproducible version of this worksheet is provided with the other teacher resources for this book available at the Brookes Download Hub.

Planning Worksheet—IEP Team Members

Student initials _____ Date _____ Grade _____

IEP Team Members				
Name	Contact information	Role/why needed on IEP team	Date contacted	Notes

Organizing IEP Preparation and Communication

With Samantha Gross Toews

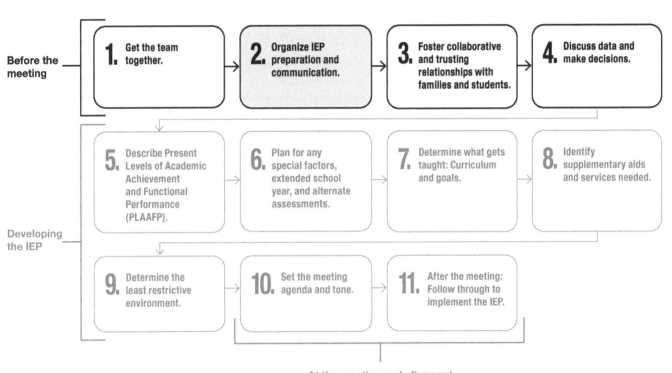

Before the meeting

1. Get the team together.

2. Organize IEP preparation and communication.

3. Foster collaborative and trusting relationships with families and students.

4. Discuss data and make decisions.

Developing the IEP

5. Describe Present Levels of Academic Achievement and Functional Performance (PLAAFP).

6. Plan for any special factors, extended school year, and alternate assessments.

7. Determine what gets taught: Curriculum and goals.

8. Identify supplementary aids and services needed.

9. Determine the least restrictive environment.

10. Set the meeting agenda and tone.

11. After the meeting: Follow through to implement the IEP.

At the meeting and afterward

A well-functioning IEP team needs a leader, and usually this responsibility falls to the special education teacher. In this role, the special education teacher functions in a managerial role, and needs to use clear and timely communication with all members of the IEP team throughout the school year. Organizational strategies are essential for keeping everyone on the large, multidisciplinary team working efficiently and effectively toward the shared goal of providing an equitable and strengths-based education for the student with complex support needs. Effective, team-wide communication prior to the annual IEP meeting is essential to ensure the legal requirements of IDEA are met, as well as to guarantee the most current information is available for the IEP team to consider during the meeting.

Communication among team members can also be challenging because of the wide variety of backgrounds various team members bring to the IEP process, as described in Chapter 1. Because of their specific areas of expertise and varied training, team members often use technical terms that are specific to their area of specialization. However, when these terms are used without explanation, misunderstandings, and ultimately mistrust, can result. For example, the term "assessment" can mean different things to different members of the team—an administrator might be thinking of a standardized statewide test, a school psychologist might be thinking of a cognitive assessment, a general education teacher might be thinking of a curriculum-based assessment, whereas a special education teacher might be imagining an authentic assessment. Being careful to use specific, descriptive language will ensure all team members are able to fully participate in the meeting. More importantly, the use of discipline-specific jargon can create a barrier between communicators, as the person who doesn't understand the terms is marked as an outsider and can feel isolated from the decision-making process (Zeitlin & Curcic, 2014).

Sometimes, communicating in plain language is more difficult than using the technical terminology in your area of expertise. For this reason, an IEP coordinator must be an excellent communicator. Continually check for understanding with individual team members, especially parents and family. Consider the following email written by a school administrator to a parent:

> *Mrs. Herman,*
> *Would this Friday, 9/17 at 10 AM work for you? We can meet in person, or via Zoom.*
> *Please let us know and I will send out a notification of conference and ask that you waive the 10 notice* [sic] *requirement.*
> *We look forward to meeting with you.*

Even though the child of the parent receiving this email had been receiving special education services for several years, some of this language was unfamiliar. Specifically, parents might be unfamiliar with the language about "notification of conference" and "10-day notice requirement," which refers to the state's requirement that families must be notified 10 days prior to the meeting, a right they can waive if they prefer an earlier time. In this situation, the administrator failed to consider the parent's point of view and familiarity with the technical language used in special education—leaving the parent utterly confused. At the same time, the administrator asked the parent to waive a right that they might not understand. Using plain language and explaining terms that might be unfamiliar is a courteous way to establish a positive rapport with families.

UNDERSTANDING THE COMMITMENT: *Managing Communication*

Good communication among IEP team members—including the student and their family, as well as educators and service providers—is essential for the team to succeed in its aims. No matter your role, you will need to be thoughtful about how you communicate with other team members. If you are leading the team, your role may also include managing and facilitating good communication among other team members.

1. Think about a recent situation where you've needed to call on good communication skills in your work. Why was good communication important in that situation? What went well in this communication? What could have been improved?

    _____

    _____

    _____

    _____

    _____

2. Now, consider the student whose IEP team you are working with. What are some essential topics you will need to communicate to staff members on the team? To the student or family? What are some potential communication challenges?

    _____

    _____

_____

_____

_____

_____

SETTING COMMUNICATION TIMELINES

Figure 2.1 provides a recommended communication timeline for IEP development. IDEA specifies that families must be notified "within a reasonable amount of time," prior to meetings and changes in services, and specific timelines for notifying families about meetings and changes in services (also known as "prior written notice") vary by state (IDEA §300.503(b)). Team members should check state regulations to be sure their meeting invitation or other prior written notice will arrive in time. In addition, written material must be provided in the parent's native language if that language is not English, and if a parent's native language or other mode of communication is a nonwritten language, schools must translate orally, or by other means, depending on the communication mode of the parents.

Universal design refers to the practice of designing environments and activities by considering the diverse needs of individuals first, reducing the need for accommodations and adaptations after the fact (CAST, 2022). Applying the principle of universal design to this scenario, it's good practice to follow up with an oral explanation, either from the special educator or interpreter, for any family member. *Remember:* Anyone unfamiliar with the special education process is bound to be confused by it! Offering this to all families ensures all families fully understand the process and have a chance to ask questions.

Finally, start planning the meeting early. Team members will need a reminder ahead of the IEP due date and will need to begin compiling data in anticipation of the meeting. Schedules will be busy, so be sure to offer a selection of times to maximize team member attendance and to be sure the family can attend. According to IDEA, the meeting must occur at "a mutually agreed upon time and place" (IDEA, §300.322, 2004), so be sure that family members are offered this flexibility, within reason.

Scheduling a Planning Meeting

One to two months prior to the IEP meeting, the IEP team leader should organize a meeting of the entire IEP team to make a comprehensive plan for data collection and collaboration activities that will occur prior to preparing or updating the IEP. It is helpful to record all information in a central location that

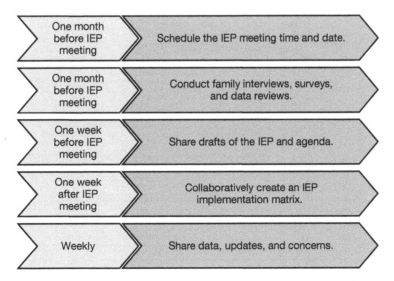

One month before IEP meeting	Schedule the IEP meeting time and date.
One month before IEP meeting	Conduct family interviews, surveys, and data reviews.
One week before IEP meeting	Share drafts of the IEP and agenda.
One week after IEP meeting	Collaboratively create an IEP implementation matrix.
Weekly	Share data, updates, and concerns.

Figure 2.1. Timeline planning checklist.

can be accessed by team members after the meeting. The creation of a shared folder on a cloud platform such as Google Drive or Dropbox can facilitate collaboration.

Figure 2.2 displays the first page of an IEP Team Data Collection Plan form that can be used during this meeting to organize the activities of each IEP team member. (A full-size, reproducible version of the complete form is provided in the Chapter 2 appendix and with the downloadable resources for this book, available at the Brookes Download Hub.) This form guides the team to discuss areas of need for the student and identify what assessment strategies will be used in each area, who will be involved, and the date when the data collection will be completed. See Table 2.1 for a list of common assessments. As shown on the IEP Team Data Collection Plan form, it is essential to plan for student and family involvement in the IEP planning process early. The date and types of person-centered planning meetings that will be used should be identified. For more information on strategies to involve students and their family in the IEP planning process, please read Chapter 3, and for more information about collecting data and using it for decision making, please see Chapter 4.

Preparing for the IEP Meeting

One week prior to the IEP team meeting, the school-based team should have all assessment data, present levels of performance narratives, suggested supplementary aids and services, a proposed service plan, and proposed goals shared in a central location. This facilitates collaborative team review of information and revisions prior to the IEP meeting. The present levels of performance and proposed IEP goals should be developed with the student and family one week prior to the IEP meeting. When requesting input from families, it is important to support their contribution by providing information that is free from confusing jargon, translated, if necessary, into the language they are most comfortable using, and welcoming many modes of feedback such as written or oral. Team members' feedback—including family feedback—should be incorporated into the IEP prior to the meeting (Harry & Ocasio-Stoutenburg, 2020).

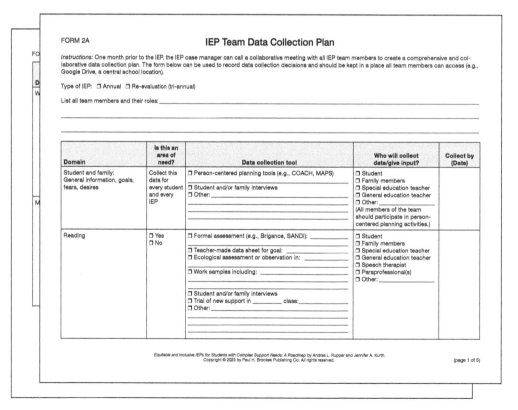

Figure 2.2. Page 1 of the IEP Team Data Collection Plan form.

Table 2.1. Common assessments and assessment resources

Assessment or Tool	URL
General person-centered planning	
McGill Action Planning Systems, also known as Making Action Plans (MAPS)	http://inclusionworks.org/sites/default/files/PlottingYourCourse.pdf
Choosing Options and Accommodations for Children (COACH) (Giangreco, Cloninger, & Iverson, 2011)	https://products.brookespublishing.com/Choosing-Outcomes-and-Accommodations-for-Children-COACH-P463.aspx
Personal Preference Indicators: A Free Guide for Planning	https://www.ou.edu/content/dam/Education/documents/personal-preference-indicator.pdf
Assessment area: Academic achievement	
Brigance Inventory of Early Development and Brigance Comprehensive Inventory of Basic Skills	https://www.curriculumassociates.com/products/brigance/special-education
Student Annual Needs Determination Inventory (SANDI)	https://www.lakeshorelearning.com/services/sandi
Kaufman Test of Educational Achievement, 3rd ed. (KTEA-3) (Kaufman & Kaufman, 2014)	http://www.pearsonclinical.com/psychology/products/100000777/kaufman-test-of-educational-achievement-third-edition-ktea-3.html
Woodcock-Johnson Test of Achievement	https://riversideinsights.com/woodcock_johnson_iv
Assessment area: Adaptive Skills	
Adaptive behavior	
Supports Intensity Scale (SIS)	https://www.aaidd.org/sis/sis-c
Diagnostic Adaptive Behavior Scale	https://www.aaidd.org/dabs
Vineland Adaptive Behavior Scale	https://www.pearsonassessments.com/store/usassessments/en/Store/Professional-Assessments/Behavior/Adaptive/Vineland-Adaptive-Behavior-Scales-%7C-Third-Edition/p/100001622.html
Functional Behavioral Assessment (FBA)	https://www.pattan.net/getmedia/eca12015-858b-4448-962d-753816d71e20/FBA_ProcessBklt0516#:~:text=Functional%20Behavioral%20Assessment%20(FBA)is,is%20serving%20for%20the%20student
Casey Life Skills (Casey Family Programs, 2012)	http://www.caseylifeskills.org
Enderle-Severson Transition Rating Scale (Enderle & Severson, 2003)	http://www.estr.net/publications.cfm
Self-determination	
AIR Self-Determination Assessment (Wolman et al., 1994)	https://www.ou.edu/education/centers-and-partnerships/zarrow/self-determination-assessment-tools/air-self-determination-assessment
ARC Self-Determination Scale (Wehmeyer & Kelchner, 1995)	http://www.thearc.org/document.doc?id=3670
Self-Determination Assessment (Hoffman et al., 2014)	http://www.ealyeducation.com/
Assessment area: Transition	
Transition Coalition New Parent Transition Survey	https://transitioncoalition.org/blog/tc-materials/the-new-parent-transition-survey/
Brigance Transition Skills Inventory	https://www.curriculumassociates.com/programs/brigance/brigance-special-education-transition-guide
O*NET Career Interest Inventory (U.S. Department of Labor, 2002)	https://www.onetonline.org/
Career Key (Jones, 2014)	http://www.careerkey.org
Career Quiz: Wisconsin Technical College System	http://bit.ly/1R5a7eJ

(continued)

Table 2.1.   *(continued)*

Assessment or Tool	URL
Assessment area: Communication	
Wisconsin Assistive Technology Initiative (WATI) Assessment	http://www.wati.org/wp-content/uploads/2017/10/WATI-Assessment.pdf
Clinical Evaluation of Language Fundamentals (CELF-4)	https://www.pearsonassessments.com/store/usassessments/en/Store/Professional-Assessments/Speech-%26-Language/Clinical-Evaluation-of-Language-Fundamentals---Fourth-Edition/p/100000442.html
Receptive One-Word Picture Vocabulary Test (ROWPVT-4)	https://www.proedinc.com/Products/13688/rowpvt4-receptive-oneword-picture-vocabulary-testfourth-edition.aspx
Expressive One-Word Picture Vocabulary Test–Fourth Edition (EOWPVT-4)	https://www.proedinc.com/Products/13692/eowpvt4-expressive-oneword-picture-vocabulary-testfourth-edition.aspx

Once the IEP has been agreed upon, the full IEP team should meet again to detail how the student will be supported to access content and make progress in their goals across the school day and at home. A common way teams choose to plan IEP implementation is the use of an IEP matrix. A sample IEP matrix and description of the planning process for this stage of the IEP can be found in Chapter 3. Establishment of these planned lines of communication supports consistency of service, enhanced opportunity for generalization with practice of skills in different settings, and family participation and satisfaction.

EFFECTIVELY INVOLVING GENERAL EDUCATION TEACHERS

Successful inclusive education depends on general educators being involved and informed IEP team members. There are different ways of thinking about the partnership between a general and special educator, but a common model is to think of the general education teacher as the expert on the general curriculum, and the special education teacher as the expert on making the general curriculum accessible (Murawski & Dieker, 2008). As a content specialist, the general education teacher can identify the key concepts to be taught and can work with the special education teacher to ensure the activities and content are accessible to students with disabilities in their classes.

Unfortunately, many general educators are reluctant or feel unprepared to participate on IEP teams (Pugach et al., 2014). It is common for general educators to take a passive role on IEP teams, especially if a student does not attend their class all day. However, students with complex support needs will, by definition, require more support in general education classes than other students with disabilities. Therefore, communication must be more frequent, and the general education teacher needs to take a more active role on the IEP team. Technology can facilitate special and general education teacher communication, especially when teachers have few opportunities for face-to-face conversations during the day. After the COVID-19 pandemic, teachers and families have experience using flexible technologies to facilitate communication.

COMMITTING TO STRENGTHS-BASED COMMUNICATION

Many special education teachers use daily or weekly written logs to communicate with general education teachers and families. For example, general educators might provide a daily or weekly written report about a student's behavior, or a special educator might provide a daily note to the family with important information about the school day. Remember that these written words, however quickly jotted down, have power to shape others' views about the student. Modeling strengths-based language, therefore, is especially important to consider.

Think about the following note home from a special education teacher to a parent:

Hi Ms. Lincoln,
Lunch was chaotic today. Henry was screeching and swinging his iPad around by its
strap. He was twirling and twirling throughout the whole day, especially in lunch. When

I scolded him he COMPLETELY ignored my comments. He made my assistant feel like he could've been physical. By the end of the day, I had warned Henry several times that he needed to be safe with his iPad. I then caught him doing it again. So, I had Henry switch to sitting alone.

What is missing from this note? What could be rephrased so that Henry is not positioned as an irrational, scary student?

Hi Ms. Lincoln,

  Henry seemed to be having a difficult time all day today, especially during lunch. I noticed that he was twirling more than usual and I was worried he might damage his iPad or hurt someone. I know we need to re-evaluate his plan so that he stays safe and gets what he needs. What do you think he might be trying to communicate when he is in this state?

In the second example, the teacher phrases her concerns as questions and prioritizes Henry's communication needs rather than her perceptions about his misbehavior. The teacher focuses on Henry's needs in the general education environment and characterizes his behavior in terms of communication rather than bodily threat.

The next example comes directly from Andrea's teaching experience and describes more extended communication over the course of a school year. Luis's story illustrates how commitment to strengths-based communication is part of advocating effectively for students with complex support needs when general education teachers are resistant to including these students in their classroom.

How I Did It: My Student's First-Grade Teacher Said, "Not in My Classroom."

Luis is my student with complex support needs. He uses a communication device, which he accesses with two switches, and we are focusing on vocabulary development to help him participate in general education activities. His kindergarten year couldn't have been better. His teacher was flexible, interested, and accommodating, he made friends in school, and his whole demeanor changed. I was so excited to build on this success in first grade. However, the principal made the wrong choice for his first-grade teacher. While the teacher had some experience in special education, it was clear that she didn't think a student like Luis should be in her classroom. This created a very unwelcoming atmosphere.

I decided I could not let this teacher make me angry, because tensions would rise to an untenable level. I knew that I had to see it as my goal to get her on my side. I shared data about Luis' progress, and I showed her how my paraprofessional and I worked with Luis to develop vocabulary during general education activities. And I tried to protect Luis from her negative attitude as much as I could. I decided I would "take" all the ableism on his behalf, or at least I would try to deflect as much as possible.

It was definitely one of my most difficult years as a teacher, but remaining focused on Luis and his needs, and modeling strengths-based language, I left the year feeling more confident about my teaching. And when he got to second grade, I was able to advocate for a more welcoming classroom teacher for Luis. While I wish all teachers would understand the importance of general curriculum access, I recognize that everyone harbors ableism in different ways. Recognizing her behavior as ableist helped me understand how to advocate for Luis in a more targeted and healthy way.

INVOLVING PARAPROFESSIONALS

Paraprofessionals are rarely thought of as relevant IEP team members, but paraprofessionals can provide a bird's-eye view of the student's participation in general education classes and can offer suggestions relevant to the day-to-day successes and challenges for a student with complex support needs. The information they provide can inform the assessment, goals, supports, and intervention plans. In addition, when paraprofessionals provide input to the IEP team, they may also increase their knowledge of the student's individualized program, in turn more effectively supporting the student (Giangreco, 2013).

However, integrating paraprofessionals' viewpoints is difficult, especially because paraprofessionals usually lack formal training for supporting students with complex support needs. Gathering information from paraprofessionals, therefore, should take a universal design approach with multiple forms of data informing decisions. Paraprofessionals should be trained to collect observational data about students' progress, which will inform the Present Levels of Academic Achievement and Functional Performance, as well as the goals and objectives. In addition, paraprofessionals can offer important qualitative data about the student's experiences in school, which should also inform the IEP.

WORKING WITH OUTSIDE SERVICE PROVIDERS

Students with complex support needs sometimes see therapists outside of school, such as physical therapists, occupational therapists, speech-language pathologists, and mental health providers. The perspectives of these providers are very important to understand. Whenever possible, ask families to allow outside providers to communicate with the school. Usually, outside providers will welcome this opportunity to share ideas and collaborate to support students with complex support needs in school. Sometimes, a family might need to sign a waiver to allow information to be shared between private providers and the school. Check on this before sharing information. Invite outside providers only with the consent of families.

INVOLVING STUDENTS IN THEIR OWN IEP

Active involvement of the student in their own IEP meeting is critical to developing an IEP that is truly individualized and reflects the interests and priorities of the student. However, according to the National Longitudinal Transition Study, while approximately 57% of students age 14–22 attended their own IEP meetings, only 12.2% participated actively (Newman et al., 2011). When students attend their own meeting, they report having more knowledge of their disability and support needs, develop better self-determination skills, and better understand the IEP purpose and process (Danneker & Bottge, 2009; Van Dycke et al., 2006). Yet, student involvement can seem prohibitive to some team members who are unsure of how to involve a student due to their age or support needs. Nevertheless, it is essential to remember that involvement is also individualized, with students taking on a variety of roles based on their age or interest, as seen in Figure 2.3. For example, Teresa, a kindergarten student with Down syndrome, attends a portion of her IEP meeting and listens to the discussion. She answers questions that are asked of her (e.g., what she likes best about school, what she wants to be when she grows up), and shares some of her classwork. On the other hand, Daniel, a 10th grader with Down syndrome, prepares a discussion of his hopes and dreams, calls on team members to provide reports and asks them questions about their recommendations, and sets the meeting agenda in collaboration with his special education teacher. These different types of involvement make sense for students of different ages with different developmental needs.

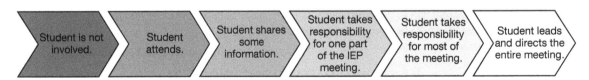

Figure 2.3. Progression of student involvement in the individualized education program (IEP) meeting. (From Thoma, C., & Wehman, P. [2010]. *Getting the most out of IEPs*. Paul H. Brookes Publishing; adapted by permission.)

Jessica Peacock, an inclusive elementary teacher in Colorado who teaches students with complex support needs, has several tips for involving students in their own IEP meeting. These are shared in Tips and Strategies to Support Student Involvement.

Tips and Strategies to Support Student Involvement

☐ Plan for all students to participate in at least a portion of their IEP meeting (with child care or entertainment set up for when the student is done).

☐ Permit students to take breaks or be excused from parts of the meeting.

☐ Use AAC and other technology, including pictures and Power Point slides, to support students in sharing their ideas and organizing their thoughts and the meeting agenda.

☐ Practice with students ahead of the IEP meeting.

☐ Record student responses on video prior to the meeting, and play them during the meeting.

☐ Share pictures from home, school, and community settings highlighting student interests and priorities.

☐ Invite friends, siblings, favorite teachers, and other school staff the student prefers.

☐ Support the student in choosing snacks to bring to the meeting.

☐ Work with the student to select the location for the IEP meeting.

☐ Make name cards.

☐ Interview classmates or other people who cannot attend the meeting.

☐ Make videos to share present levels, mastered goals, and favorite parts of the day.

For further resources and ideas for involving students in their IEP meeting, be sure to review other resources listed in Table 2.2.

CONCLUDING THOUGHTS: MANAGING COMMUNICATION

Clear communication is necessary when planning for an effective IEP meeting. Given the number of team members usually present on IEP teams for students with complex support needs, this communication and planning is especially important to ensure all team members are prepared to fully

Table 2.2. Resources to support student involvement in the individualized education program (IEP) meeting

Resource	Website
I'm Determined	https://imdetermined.org/resource/student-led-iep/
IRIS Center	https://iris.peabody.vanderbilt.edu/module/tran-scp/cresource/q1/p01/
Include NYC	https://includenyc.org/help-center/resources/tips-for-encouraging-student-participation-in-iep-meetings/
Washington, DC, Office of the State Superintendent of Special Education	https://osse.dc.gov/sites/default/files/dc/sites/osse/documents/Facilitating%20Student-led%20IEPs.pdf
Student-Led IEP Meetings: Planning and Implementation Strategies	https://files.eric.ed.gov/fulltext/EJ967458.pdf

participate, including families and students. By working on clear communication and using online and in-person tools, as described in this chapter, you increase the likelihood IEP meetings will be effective and efficient.

REVIEWING THE COMMITMENT: *Managing Communication*

This chapter discussed the importance of good communication among IEP team members.

Now, consider a student with complex support needs whose IEP team you are working with. What aspects of communication are going well?

_____

_____

_____

_____

_____

In what ways could communication be tweaked to improve it?

_____

_____

_____

_____

_____

ACTING ON THE COMMITMENT: *Managing Communication*

At this time, get started completing the IEP Team Data Collection Plan form provided in the appendix to this chapter. (You may also obtain an electronic copy of this form at the Brookes Download Hub.)

What other tools or strategies can you use to manage communication? List them here.

_____

_____

_____

_____

_____

FORM 2A

IEP Team Data Collection Plan

Instructions: One month prior to the IEP, the IEP case manager can call a collaborative meeting with all IEP team members to create a comprehensive and collaborative data collection plan. The form below can be used to record data collection decisions and should be kept in a place all team members can access (e.g., Google Drive, a central school location).

Type of IEP: ☐ Annual   ☐ Re-evaluation (tri-annual)

List all team members and their roles: _____

_____

Domain	Is this an area of need?	Data collection tool	Who will collect data/give input?	Collect by (Date)
Student and family: General information, goals, fears, desires	Collect this data for every student and every IEP	☐ Person-centered planning tools (e.g., COACH, MAPS) ☐ Student and/or family interviews ☐ Other: _____ _____ _____	☐ Student ☐ Family members ☐ Special education teacher ☐ General education teacher ☐ Other: _____ (All members of the team should participate in person-centered planning activities.)	
Reading	☐ Yes ☐ No	☐ Formal assessment (e.g., Brigance, SANDI): _____ ☐ Teacher-made data sheet for goal: _____ ☐ Ecological assessment or observation in: _____ ☐ Work samples including: _____ _____ ☐ Student and/or family interviews ☐ Trial of new support in _____ class: _____ ☐ Other: _____ _____	☐ Student ☐ Family members ☐ Special education teacher ☐ General education teacher ☐ Speech therapist ☐ Paraprofessional(s) ☐ Other: _____	

FORM 2A **IEP Team Data Collection Plan** (continued)

Domain	Is this an area of need?	Data collection tool	Who will collect data/give input?	Collect by (Date)
Writing	☐ Yes ☐ No	☐ Formal assessment (e.g., Brigance, SANDI): _____ ☐ Teacher-made data sheet for goal: _____ ☐ Ecological assessment or observation in: _____ ☐ Work samples including: _____ ☐ Student and/or family interviews ☐ Trial of new support in _____ class: _____ ☐ Other: _____	☐ Student ☐ Family members ☐ Special education teacher ☐ General education teacher ☐ Speech therapist ☐ Occupational therapist ☐ Paraprofessional(s) ☐ Other: _____	
Math	☐ Yes ☐ No	☐ Formal assessment (e.g., Brigance, SANDI): _____ ☐ Teacher-made data sheet for goal: _____ ☐ Ecological assessment or observation in: _____ ☐ Work samples including: _____ ☐ Student and/or family interviews ☐ Trial of new support in _____ class: _____ ☐ Other: _____	☐ Student ☐ Family members ☐ Special education teacher ☐ General education teacher ☐ Paraprofessional(s) ☐ Other: _____	

FORM 2A **IEP Team Data Collection Plan** *(continued)*

Domain	Is this an area of need?	Data collection tool	Who will collect data/give input?	Collect by (Date)
Adaptive skills (e.g., self-determination, self-care, completing multi-step tasks)	☐ Yes ☐ No	☐ Formal assessment (e.g., SIS, Adaptive behavior scales, AIR Self-Determination Assessment): _____ ☐ Teacher-made data sheet for goal: _____ ☐ Ecological assessment or observation in: _____ ☐ Work samples including: _____ ☐ Student and/or family interviews ☐ Other: _____	☐ Student ☐ Family members ☐ Special education teacher ☐ General education teacher ☐ School psychologist ☐ Physical therapist ☐ Occupational therapist ☐ Adaptive PE/PE coach ☐ Other: _____	
Social-emotional and behavioral (e.g., self-regulation, peer interaction)	☐ Yes ☐ No	☐ Formal assessment (e.g., functional behavioral assessment): _____ ☐ Teacher-made data sheet for goal: _____ ☐ Ecological assessment in _____ ☐ Antecedent, behavior, consequence observation in: _____ ☐ Student preference assessment or interview ☐ Family interviews or surveys ☐ Trial of new support in _____ class: _____ ☐ Other: _____	☐ Student ☐ Family members ☐ Special education teacher ☐ General education teacher ☐ School psychologist ☐ BCBA ☐ Social worker ☐ Other: _____	

FORM 2A IEP Team Data Collection Plan *(continued)*

Domain	Is this an area of need?	Data collection tool	Who will collect data/give input?	Collect by (Date)
Transition (required for students age 16 and older)	☐ Yes ☐ No	☐ Formal assessment (e.g., Brigance Transition Skills Inventory): ___ ☐ Student-driven person-centered planning (e.g., Career interest questionnaire, MAPs, preference assessment): ___ ☐ Teacher-made data sheet for goal: ___ ☐ Ecological assessment or observation in: ___ ☐ Student and/or family interviews ☐ Trial of new support in ___ class: ___ ☐ Other: ___	☐ Student ☐ Family members ☐ Special education teacher ☐ General education teacher ☐ Speech therapist ☐ Occupational therapist ☐ Transition/job coach ☐ Other: ___	
Communication	☐ Yes ☐ No	☐ Formal assessment (e.g., Receptive and Expressive One-Word Picture Vocabulary Test): ___ ☐ Assistive technology evaluation (e.g., WATI): ___ ☐ Teacher-made data sheet for goal: ___ ☐ Ecological assessment or observation in: ___ ☐ Student and/or family interviews ☐ Trial of new support in ___ class: ___ ☐ Other: ___	☐ Student ☐ Family members ☐ Special education teacher ☐ General education teacher ☐ Speech therapist ☐ Other: ___	

FORM 2A **IEP Team Data Collection Plan** (continued)

Domain	Is this an area of need?	Data collection tool	Who will collect data/give input?	Collect by (Date)
Physical and sensory needs (e.g., fine motor, gross motor)	☐ Yes ☐ No	☐ Formal assessment (e.g., Vineland): _____ ☐ Teacher-/therapist-made data sheet for goal: _____ ☐ Ecological assessment or observation in: _____ ☐ Work samples including: _____ _____ ☐ Student and/or family interviews ☐ Trial of new support in _____ class: _____ ☐ Other: _____	☐ Student ☐ Family members ☐ Special education teacher ☐ General education teacher ☐ Physical therapist ☐ Occupational therapist ☐ Adaptive PE/PE coach ☐ Other: _____	
Vision and/or hearing	☐ Yes ☐ No	☐ Formal vision and/or hearing screening ☐ Meeting vision and/or hearing specialist ☐ Trial of new support in _____ class: _____ ☐ Student and/or family interviews	☐ Student ☐ Family members ☐ Special education teacher ☐ General education teacher ☐ Vision specialist ☐ Hearing specialist ☐ Other: _____	
Health care	☐ Yes ☐ No	☐ Review of medical records ☐ Meeting with health care professional ☐ Student and/or family interviews	☐ Student ☐ Family members ☐ Special education teacher ☐ General education teacher ☐ School nurse ☐ Other: _____	

Fostering Collaborative and Trusting Relationships with Families and Students

With Samantha Gross Toews and Jessica A. McQueston

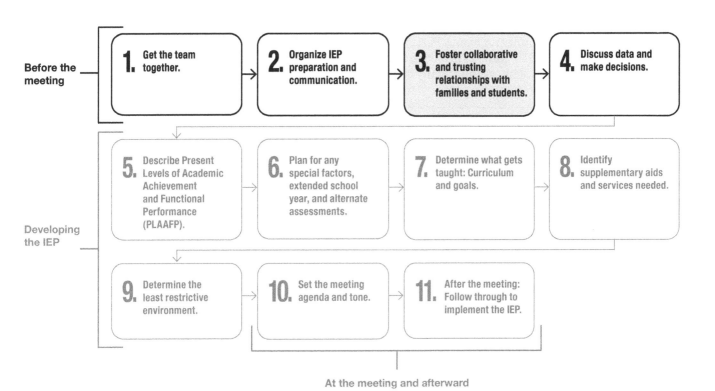

Before the meeting

1. Get the team together.

2. Organize IEP preparation and communication.

3. Foster collaborative and trusting relationships with families and students.

4. Discuss data and make decisions.

Developing the IEP

5. Describe Present Levels of Academic Achievement and Functional Performance (PLAAFP).

6. Plan for any special factors, extended school year, and alternate assessments.

7. Determine what gets taught: Curriculum and goals.

8. Identify supplementary aids and services needed.

9. Determine the least restrictive environment.

10. Set the meeting agenda and tone.

11. After the meeting: Follow through to implement the IEP.

At the meeting and afterward

A Parent's Perspective: Learning to Advocate

Joanne Juhnke, a family member we know, recounts her experiences learning to advocate for her daughter during IEP team meetings:

I remember vividly my first IEP meeting, when my husband and I went nervously in to sit down with a table full of people we didn't know, to embark on a process we didn't understand, on behalf of our just-turned–3-year-old daughter, Miriam, whom we didn't know how to educate. It would be hard to call that first IEP a collaboration. We knew we were supposed to advocate for Miriam, but we were outnumbered and underinformed, and we didn't even know what a "good" IEP in that situation was supposed to look like.

That 3-year-old is now a high school junior, and now we collaborate for real. I've become involved in education and disability advocacy professionally, which has improved our power dynamics. The degree of collaboration versus flailing or confrontation has varied from year to year, though, depending on the approach and willingness of the school folks around the table. When the team is invested in collaboration, parents and school and all, it can be a beautiful thing! I find myself advising parents to keep bringing their love and knowledge of their student to the table, and to keep looking for creative problem-solving possibilities and areas of agreement to build on. And, as Fred Rogers famously said: "Look for the helpers."

–Joanne Juhnke, Mother of Miriam Oakleaf

Families have deep knowledge of their child, and each family is the most important stakeholder in the child's long-term success (Kurth, Ruppar, et al., 2019). Expert special education teachers have been found to collaborate closely with families of students with complex support needs, treating them as valued colleagues (Ruppar et al., 2017). Although families' and school team members' perspectives might not always align, families are, nevertheless, a special educator's most important ally.

Furthermore, research shows that the interventions teachers and other team members use are more likely to be aligned with student needs when their families have collaborated in the design of the program (Chen & Gregory, 2011). When families merely attend the IEP meeting and sign required forms, this is a missed opportunity for teams. Partnering with families includes 1) ensuring families understand their role on the IEP team; 2) involving families in the IEP data collection process as experts on their child's needs; and 3) integrating family input throughout the final IEP.

A Note on Terminology: Families

In this book, we refer to "families" rather than "parents" in acknowledgment that many people take on parenting roles, including grandparents, aunts, uncles, stepfamilies, committed partners, and biological parents, among others. A family consists of two or more people related by birth, marriage, or adoption who reside together *or* who consider one another family (Turnbull et al., 2016).

Many families feel alienated because educators dominate the decision-making process (Vaughn et al., 1988), typically speaking more often than families by a factor of 8:1 (Ruppar & Gaffney, 2011). Consequently, families often feel that decision making during the IEP meeting is much more influenced by educators than by families (Kalyanpur et al., 2000). Families feel that they are merely recipients of information, and their primary role is to agree to and sign IEP documents (Garriott et al., 2000; Love et al., 2017). Families also report being dissatisfied with IEP meetings because they have had negative experiences with educators over many years. As a result, they often report feeling IEP meetings are traumatic, confusing, and complicated (Fish, 2006).

School hierarchies can also be a barrier to family–school partnerships. Often, families feel that educators do not have "power of the purse," and therefore the real decisions are made by administrators who know the student the least (Love et al., 2017). In some cases, this is true. However, consider the perspective of Heather Danser, a special educator in Las Vegas, NV:

> Make it your life mission to really hear their side and validate their concerns. I have at least one [difficult IEP meeting] every year. It works best if administrators are there, so they can be the "bad guy" and you can ally with the parent. This preserves the relationship and helps them to not feel so backed in a corner, or ignorant, or helpless.

Therefore, being strategic as you weigh the parents' or caregivers' concerns with the realities of the school district can help ensure that the school team has a positive relationship with the family. As research shows, this relationship can make or break a student's educational outcomes.

UNDERSTANDING THE COMMITMENT:

Supporting, Advocating for, and Empowering Families and Students

For any student you work with, your top source of expert information is the family and the student themself. Supporting the student and family, advocating for their wants and needs, and empowering them in the decision-making process are at the heart of creating an equitable and inclusive IEP.

1. Think about the family of a student with whom you work. What are their priorities for their student's education? What are their concerns? What strengths and insights do they bring to the planning process?

_____

_____

_____

_____

_____

2. What has the student expressed to you about their own priorities, goals, and hopes for the future? About their concerns and needs? What strengths does the student bring to the planning process?

_____

_____

_____

_____

_____

UNDERSTANDING AND FACILITATING THE ROLE OF FAMILIES

IDEA 2004 requires family participation in IEP teams and approval of all team decisions before the IEP is put into place (20 U.S.C. § 614 (e)). As equal members of IEP teams, families are tasked with providing critical information about students receiving special education services, while partnering with schools to make decisions about those services and how they will be delivered, including goals, supports, and the placement in which the student will receive services (Sec. 300.306I(1)(i)).

Supporting Families to Understand Their Roles

In addition to mandating families co-develop the IEP, IDEA further requires school personnel to ensure meaningful family involvement and active participation in the IEP process (Salas, 2004). Educators must establish clear lines of communication with families and explicitly share expectations for co-development and co-implementation of the IEP well before the IEP meeting. During initial communication with each family, educators should ask them to share their preferred methods of communication. Options may include email, text messaging, in-person conversations, home–school communication notebooks, phone calls, and online meetings. Likewise, expectations about when communication works best for each team member should be shared to avoid any misunderstandings or flawed assumptions, such as assuming the family or educator is choosing not to respond or is too busy to respond. For example, an educator might respond to messages between 3 and 5 p.m. Monday through Friday, whereas families might send messages on Sundays. Note the partners are available at different times; this is perfectly fine, as a message can be sent on Sunday evening and responded to on Monday evening, thus keeping channels of communication open and clear. Conversations about communication preferences should also be mindful of cultural values around schooling and communication with the IEP team (Rossetti et al., 2017), as discussed later in this chapter. Briefly, however, family preferences for communication might vary based on their familiarity with written or spoken English, their immigration status, and cultural norms around how families and school personnel interact. Once the preferred frequency and method of communication for each family has been identified, educators should build these communications into their schedule or calendar to support the development and maintenance of a trusting relationship.

A Parent's Perspective: A Day in the Life

As a parent, I want to do everything I can to support my son, Jose, to grow into a happy adult with friends who is as supported to pursue his dreams and interests. I am extremely grateful to his teachers at school who work hard to teach him important skills, but when it comes to Jose's vocational goals, I have not always agreed with what they focused on. His goals always seem to be about specific tasks like recycling or delivering materials around campus with fewer and fewer prompts needed. I wanted them to work with Jose on advocating for himself by asking for help or more support when needed, but my background is not in education, and I grew up learning to respect the expertise of teachers, so I never said anything about it. That is, until this year! This year Jose's teacher set up a meeting with me to ask me about my goals for him and any suggestions I had. I shared my ideas with her and now Jose has a self-advocacy goal in his IEP. I was nervous to share my ideas, but the teacher made me feel like I was a part of the team.

—Sofia, Parent of Jose

Removing Barriers to Family Participation

At the start of this chapter, we identified several barriers to family involvement, including the tendency of school personnel to dominate meetings and provide limited information to families. These barriers are persistent but not intractable. Some rather simple solutions exist to remove these barriers and improve family–school partnerships.

Communicate Clearly and Frequently   A first key strategy centers on effective, quality communication. Educators should use clear, jargon-free language when communicating with families. Often, jargon and acronyms become second nature to educators. For example, "Jessica needs access to her AAC in all Gen Ed classes with push-in support from the SLP to receive FAPE." This sentence might be perfectly understandable to another special educator but could be completely baffling to somebody unfamiliar with this lingo.

School teams should create a welcoming environment with families, and educators should find ways to learn about the student and family. One step toward this is establishing frequent communication. Home–school communication notebooks can be used for this purpose (see Figures 3.1 and 3.2; full-size, reproducible versions of these forms are available in the appendix to this chapter and on the Brookes Download Hub). Sharing data (see Chapter 4), along with frequent informal meetings and conversations, can also support positive relationships. Too often, educators lead interactions, using meeting time to "tell the family" something rather than learning from the deep knowledge and experiences of families.

Encourage Families to Bring an Ally to Meetings   Usually, family members are outnumbered during meetings, are overwhelmed with information and jargon, and yet are expected to make critical decisions. Inviting families to bring an advocate, a trusted friend, or another ally to meetings can be enormously helpful to families. This friend or advocate can discuss ideas with families, ask questions of all IEP team members, and support families in ensuring their priorities and interests are foregrounded.

Adhere to Mutual Decisions Finally, educators must be trustworthy partners. Families must trust educators to adhere to decisions made during the meeting and documented in the IEP itself. Frequent communication and status updates throughout the year can facilitate this, with meetings focused on problem-solving implementation of the IEP and discussing data with families as educators make educational decisions. Educators must also avoid predetermination—that is, decisions being made outside of the meeting or without the family present. Predetermination is a violation of IDEA and erodes trusting relationships by making families feel their input is not needed or valid.

As team members deeply vested in improving student outcomes and supporting family–school partnerships, educators are encouraged to reflect on their practices regularly, with "gut checks" along the way to ensure family partners feel as supported by the educator as intended. Ask yourself: How would you want families to feel when they are partnering with you to develop and implement plans for students with disabilities? Do families feel:

- They are treated with respect?

- They are treated as equal decision makers?

- They have freedom to discuss topics?

- They have knowledge to discuss topics?

- Their contributions are valued by educators?

- Their contributions are equally considered as other team members'?

- They are welcomed by educators?

In this vein, educators might take steps beyond self-reflection to ensure families they partner with feel empowered and supported. A questionnaire, such as the one shown in Figure 3.3, can be used to get regular feedback from families and allow educators to adjust their approach to better support families. In fact, simply surveying families about their experiences with the IEP process can be viewed as an invitation to partnership and an indicator of educator openness and approachability. (A full-size, reproducible version of this questionnaire is provided in the appendix to this chapter and is available for download on the Brookes Download Hub.)

FORM 3A

Elementary Level Home–School Communication Notebook

Prompt	Response
Today in class, I enjoyed:	
Today in class, we worked on:	
My peer buddy today was:	
At recess, I:	
I used my self-determination, communication, or problem-solving skills today to:	
Today I also did:	☐ Speech ☐ OT ☐ PT ☐ APE ☐ Lunch Bunch ☐ Other
News from my teacher:	
Comments from my team:	
News from home:	
Comments from home:	

Source: Voss, 2000.

Equitable and Inclusive IEPs for Students with Complex Support Needs: A Roadmap by Andrea L. Ruppar and Jennifer A. Kurth. Copyright © 2023 by Paul H. Brookes Publishing Co. All rights reserved. (page 1 of 1)

Figure 3.1. Elementary Level Home–School Communication Notebook. (*Source:* Voss, 2000.)

Improving Family Partnerships

To this point, we have focused on how educators can support the family–school partnership. There are also steps families can employ to improve the partnership, and educators should make sure that families are supported to engage before, during, and after the meeting. Prior to the meeting, some families

FORM 3B

Secondary Level
Home–School Communication Notebook

Class	What I did in class today	Homework	Upcoming tests, long-term assignments
Math			
English			
Science			
Social studies			
Art			
PE			
Today I also did:	☐ Speech ☐ OT ☐ PT	☐ APE ☐ Lunch Bunch	☐ Other:
Lunch/social events today:			

Source: Voss, 2000.

Figure 3.2. Secondary Level Home–School Communication Notebook. (*Source:* Voss, 2000.)

create mini-presentations about their child, and their hopes and dreams for the child to share during the IEP meeting. Families can also be invited to add items to the meeting agenda. They can also commit to being proactive during meetings and to ask questions or make suggestions. Requesting that statements be rephrased, asking for a break to read or think, or asking any question about what is being said or assumed are all key. Finally, families should feel confident in bringing a trusted ally or advocate to any meeting with them who can support the family in listening, asking questions, and rephrasing what educators have said to support the family in making fully informed decisions. Certainly, education team members must be supportive of these strategies and suggest them, as needed, to facilitate family involvement and empowerment. A sample timeline for communicating with families is shown in Figure 3.4.

DIRECTLY INVOLVING FAMILIES IN IEP DEVELOPMENT

The previous sections discussed the family's role in the IEP process and what general practices you can follow to support them in their role and form a strong partnership. The sections that follow present strategies for managing the logistics of involving families directly in developing the IEP. This includes scheduling the meeting with them, gathering information from the family about the student, drafting the agenda and the IEP together, and creating a goal activity matrix after the IEP meeting to help everyone follow through on the decisions you made.

Scheduling the IEP Meeting With Families

Most students with complex support needs have large IEP teams, consisting of families, administrators, special educators, at least one general educator, assessors, and related services providers. Finding a date and time when all team members are available can be a significant challenge and can place an undue burden on families. Most families want nothing more than to support their child's education and growth, but typically IEP meetings are held during working hours. For working families, this puts them in a difficult position of needing to decide to go to work or go to their child's IEP meeting. For many families, attending an IEP meeting means the family is not paid for the hours they missed work, which can have serious consequences for the family finances. Parents could be fired due to frequent absences to care for their child with a disability. Children with disabilities often need medical care and miss school due to illness. Families may lack transportation, child care for other children at home during the IEP meeting, or any number of other factors, which can make attending an IEP meeting difficult or even impossible. In short, a family might not be able to attend the IEP meeting when it is convenient for the school. Difficulty in scheduling an IEP meeting does not reflect a lack of interest on the part of the family. The least dangerous assumption a school team can make about family involvement is that family members want to attend and participate meaningfully but may lack the resources or flexibility to do so.

The Least Dangerous Assumption

The Least Dangerous Assumption states that in the absence of conclusive evidence, educational decisions should be based on assumptions that, if incorrect, would have the least harm for the student or their family (Donnellan, 1984). When applied to families, in the absence of evidence conclusively demonstrating families are disinterested in participating in their child's education or somehow do not care to be involved, the least dangerous assumption is that families are committed, knowledgeable, caring, and seeking to be involved in ways that are feasible for them. Following this principle is important not only in working with students with complex support needs but also in working with their families. It will help you to seek strategies to support families in being involved and advocating for their children, strengthening your capacity for a partnership that can enhance student outcomes. It will further help you to avoid mistaking lack of involvement for lack of care; instead, it will support you to find ways to build on family preferences and needs and enable them to be involved in meetings that are scheduled at times that work well for them and be involved in communicating in ways that match their preferences and timelines.

Legally, school personnel must notify families about the IEP in advance of the date of the IEP meeting and allow families the opportunity to agree on a date. Meeting times and places should be convenient for all IEP team members, including families (IDEA 2004, Sec. 300.322). For example, the IEP meeting could be held at the school, but it could also be held at the family's home. Meetings have been held in even less conventional places, such as a fast-food restaurant during the family's lunch break at work. Meetings might also be held over the phone or by video conference if doing so facilitates family involvement. In sum, school personnel should be flexible in their meeting location to best support meaningful and thorough family involvement. Privacy and distractions should be considered when selecting meeting locations, ensuring that all team members feel comfortable speaking in the location and that they will not be interrupted or distracted.

School personnel must also allocate enough time to conduct an IEP meeting so that families do not feel rushed or uncomfortable. Triennial evaluations, in which major assessments are discussed, require more time than annual reviews, which in turn will usually require more time than IEP amendment meetings. Likewise, school personnel must ensure all team members are present at the scheduled IEP meeting.

FORM 3C   **Family Survey**

For the following questions, please answer according to your experiences with this IEP meeting only. Please rate your level of agreement with each statement using the following scale:

Rating	1	2	3	4	5
	Strongly Disagree	Disagree	Neither Agree nor Disagree	Agree	Strongly Agree
I understand the reason for having the IEP meeting.					
I talked frequently during the IEP meeting.					
I understood what was said (including school terminology) in the meeting.					
I helped make decisions in the IEP meeting.					
I was able to contribute to my child's IEP.					
My contributions were valued by other IEP team members.					
I felt welcomed as an IEP team member.					
I felt informed/prepared for the IEP meeting.					
I am satisfied with the outcome of the IEP meeting.					

From Jones, B. A., & Gansle, K. A. (2010). The effects of a mini-conference, socioeconomic status, and parent education on perceived and actual parent participation in individual education program meetings. *Research in the Schools, 17*(2), 23–28; adapted by permission.

Equitable and Inclusive IEPs for Students with Complex Support Needs: A Roadmap by Andrea L. Ruppar and Jennifer A. Kurth.
Copyright © 2023 by Paul H. Brookes Publishing Co. All rights reserved.   (page 1 of 1)

Figure 3.3. Sample Family Survey. (From Jones, B. A., & Gansle, K. A. [2010]. The effects of a mini-conference, socioeconomic status, and parent education on perceived and actual parent participation in individual education program meetings. *Research in the Schools, 17*(2), 23–28; adapted by permission.)

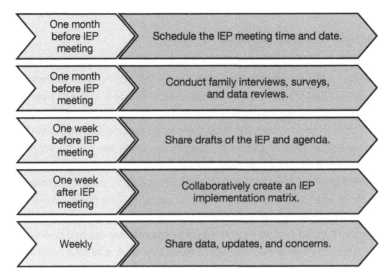

Figure 3.4.   Timeline for communicating with families.

All IEP team members should attend the duration of the IEP meeting. In specific circumstances, an IEP team member can be excused from all or part of the IEP meeting. If a team member's area of expertise *is not* going to be discussed or modified, they may be excused from all or part of the meeting if the family and the school both agree in writing that the team member's attendance is not necessary. If the team member's area of expertise *is* going to be discussed or modified, a required team member may be excused if the following conditions are met:

1. The family, in writing, and the school consent to the excusal.

2. The team member submits written input into the development of the IEP prior to the meeting, and this input is considered by the family and school team during the meeting.

Partially missed meetings result in incomplete information being shared, and also send the message to the family that their child is not a priority for the team member. Overall, the IEP team is expected to act in the best interest of the child. Therefore, if inadequate time has been allocated to a meeting, if team members are not present who would be needed to act in the best interest of the student, or other issues arise, the IEP team may reconvene the meeting again at another time, extend the length of the meeting, or request that the meeting be rescheduled (Assistance to States for the Education of Children With Disabilities, 71 Fed. Reg. at 46676).

Conducting Pre-IEP Surveys, Interviews, and Data Reviews

Approximately 1 month before the planned IEP date, educators should reach out to the family and student to begin discussing priorities for the new IEP using a person-centered approach. Person-centered planning involves bringing together a collaborative team of family members, educators, friends, and the student themselves to design goal-oriented, individualized programs that are focused on community presence, community participation, positive relationships, respect, and competence (Claes et al., 2010). Part of a person-centered approach to IEP planning involves interviewing or otherwise communicating with key stakeholders about their goals (long- and short-term), dreams, and nightmares for the student (O'Brien & O'Brien, 2002). In doing so, the entire team is better aware of the dreams, hopes, and priorities of the family and student to strive for, as well as the nightmares to avoid. Educators should ensure they respect family communication preferences when planning these important discussions. For example, some families may prefer to meet in-person for a discussion while others may prefer to fill out a written survey. Gaining valuable information about family goals and desires for their child's educational program early in the IEP planning process will allow the IEP team to consider

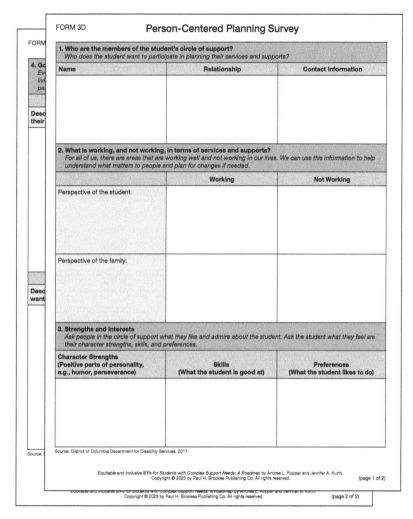

Figure 3.5. Person-Centered Planning Survey. (*Source:* District of Columbia Department for Disability Services, 2017.)

these requests from the beginning. A sample person-centered planning survey is shown in Figure 3.5. (A full-size, reproducible version of this survey is provided in the appendix to this chapter and is available for download on the Brookes Download Hub.)

As noted in Chapter 4, families, and students themselves, collect student progress data throughout the school year, and these data are reviewed regularly to make instructional decisions. In the weeks leading up to an IEP meeting, data from all team members should be compiled and shared with all team members so all participants have equal information with which to make decisions when drafting and finalizing the next IEP.

Co-drafting the Agenda and IEP

With a robust set of information gathered from a review of data and person-centered planning information, teams should co-construct an IEP meeting agenda and draft the IEP at least one week prior to the IEP meeting. As noted previously, this must be done with care to avoid predetermination. As a reminder, predetermination is a serious procedural violation of IDEA, often resulting in mediation and due process while also sabotaging family–school partnerships. Predetermination occurs when school personnel make, or appear to make, decisions about IEP content outside of the meeting. Predetermination occurs when school personnel make unilateral decisions prior to an IEP meeting. Making few or no substantial changes from a draft to final IEP is a clear example of predetermination because it documents that families had very little or no input in the final draft.

However, some planning is needed ahead of the meeting. One option is to send a draft of the proposed IEP for the family to review prior to the meeting. This is often done with the intent to allow families to get a sense of what the school team is thinking and be prepared to discuss the IEP in more detail. Many parents may also request an IEP in advance of the meeting, and such requests should be accommodated. There are also drawbacks to sending home a draft IEP ahead of a meeting. First, it can unintentionally send a message to the family that their input is unimportant—they are expected to show up and agree to what was drafted, or at best, tinker with what the school has proposed versus discussing their own goals, services, and supports in collaboration with other IEP team members. IEP drafts can also imply that decisions about the IEP have been made prior to the IEP meeting, limiting the discussion to what the team has already thought about and minimizing substantive family input.

As an alternative to a draft IEP, educators and families can share data in advance of the meeting and communicate how each are interpreting that data, as well as what each team member thinks the data means in terms of progress and needs for the next year. Using these data, each team member should indicate their agreement that a goal or service is needed for the skill. If a team member believes a goal or service is needed, they should provide a draft and share it with all other team members. Online collaboration tools, such as Google docs, can be very useful for this task. A sample document is shown in Figure 3.6. (A full-size, reproducible version of this survey is available in the appendix to this chapter and on the Brookes Download Hub.) Similarly, educators could request that families share their input orally to be recorded and incorporated into the IEP. When discussing the draft IEP goals, services, and supports, it is important to solicit true drafts and encourage out-of-the-box thinking. Ask team members for their most creative or flexible ideas, and do not insist that they provide measurable, objective, or other technically adequate statements (as discussed in Section II). The idea here is to brainstorm; goals, services, and supports that are agreed upon by all team members following this brainstorming activity and reviewed at the IEP meeting can be made technically correct at that time.

Educators should similarly solicit co-creation of the meeting agenda. An agenda is a valuable tool to ensure all necessary content is covered and that enough time is allocated for the meeting. All team members whom families and school personnel expect to be in attendance should be noted on the agenda, as well as what each team member wants to discuss or their role in the meeting (e.g., family ally). This simple act supports each team member in knowing what to expect and to ensure their required or desired team members are present. Adequate time for discussion should be allocated for the full agenda, recognizing that by co-drafting the IEP ahead of time, less time will need to be used to share reports, data, and proposed goals and services. Instead, discussion can focus on finalizing the specifics of each. A sample agenda is shown in Figure 3.7.

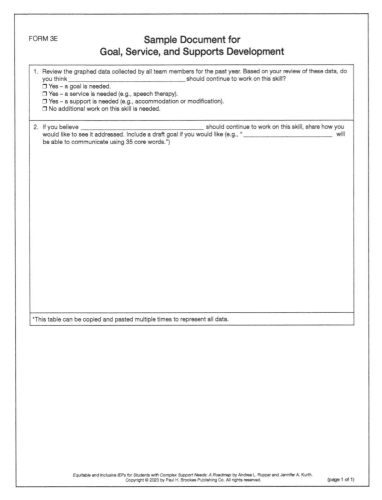

FORM 3E

**Sample Document for
Goal, Service, and Supports Development**

1. Review the graphed data collected by all team members for the past year. Based on your review of these data, do you think _____ should continue to work on this skill?
   ❏ Yes – a goal is needed.
   ❏ Yes – a service is needed (e.g., speech therapy).
   ❏ Yes – a support is needed (e.g., accommodation or modification).
   ❏ No additional work on this skill is needed.

2. If you believe _____ should continue to work on this skill, share how you would like to see it addressed. Include a draft goal if you would like (e.g., "_____ will be able to communicate using 35 core words.")

*This table can be copied and pasted multiple times to represent all data.

Figure 3.6. Sample Google Document for Goal, Service, and Supports Development.

1. Introductions
2. Review purpose of the IEP meeting
3. Review and agree to the agenda
4. Discuss likely length of meeting and confirm if any team member will miss part or all of the meeting
5. Family and student discussion of priorities and preferences for upcoming IEP
6. Review data from previous IEP
7. Review assessment results
8. Review proposed present levels statements from all team members
9. Review proposed IEP goals from all team members
10. Review proposed services and accommodations from all team members
    a. Related services
    b. Supplementary aids and services
    c. Extended school year
    d. Transportation
    e. Assistive technology
    f. Accommodations and modifications
11. Discuss placement options that ensure student free and appropriate public education in the least restrictive environment
12. Determine placement for special education services
13. Review and approve minutes
14. Signatures
15. Plan for next meeting (date, time, content)

Figure 3.7. Sample IEP meeting agenda.

This is also an important checkpoint for the school-based members of the IEP team to ensure their communications with families, both written and verbal, are respectful of how the family communicates. Many families speak a language other than English as their preferred or only language, and school–family communications must acknowledge this and seek the support of translators and interpreters as needed. Interpreters translate spoken language in real time, whereas translators interpret written text. In partnering with families who do not communicate in English, the services of both will be needed. For example, a translator will provide data, summary statements, and proposed IEP language to families. An interpreter will be available for phone, online, or in-person meetings with families to discuss IEP content and progress updates. A variety of certified translation and interpretation services are available for hire by schools; these services might be especially necessary for families who speak languages or dialects that are uncommon in their community. We will revisit the issue of translators and interpreters later in this chapter.

Co-developing a Goal Activity Matrix After the IEP Meeting

Family–school partnership does not end after the IEP has been signed. After the IEP meeting, the team works together to plan how to embed supports, goal-related teaching, and practice into everyday instruction. Years of educational research indicates that students learn new skills and content best when teaching and practice opportunities are embedded into natural environments and routines rather than taught in isolation (Johnson et al., 2004). For example, a teacher might find 15 times throughout the school day to point out a small quantity of items and discuss their quantity. This practice has been shown to lead to better generalization and maintenance of learned skills (Polychronis et al., 2004) and is more likely to be generalized and mastered than embedded instruction. Students are also more likely to master skills when they are supported to use them across a variety of settings. For this reason, it is beneficial for the IEP team to continue to collaborate after the IEP meeting to design opportunities for the student to work toward their goals throughout the school day, at home, and in their community (Hanreddy, 2021).

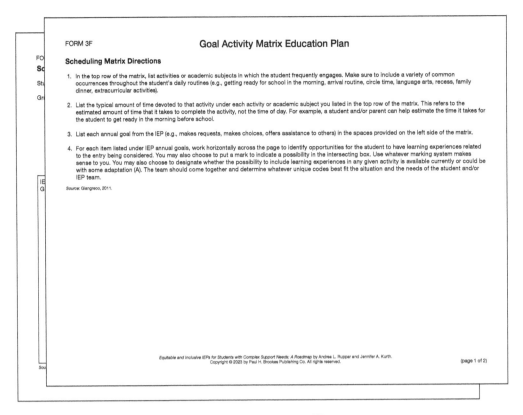

Figure 3.8.   Goal Activity Matrix Education Plan. (*Source:* Giangreco, 2011.)

One way to plan opportunities for goal practice and instruction is a goal activity matrix. This planning form can guide a discussion between family members and educators on how they can support student goal acquisition in school, home, and community settings. Figure 3.8 provides an example of a goal activity matrix. (A full-size, reproducible version is included in the appendix to this chapter and on the Brookes Download Hub.) Educators should consider drafting their plan for how to address each goal before setting up a meeting with the family to discuss the implementation plan and ways the family may be able to work on the goals at home. This meeting provides an opportunity for the team to open their line of communication surrounding IEP implementation from day one.

As we conclude this section of the chapter, we acknowledge that many myths and misunderstandings persist about families and their involvement in the IEP meeting and implementation. Some of these are noted in Table 3.1. Can you think of other myths and facts?

CULTURE AND CROSS-CULTURAL COMMUNICATION

Families from culturally and linguistically diverse backgrounds face additional barriers to their partnership with schools (Love et al., 2017). These barriers can include lack of access to adequate translation and interpretation services (Cheatham, 2011), school personnel use of deficit perspectives towards diverse families (Lalvani, 2012), and a lack of cultural responsiveness among school personnel (Harry, 2008). As such, considering cultural and cross-cultural communication when developing IEPs is crucial for educators. Infusing cultural competence is more than checking a box; it depends on creating authentic bonds and development of ongoing partnerships with families. Developing partnerships is more than establishing contact. All members of the IEP team should be collaborating with families in relation to goals, supplementary aids and services, and other IEP decisions before, during, and after IEP meetings.

Table 3.1. Individualized education program (IEP) team myth and fact

Myth	Fact
The family can be "out-voted" by other members of the IEP team when making decisions.	The IEP team is not a democracy; there is no majority rules when it comes to making decisions. Consensus decisions are required instead.
A family who brings an advocate to an IEP meeting is upset and likely difficult to work with.	An advocate is a great resource for families to assist in gathering and sharing information. Bringing an advocate only means that the family is interested in participating to the best of their ability.
Sending a draft of the IEP home for families to review ahead of the meeting is a useful strategy to facilitate participation.	Sending home a draft of the IEP, written by school personnel, can be an indication of predetermination of decisions. Be sure to invite family input before sending a draft IEP.
The best way for families to participate in the IEP meeting and document is for them to report their needs and concerns in the "parent input" section of the IEP.	Families should contribute to every component of the IEP in a substantial way; the "parent input" section of an IEP is simply a summary of the family's concerns and priorities.
Families are not responsible for implementing the IEP.	Skill development is enhanced when students practice skills across home, school, and community settings, making families valuable partners in teaching skills.

Defining Culture

Many of us may have grown up thinking culture was just reflected in the food we ate, holidays we celebrated, and clothing we wore. While these characteristics are observable, these are not the only form of culture we experience. In fact, as Hammond (2014) says, "Culture . . . is the way that every brain makes sense of the world. That is why everyone, regardless of race or ethnicity, has a culture" (p. 22). Hammond refers to three levels of our culture tree—surface, shallow, and deep. Surface-level culture includes observable things like hairstyles, talking styles, food, music, clothing, and holidays. Shallow culture contains unspoken rules, such as nonverbal communication, social interactions, ways of handling emotions, and eye contact. Deep culture centers around the norms and beliefs of the larger group.

Relationship building is part of culture, and educators must work to understand the unique culture and background of each student and their family. In doing so, cultural insensitivities and misunderstandings can be avoided. For example, in mainstream Western culture, eye contact is considered an important way to establish a bond between a speaker and a listener. Use of eye contact is not only deemed appropriate but is desired. However, eye contact is thought to be disrespectful and rude in many cultures, including some Hispanic, Middle Eastern, Asian, and Native American cultures. Without this understanding, a white teacher may be frustrated that their student does not maintain eye contact during conversation and seek to provide an intervention to teach eye contact. This intervention could be considered inappropriate or unnecessary by the family. However, the same family may come from a culture in which educators are honored and respected, making them unlikely to disagree with the recommendation of an educator out of concern of being disrespectful to school personnel. As a consequence, the teacher will inadvertently teach the student a skill that is considered rude or inappropriate by other members of the student's family and larger cultural heritage.

Funds of Knowledge

"Funds of knowledge" refers to the knowledge and expertise that students and their family members have due to their membership in families, communities, and cultures. Educators should consider their own cultural beliefs and assumptions in interactions with others, including families. When educators challenge their own assumptions about other cultures, identities, and individuals, it becomes easier to recognize the expertise that others bring to the IEP table. On IEP teams, educators are sometimes implicitly positioned as "experts," and do most of the talking during meetings (Ruppar & Gaffney, 2011). However, most school staff have known the student for far less time than the family. The family and student themselves should be treated as experts in this situation. Truly valuing family input helps develop collaborative and trusting relationships and discussions. Allying with the student and family is the most important thing an educator can do to facilitate positive IEP outcomes.

Strategies to Build Relationships With Culturally and Linguistically Diverse Families

Given the importance of establishing positive, productive, and trusting relationships between school personnel and families, efforts must be made to create and sustain these relationships with culturally and linguistically diverse families. In this section, we describe two such strategies: working with translators and interpreters and completing home visits.

Working With Translators and Interpreters   The use of complex terms in meetings and in documents causes significant difficulty and stress for families (Jegatheesan, 2009). Families with limited English language proficiency, however, face even greater obstacles. Interpreters, too, might lack adequate background knowledge of special education processes and terms to result in good experiences for family members, leading them to skip important information or summarize them briefly. This obviously results in confusion and can break down trust and understanding among all involved.

Other times, cultural considerations are not adequately addressed by interpreters and translators. For example, the use of "はい" by Japanese speakers is a well-documented source of misunderstanding. Pronounced "hai" and typically assumed to mean "yes," the term can also mean "I understand" or "I am listening" (Cheatham, 2011). A Japanese parent might use "はい" to indicate they understand a recommendation, and not that they agree. In fact, "I disagree" might be considered rude for a Japanese parent to say during an interaction with a teacher. However, an interpreter who is unaware of these cultural considerations could misinterpret the family, leading to a significant family–educator misunderstanding and result in the family's inability to be fully informed and provide consent for their child's IEP services.

To avoid these concerns, professional interpreters should be used whenever possible. School personnel can also support quality interpretation and translation services by doing the following:

- Providing adequate time for the translator or interpreter to prepare for meetings (e.g., reviewing previous IEP documents and proposed IEP drafts)

- Preparing the translator or interpreter ahead of time to ask for clarification as needed and to learn technical terms

- Providing time for the family and interpreter to meet and establish rapport

- Introducing team members to the interpreter

- Clarifying that everything that is said by anyone is interpreted

- Speaking directly to the family, not to the interpreter

- Speaking in short segments and pausing for interpretation.

- Avoiding idioms (e.g., "the cat's out of the bag")

- Considering connecting families to members of their own community who also have children with disabilities

Home Visits   One way to begin to understand the culture and embrace the funds of knowledge each family offers is by completing visits to the homes of students. Home visits allow educators to see the everyday family context, child engagement, parent/family engagement, and parent/family competence and confidence (Keilty, 2008). There are many advantages to home visits; however, there are several considerations before starting this process. First, before completing a home visit, school personnel should determine if their school district has policies about home visits. A school district may require two staff members to go together or may not allow home visits at all. Asking colleagues who have been at the school for several years may also be an additional source for useful information about home visits. A quick email or text to a colleague saying you are leaving one home and heading to another ensures that someone knows your whereabouts.

Secondly, consider the needs of the families during this process. The purpose and benefits of home visits should be clearly communicated before families agree to a visit. If families do not want you to visit their home or do not have a stable home, meeting in a public place (e.g., park) or via online meeting platforms (e.g., Zoom) offers some of the same benefits as a physical home visit in terms of establishing rapport and understanding the family's culture. When offering times for a home visit, offer several times in the evening or weekends as it may work better for families and students. Upon arrival at the family home, respect any cultural norms or preferences of the house. In many households, taking shoes off before entering or immediately upon entering is expected. If you are unsure, ask if the family has a preference or look to see how other members of the household are responding.

Lastly, consider your own needs during this process. Visiting the homes of students is not something everyone is used to. If you are unsure about making a home visit, it might be helpful to understand and work through any feelings or doubts. Finding a mentor or partner to begin this process with may help with feeling more confident while planning and completing home visits. Connecting with families and establishing a partnership is the most important part of home visits, meaning "home visits" can occur anywhere. We offer six tips for educators to consider in Figure 3.9, along with questions to ask yourself in Figure 3.10.

CONCLUDING THOUGHTS: PARTNERING WITH FAMILIES

Throughout this chapter, we have emphasized the importance of family–school partnership in enhancing student learning and developmental outcomes. The cultural funds of knowledge of families must be considered in these partnerships, and efforts must be made by school personnel to reflect on their

---

- *Consider the reasons for the home visit. Ask yourself, "Why do I want to do home visits?"* Thinking about what you hope to gain from doing home visits is important. Do you want to improve family partnerships? Maybe you want to discuss generalization of skills with the family. Understanding the reason why you want to do home visits is the first step.
- *Is there someone at my school or district who can mentor me while I make my first home visit? If not, where can I get additional support and guidance to implement home visits in my practice?* If you did not complete a home visit during your teacher preparation program or from previous experiences, ask someone to help you. Connecting with teachers via social media who do home visits is a way to expand your network and find a mentor. Think about the local context and community if you are new to the district. Make sure you know the history of home visits in the local context.
- *Check the policies at your school and district.* Consult the policies of your district and check in with your administrators to see if there are policies about home visits. Policies may include taking an additional staff member, sharing the schedule with administrators, or may even forbid the practice. Know the policies completely before beginning this practice.
- *Do I feel comfortable going to the homes of my students?* Home visits can be an asset to school and family partnerships, but it is also important to consider your comfort level. If you are uncomfortable, consider meeting in a public place, virtually, or shadowing another staff member as they do a home visit to build up your confidence.
- *Do I need to ask about the accessibility of the home?* You know your body and its needs the best. Be sure to plan for and ask about any accessibility accommodations you may need to complete the home visit. For example, it is okay to ask if there are elevators to an apartment or a ramp to a home. Knowing this ahead of time lets you plan accordingly.
- *What are the school resources, community resources, or reporting obligations after the home visit?* During home visits, you may visit a family who could benefit from additional community or school resources. Know what resources (e.g., food, housing) are in your local community and what resources your school or district can help with. Although not as likely, you may witness neglect or abuse in the home. If so, be sure to follow the reporting obligations of your district or state. Consider what supports you may need if you are witness to neglect or abuse.

Figure 3.9. Considerations in a home visit.

Ask Yourself!
Consider the following questions as you approach partnering with families.

- Have you ensured parent, family, and student input is included in all aspects of the IEP? Is this a collaborative process from the beginning?

- Have you asked families, including the student, what information, preferences, and priorities (including what is happening at home) that they would like to share prior to the meeting?

- What considerations have you made to address cultural diversity and include families as members of the IEP team?

- Are you acting as an ally for families?

- Are you supporting families and educating them on their individual rights? Are you working as an advocate for and with the families?

- Do you consider families and students as equal stakeholders and collaborative members in decision making during the IEP process?

Figure 3.10. Questions to ask yourself about partnering with families.

practices to best understand how their behaviors welcome, or rebuff, families. Consider these questions and how values around partnership can be enacted and made visible to others.

REVIEWING THE COMMITMENT:

Supporting, Advocating for, and Empowering Families and Students

This chapter discussed the importance of building a strong relationship with families and making the family, and the student, true partners in creating the IEP. Now, think back to the student and family you identified at the beginning of the chapter.

What barriers or challenges exist that the IEP team must consider to facilitate the family's involvement in the process? (For example, scheduling challenges, language or cultural barriers, past experiences that weakened the school–family partnership.)

_____

_____

_____

_____

_____

_____

Are there other changes you could make to build a stronger partnership with this family? If so, jot down ideas here.

_____

_____

_____

_____

_____

_____

ACTING ON THE COMMITMENT:

Supporting, Advocating for, and Empowering Families and Students

This chapter provides several resources for you to use to gather input from the families of the students with whom you work:

Full-size, reproducible copies are included in the appendix at the end of the chapter and are also available at the Brookes Download Hub with the other downloadable resources for this book. Take a moment now to gather the resources you want to use and plan how you will share them with families.

Resources for Communicating with Families

1. Elementary Level Home–School Communication Notebook 47

2. Secondary Level Home–School Communication Notebook 48

3. Family Survey 49

4. Person-Centered Planning Survey. 50

5. Sample Document for Goal, Service, and Supports Development 52

6. Goal Activity Matrix Education Plan 53

Elementary Level
Home–School Communication Notebook

Prompt	Response	
Today in class, I enjoyed:		
Today in class, we worked on:		
My peer buddy today was:		
At recess, I:		
I used my self-determination, communication, or problem-solving skills today to:		
Today I also did:	❒ Speech ❒ OT ❒ PT	❒ APE ❒ Lunch Bunch ❒ Other
News from my teacher:		
Comments from my team:		
News from home:		
Comments from home:		

Source: Voss, 2000.

Secondary Level
Home–School Communication Notebook

Class	What I did in class today	Homework	Upcoming tests, long-term assignments
Math			
English			
Science			
Social studies			
Art			
PE			
Today I also did:	❒ Speech ❒ OT ❒ PT	❒ APE ❒ Lunch Bunch	❒ Other:
Lunch/social events today:			

Source: Voss, 2000.

Family Survey

For the following questions, please answer according to your experiences with this IEP meeting only. Please rate your level of agreement with each statement using the following scale:					
Rating	**1**	**2**	**3**	**4**	**5**
	Strongly Disagree	**Disagree**	**Neither Agree nor Disagree**	**Agree**	**Strongly Agree**
I understand the reason for having the IEP meeting.					
I talked frequently during the IEP meeting.					
I understood what was said (including school terminology) in the meeting.					
I helped make decisions in the IEP meeting.					
I was able to contribute to my child's IEP.					
My contributions were valued by other IEP team members.					
I felt welcomed as an IEP team member.					
I felt informed/prepared for the IEP meeting.					
I am satisfied with the outcome of the IEP meeting.					

From Jones, B. A., & Gansle, K. A. (2010). The effects of a mini-conference, socioeconomic status, and parent education on perceived and actual parent participation in individual education program meetings. *Research in the Schools, 17*(2), 23-28; adapted by permission.

Person-Centered Planning Survey

1. Who are the members of the student's circle of support?		
Who does the student want to participate in planning their services and supports?		
Name	**Relationship**	**Contact Information**

2. What is working, and not working, in terms of services and supports?
For all of us, there are areas that are working well and not working in our lives. We can use this information to help understand what matters to people and plan for changes if needed.

	Working	**Not Working**
Perspective of the student:		
Perspective of the family:		

3. Strengths and Interests
Ask people in the circle of support what they like and admire about the student. Ask the student what they feel are their character strengths, skills, and preferences.

Character Strengths (Positive parts of personality, e.g., humor, perseverance)	**Skills (What the student is good at)**	**Preferences (What the student likes to do)**

Source: District of Columbia Department for Disability Services, 2017.

4. Goals and Preferences
Everyone wants a good life. Find out what a good life means to the student, and what they don't want. For example, living in your own home, having a good job, and having a healthy relationship with a significant other might be how a person defines a good life.

Vision for a Good Life		
Describe what the student wants their "good life" to be like:	**Perspective of the Family (if applicable)**	**Perspective of the Circle of Support (if applicable)**

What the Student Does Not Want		
Describe what the student does not want in their overall life:	**Perspective of the Family (if applicable)**	**Perspective of the Circle of Support (if applicable)**

Source: District of Columbia Department for Disability Services, 2017.

Sample Document for
Goal, Service, and Supports Development

1. Review the graphed data collected by all team members for the past year. Based on your review of these data, do you think _____ should continue to work on this skill? ❐ Yes – a goal is needed. ❐ Yes – a service is needed (e.g., speech therapy). ❐ Yes – a support is needed (e.g., accommodation or modification). ❐ No additional work on this skill is needed.	
2. If you believe _____ should continue to work on this skill, share how you would like to see it addressed. Include a draft goal if you would like (e.g., "_____ will be able to communicate using 35 core words.")	
*This table can be copied and pasted multiple times to represent all data.	

Goal Activity Matrix Education Plan

Scheduling Matrix Directions

1. In the top row of the matrix, list activities or academic subjects in which the student frequently engages. Make sure to include a variety of common occurrences throughout the student's daily routines (e.g., getting ready for school in the morning, arrival routine, circle time, language arts, recess, family dinner, extracurricular activities).

2. List the typical amount of time devoted to that activity under each activity or academic subject you listed in the top row of the matrix. This refers to the estimated amount of time that it takes to complete the activity, not the time of day. For example, a student and/or parent can help estimate the time it takes for the student to get ready in the morning before school.

3. List each annual goal from the IEP (e.g., makes requests, makes choices, offers assistance to others) in the spaces provided on the left side of the matrix.

4. For each item listed under IEP annual goals, work horizontally across the page to identify opportunities for the student to have learning experiences related to the entry being considered. You may also choose to put a mark to indicate a possibility in the intersecting box. Use whatever marking system makes sense to you. You may also choose to designate whether the possibility to include learning experiences in any given activity is available currently or could be with some adaptation (A). The team should come together and determine whatever unique codes best fit the situation and the needs of the student and/or IEP team.

Source: Giangreco, 2011.

Equitable and Inclusive IEPs for Students with Complex Support Needs: A Roadmap by Andrea L. Ruppar and Jennifer A. Kurth.

FORM 3F Goal Activity Matrix Education Plan (continued)

Scheduling Matrix

Student Name: _____

Grade: _____

Class Activities

Minutes											

IEP Annual Goals								

Source: Giangreco, 2011.

Equitable and Inclusive IEPs for Students with Complex Support Needs: A Roadmap by Andrea L. Ruppar and Jennifer A. Kurth.

Discussing Data
and Making Decisions

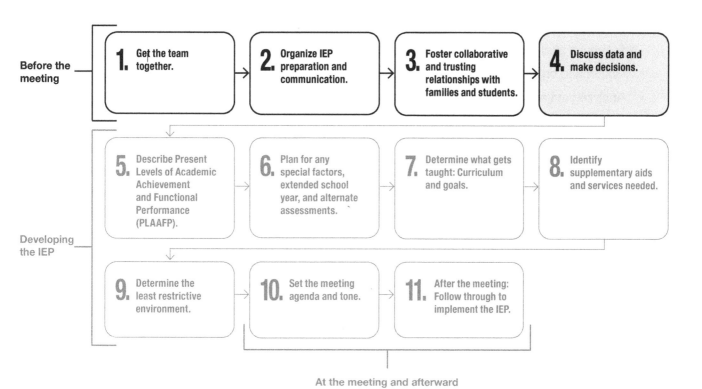

Before the meeting

1. Get the team together.

2. Organize IEP preparation and communication.

3. Foster collaborative and trusting relationships with families and students.

4. Discuss data and make decisions.

Developing the IEP

5. Describe Present Levels of Academic Achievement and Functional Performance (PLAAFP).

6. Plan for any special factors, extended school year, and alternate assessments.

7. Determine what gets taught: Curriculum and goals.

8. Identify supplementary aids and services needed.

9. Determine the least restrictive environment.

10. Set the meeting agenda and tone.

11. After the meeting: Follow through to implement the IEP.

At the meeting and afterward

Improving student outcomes and promoting student achievement are important goals for all teachers, including special education teachers. The increased focus on accountability mandated by the No Child Left Behind Act (NCLB) of 2001 (PL 107-110), now known as the Every Student Succeeds Act (ESSA) of 2015 (PL 114-95), only reinforce these notions. Further, the IDEA 2004 stipulates students with disabilities must have IEP goals written for each area of need, with progress monitoring completed to enable effective reporting and monitoring of progress toward these goals. However, many special education teachers lack the tools needed to determine if students are making adequate progress in their learning. Consequently, teachers often rely on vague notions of "knowing a student" to make instructional decisions (Grigg et al., 1989). What teachers do know about data collection was usually learned in their teacher preparation programs, which often did not include instruction in how to make data-based decisions (Jimenez et al., 2012). As articulated by Jimenez and colleagues (2012), data-based decisions are defined as a teacher using student performance data to make instructional decisions.

Research demonstrates that when teachers collect and analyze data, student performance improves (Shapiro et al., 2016). Further, students make *more progress* when teachers follow decision-making guidelines when reviewing data (Browder et al., 1989). Data-based decision guidelines have been well researched, with findings consistently demonstrating students make improved progress when teachers follow these guidelines (e.g., Belfiore & Browder, 1992; Browder et al., 1989; Jimenez et al., 2012). For example, most recently Jimenez and colleagues found teachers learned data-based instructional guidelines in an online professional development setting and were able to identify data patterns and use them to make data-based decisions. Others have found pre-service teachers can use these guidelines effectively (e.g., Browder et al., 1986) as can in-service teachers (Browder et al., 2005).

UNDERSTANDING THE COMMITMENT: *Making Decisions Based on Data*

Decisions about a student's education should not be based solely on your impressions of the student, or on what teaching practices are currently in vogue or easiest to implement. To make sound decisions for your student, you will need to collect and analyze progress monitoring data.

Think about a student with whom you work. What questions or concerns do you have about how to

- Gather and organize relevant data about this student?

- Analyze data and identify patterns?

- Use what you have determined to make good decisions for this student?

_____

_____

_____

_____

_____

_____

_____

_____

_____

_____

_____

_____

WHAT IS DATA?

Education data are facts and figures that are collected for analysis by educators to guide instruction, evaluate student progress, and are used to make decisions about student progress. All types of data are collected about students, including attendance, assessment scores, homework completion, grades, and tests, among others. For IEP teams, data are essential for understanding the student's current performance and are used as a benchmark to evaluate progress. Data collection is therefore the systematic approach of measuring and gathering information. To obtain useful data, learning objectives must be measurable and objective; in making them so, it is clear what data should be collected and how those data will inform student progress. Consider the following example: "By the end of the school year, Jesse will type a passage of text at a speed of 20 correct words per minute with no more than 5 errors, with progress measured on a two-minute timed test." In this goal, it is clear what Jesse is expected to do (type 20 words), what data will be needed to evaluate progress on the goal (number of words typed correctly), and how these data will be obtained (a timed test).

Avoid Pseudo-data

In reporting data or developing goals, teams can inadvertently use pseudo-data. Pseudo-data are pieces of information presented as data, but which are in fact not measurable or objective (Ruppar et al., 2019) and/or are not relevant. A hallmark of pseudo-data is a lack of context with which to interpret the information presented. For example, a team might report a student can "engage in a reciprocal social exchange", yet it remains unclear under what conditions that skill is demonstrated. In this example, measurable and objective data are reported, but the contextual information is missing that explains how and when the skill is demonstrated. Similarly, pseudo-data may include information about student dispositions; for example, "Tom can be stubborn and will do what he wants." Or "James is a friendly, happy child." These are not measurable and objective data but are reported as facts that would presumably guide team decisions. Finally, Ruppar and colleagues (2019) describe how adult supports can be presented as data, such as, "She requires maximum assistance to complete all activities." This statement reports the behaviors of the professional, rather than the student, and is therefore pseudo-data.

Commit to Strengths-Based Data Collection

Throughout this book, we have emphasized the importance of developing strengths-based, inclusive IEPs. Data collection is an important component to ensuring students that this type of IEP is developed. Before we discuss types of data, we first consider how data are used and how these data can position students.

As will be discussed in Chapter 5, baseline, assessment, and progress monitoring data are used to develop Present Levels of Academic Achievement and Functional Performance (PLAAFP) statements about students. These statements tell a narrative about students and can position them as a capable or incapable learner. The type of data reported in the PLAAFP also suggests the types of data to be collected to monitor student progress in achieving IEP and curricular goals; this alignment across sections of the IEP is essential for development of a logical and meaningful IEP. The data collected and reported in the PLAAFP also dictate IEP implementation: data on present levels forecast goals, which in turn forecast instructional strategies and progress monitoring decision making across the school year.

Data are consequential in determining not only how IEPs are developed and implemented, but also how students are positioned. Data can highlight student deficits or can position students as innovative and resourceful people who positively affect their own lives. Therefore, when deciding what skills or behaviors to take data on, as well as what type of data to collect, IEP teams should check that the data collection process seeks strengths and interests and reflects student priorities.

FORMS OF DATA: QUANTITATIVE AND QUALITATIVE

Data collection can and should occur in many different formats. Quantitative data reveal information on discrete student skills by quantifying information. Quantitative data answer questions like, "How much?" "How often?" and "How accurately?" These questions can be answered with numbers. This information may include

- Frequency with which a student performs a task (e.g., uses an AAC device to make a comment, enters a classroom, and gets out the appropriate materials independently)

- Accuracy (e.g., number of sight words student reads independently, number of oral vocabulary words student uses)

- Percentages (e.g., percent steps completed independently in specified multi-step tasks, rate of accuracy responding to comprehension questions)

- Standardized assessment results.

These data support the IEP team to gain a basic understanding of skills the student has mastered, emerging skills, and areas of challenge.

Although quantitative data can be useful for understanding a student's skills and needs for support, qualitative data provide rich descriptions of characteristics, settings, and materials that facilitate the design and delivery of effective supports. In addition, qualitative data illuminate student and family preferences and goals. Qualitative data include activities such as observations, interviews, and student interest inventories. All IEPs should include both qualitative and quantitative forms of data. The type of data used, however, will depend on how information is best gathered. For example, family priorities are likely best gathered from an interview (qualitative), whereas student progress toward a reading goal is best measured by student reading accuracy data (quantitative). See Table 4.1 for a comparison of quantitative and qualitative approaches to data collection.

Qualitative Data

Qualitative data help members of the team understand the students' school experience, strengths, needs, desires, and barriers to access. There are many forms of qualitative data, but some common sources are observation and interviews. All data collected should focus on identifying student strengths, interests, and priorities, and qualitative data are uniquely able to recognize these. Two common forms of qualitative data, observations and interviews, are discussed next.

Observations   Observational data in natural, inclusive environments provide valuable information about the demands of the environment and how the student responds to those demands, as well as what supports are accessed by the student (Downing, 2010). Understanding the unique characteristics of each school environment and how those characteristics impact student access or reaction to content can help the IEP team adapt the environment and supports available to increase student access and progress. There are multiple ways to collect observational data, including journal notes. However, applying structure to observation improves the usefulness of data collected, and one of the most valuable observation assessments is ecological assessment. In brief, an ecological assessment involves observing the routines of a classroom activity and documenting what performance is expected, how the student with disabilities performs, and what skills need to be taught or supports provided to facilitate the involvement and learning of the student with disabilities.

Ecological assessments can, and should, be conducted in any environment or common instructional scenario the student engages in. Completing ecological assessment of a wide variety of locations, social scenarios, and academic content areas will give the IEP team detailed information about student strengths and needs for support. Any member of the IEP team can complete an ecological assessment. It can be particularly helpful for related services providers to complete ecological assessments for students with complex support needs in natural settings rather than therapy room settings so they may understand student needs in context and plan for integrated service delivery. The ecological assessment form has six components that are organized by columns. Table 4.2 shows an example of an ecological assessment. (See Chapter 7 for more detail. A blank form for conducting an ecological assessment is provided in the Chapter 7 Appendix and with the downloadable resources for this book.).

Table 4.1. Quantitative versus qualitative data collection

Quantitative	Qualitative
Teacher-created data collection sheets (e.g., frequency, accuracy, duration)	Observations (e.g., ecological assessment; antecedent, behavior, consequence [ABC])
Scores on curriculum-based assessments	Interviews (e.g., person-centered planning meetings)
Running records	Student interest inventories
Standardized or formal assessment scores	

Table 4.2. Ecological assessment example for Jake

1. List each step in the activity	2. Cues	3. Skill(s) needed	4. Discrepancy	5. Supplementary aid and service needed	6. Action plan (what to teach or how to embed supports)
Getting ready for class: Students take out their language arts book, turn to page 65, and listen as the teacher introduces the story.	*Hear* the teacher's instruction to take out materials *See* other students taking out their books *Want* to hear the details of the story	Fine and gross motor Receptive language Math: number identification	Jake sits quietly and watches peers as they take out materials. He struggles to comprehend the directions and has not developed the fine motor skills to flip book pages unassisted. He is working on identifying numbers 1–10 and does not independently find 65.	Peer or adult assistance to select and open correct book Access to big-button switch Provide objects that represent key events and characters in the story Key numbers on pages highlighted to provide identification opportunity	Jake should learn to select the correct book for class when shown a sample of the correct book and asked to gesture toward the correct book from a field of two books. A peer can present the book choices to increase peer interaction. The page number can be programed onto Jake's big-button, and the general education teacher can ask him to tell the class the page to go to for an embedded communication opportunity. An adult can embed number identification into practice by asking Jake to read the highlighted number on the page by gesturing toward the matching number from a field of three options.
Read aloud and book discussion: Students continue to listen to the story, respond to questions from the teacher, or share predictions about the story with a peer.	*Hear* a peer talking *See* other students raising their hands or turning to their table partners *Want* to talk with a friend	Expressive language Social: turn taking Social: confidence	Jake sits quietly and listens while the teacher reads and peers share. He does not communicate with oral language. Jake struggles to comprehend the story in order to make predictions.	Provide objects that represent key events and characters in the story Peers receive information on how to be responsive communication partners for Jake	To work on communication and choice making skills, the general educator can call on Jake to point to a student with their hand up to share their answer. Special education teacher, peer, or paraprofessional present object representation of key vocabulary from the story as it is read. Teach relevant cues of the object (e.g., color, size). During peer share times, a peer can ask Jake a question using previously reviewed object options as answers.
Independent work: Students take out spiral notebooks and complete a handwritten reading reflection.	*Hear* assignment directions from the teacher *See* students taking out notebooks and writing *Want* to get a good grade on assignment	Fine motor Literacy: independent reading Literacy: handwriting Literacy: comprehension	Without support, Jake sits and watches other students write and pushes school supplies off the desk. He does not write about the story due to fine motor delays and limited story comprehension. He currently writes via gestures, object selection, and big-button switches.	Adapted version of story that targets key vocabulary and concepts Multiple big-button switches to present object answer options Place Dycem (nonstick mat) on table to support objects from falling	Special educator, general educator, or paraprofessional use independent work time to deliver individualized literacy intervention using adapted version of book and objects to support comprehension. Teach communication and writing by promoting Jake to comment on book content or answer questions using object on switches.

Person-Centered Planning   Useful qualitative data about student skill development can also be obtained through conversations or interviews with others. Person-centered planning (PCP) is a type of structured conversation in which people who are very familiar with the student come together to consider options, express a vision for the future, identify potential barriers to achieving that vision, determine supports, and design an action plan to reach desired goals (Downing, 2010). The data gathered from PCP meetings are used to develop goals and supports, but also to focus the team on how to achieve outcomes that are of high priority and personally relevant to the student. The steps of a PCP interview are explained next.

1. *Gather the team:* People who are most familiar with the student, including family members, friends, neighbors, teachers, paraprofessionals, and community members (e.g., piano teacher, pastors, baseball coach) gather together. The number or roles of people are not important; it is important that the people who come together truly know the student well and care about their current and future successes.

2. *Vision sharing:* The team, including and especially the student, develop a vision of how the student will live an enviable, thriving life into the future. This vision is the "dream" scenario and may include details such as where the student will live as an adult (e.g., their own house with support), their work (e.g., competitive, integrated employment), their relationships (e.g., spouses, friends, coworker relationships), and the skills the student will have (e.g., to direct their own supports, to be able to read for information and for pleasure). By sharing visions from multiple perspectives, a clear picture will emerge of who the student can become as they age. This is the vision the team will seek to realize through teaching skills and providing supports now and into the future.

3. *Barrier identification:* Any barriers that stand in the way of realizing the team's vision for the student are identified next. These barriers might be any type; for example, lack of communication skills might be a barrier to realizing the dream of being in a loving relationship, lack of reading instruction might be a barrier to a dream of reading for fun and information, and lack of affordable housing might be a barrier to living on one's own. The team should think of any and all potential or actual barriers to realizing the student's vision for the future; by identifying these barriers, they can be systematically addressed. For example, emphasizing academic and nonacademic instruction that result in academic, social, and communication skills and relationships needed for competitive, integrated employment might position a student to be better able to afford housing in the future.

4. *Determine supports:* Any supports needed to achieve the vision are also identified. During the school years, various supports should be trialed so the student has a robust set of personally relevant supports that reflect their preferences for support (e.g., human versus technological supports) and reflect their preferred activities, relationships, and skills (i.e., supports are identified to support the student in their individual lifestyle). By identifying supports that are personally relevant, the student can also learn how to advocate for, select, and modify their own supports to best suit their preferences and lifestyle.

5. *Develop an action plan:* Finally, the team creates a plan for how to achieve their vision. The action plan must be detailed, including IEP goals to be developed, IEP supports and services to provide, how progress towards the vision will be measured, and who will be responsible for carrying out various parts of the plan. The role of the student as an active participant in achieving their own vision should be emphasized, including how the student will set their own goals, monitor their goal progress, and seek supports as needed.

Interviews   Interviews with families can also be a valuable source of information. Understanding the routine activities of students and families can be useful in determining IEP goals and services, including transition-related goals and services. The routine-based assessment interview (RBI) is an interview in which families report the typical routines of the family, how the student is involved in those routines, and their priorities related to the participation of their child in typical routines (McWilliam et al., 2009). The RBI is to get to know the family and to identify their priorities for their child by discussing their daily routines. The interviewer then asks the family a series of questions:

1. *Does the family have any major concerns?* The interviewer then writes these down and acknowledges these concerns to emphasize the interview is about them, the family, and their priorities. Often, these initial concerns are brought up again throughout the interview, and sometimes new concerns emerge through the questioning. Either way, by identifying major concerns, they can be discussed more thoroughly and then addressed.

2. *Describe a typical day for your family.* The family should be prompted to describe typical activities, such as who wakes up first and how the day unfolds until the last person goes to bed. During each routine, the interviewer seeks to learn:

   - What does each person in the family do during the routine?

   - What does the student/child do during the routine?

   - How does the student/child participate in the routine?

   - What can the student/child do independently during the routine?

   - How does the child communicate and get along with others as part of this routine?

   - How satisfied is the family with the routine?

In gathering this information, needed skills to learn, supports to use, and relationships to build emerge that can strengthen the child's engagement in family routines. Because these same skills, supports and relationship needs also occur at school, an opportunity for triangulation can also occur. In that vein, teachers might also be interviewed to gather information about how the student engages at school. Questions may include:

1. What does the class, as a whole, do during this time?

2. What does the student do during this time?

3. How does the student participate in the activity?

4. What can the student do on their own during the activity?

5. How does the student communicate and get along with others during this activity?

As with the family interview, asking teachers their major concerns and listening for common concerns across different teachers or activities is also important to identify those that must be addressed as priorities, along with any new concerns that emerge and should be taught or provided for either the student or the teacher. For example, responses may indicate the teacher needs additional support in the classroom during certain routines, or that the teacher needs to learn how to program a communication device.

Student Interest Inventories

Gathering information about interests and priorities directly from students is another valuable source of data that can inform IEP development and implementation. Student interest inventories ask students to state their preferences in academic and nonacademic areas, as well as interests related to life after high school. For example, asking students "What is your favorite subject at school?" or "When you are learning something new, what best helps you learn?" can help teams identify academic interests and preferred supports. Asking students about their friends, favorite activities outside of school, and things they are good at can generate information about nonacademic strengths and interests. Finally, asking students about their dream job can help to identify post-school goals. Students can respond to these types of questions verbally, in writing, using AAC supports, by pointing to pictures or diagrams representing their choice, and in many other individualized manners to gather information.

Quantitative Data

Other data can be collected that are quantitative. Quantitative data result in numbers that can be graphed. Many types of data can be collected using quantitative techniques. Collecting data that seek strengths and priorities relies on collecting the correct type of data. It is also important to keep in mind that IEP teams must collect data for each IEP goal, including any behavior intervention plans (Etscheidt, 2006). How does one know what type of data to collect? This is determined from the desired outcome specified in the particular IEP goal. In each case, a raw number is derived from collecting data which can later be graphed.

Duration Recording   Duration data are needed if one is interested in knowing either how long a behavior occurs or the percentage of time a behavior occurs during an observation period (Snell & Brown, 2011). The length of the observation period must always be specified. This type of data is collected for behaviors that last more than a few seconds, such as looking at the teacher to pay attention, in-seat behavior, or engaging in self-injurious behavior. For example, a goal to increase the length of social interactions from 3 to 5 minutes might best be measured using duration recording. In this instance, the teacher would use a timer to keep track of how long the student interacted with peers during the observation period.

Frequency Recording   Frequency data describe how many times a behavior occurred during the observation period (Snell & Brown, 2011). This type of data is best used for behaviors that are very brief and discrete, such as number of times a student hits or turned in homework on time, or number of problems completed correctly. The teacher only needs to determine the observation period ahead of time (e.g., 5 minutes, 1 week) and then count the frequency of the targeted behavior. For example, a goal to decrease the number of prompts a student requires to come in from recess might be measured using frequency recording.

Interval Recording   A variety of types of interval recording exist, but it is sufficient to know that interval recording is a method to estimate the occurrence of a behavior. Using interval recording, a teacher predetermines an observation window (i.e., interval) and then marks whether the behavior occurred at all during that interval (Snell & Brown, 2011). Like frequency recording, it is best used for discrete behaviors. For example, a goal to ask for help during instruction might be tracked using interval recording. In this case, the teacher might choose a difficult task (i.e., a task the teacher expects a student would need assistance with) and then track if the student asked for help during 5-minute intervals.

Task-Analytic Recording   In some cases, it is important that a student learns to complete a skill that requires correct completion of several discrete steps (Snell & Brown, 2011). For example, tying shoes requires a series of steps done correctly and in a certain order. If a step is skipped or done incorrectly, the student would not have safely tied shoes. Teachers can record the number of steps completed correctly by the student on a given observation day to determine overall accuracy in completing a skill.

Latency Recording   In other instances, educators need to know how long it takes a student to initiate a skill or behavior after a cue or prompt (Downing, 2010). For example, a student might be told "Hi" from a peer. Teachers can record the time it takes the student to responds to this greeting. If the student responds 5 minutes later, it is likely too late and their peer will have ventured off. Teaching students to respond to a cue or prompt in a timely manner is often very important.

Accuracy Recording   The final type of data recording we consider is accuracy, which is also likely the most familiar to educators. Accuracy data reports just that: how accurately a student completes an activity. For example, a team might be interested in knowing how often the student accurately responds to comprehension questions from their science book. Similarly, accuracy data might report the number of items a student retrieves from their backpack correctly at the start of a class.

Deciding What Type of Data to Use

As you read these examples of types of data, you may have recognized that a similar goal or skill could be measured in a variety of ways. For example, responding to a greeting from a peer could be measured using latency data if the team is interested in how quickly a student responds to a greeting. However, a team might also report accuracy data to indicate how accurately a student responds (or fails to respond) to a greeting. In a similar way, a team might report the frequency with which a student responds to greetings from different peers. In other words, the type of data used will always depend on the information the team is interested in knowing. When writing goals and determining data types, discussing the purpose of the goal and data will be necessary in identifying which type(s) of data to collect, analyze, and report.

Data Collection Resources   As you develop an IEP and instructional goals, drawing upon resources to support your good habits as a data collector is important. Data collection forms can be gathered from various sources and customized to your own needs. *The Data Collection Toolkit* (Golden, 2018) is one such resource that contains numerous forms that can be individualized for specific students.

MANAGING THE PROCESS OF COLLECTING DATA

Deciding what data to collect and why is important. It is also important to plan how you will manage the process of collecting data—how often it will be done; who will do it, where, and when; how data will be shared; and how to deal with conflicting data from different sources. The sections that follow discuss these aspects of the process.

How Often to Collect Data

Data collection can be time consuming, and thus has the potential to interfere with instruction (Munger et al., 1989). As a result, education teams often wonder how much data to collect and analyze for each student. A general maxim is "Teams should collect enough data to make an informed decision, but not so much that data collection and analysis becomes overwhelming and interferes with their instructional and other duties." So, what is this "Goldilocks" amount—enough data, but not too much? In general, teachers who collect data more than once per week are more accurate in making data-based decisions (Munger et al., 1989). Further, teachers must have at least six total data points to make data-based decisions (Browder et al., 2011). Thus, to ensure timely data-based decisions, collecting and graphing data for each IEP goal twice a week is recommended. However, high priority objectives (i.e., related to health and safety) must be monitored frequently (e.g., daily), as would new programs (Snell & Brown, 2011). IEP goals that are in maintenance conditions or reflect skills taught infrequently (e.g., using public transportation) might be monitored less often, such as weekly or even monthly.

Who Collects Data

Once teams decide what data to collect and how often, they need to next determine who will collect data, where, and when. Any IEP team member can provide data with which to make educational decisions, including paraprofessionals, family members, and the students themselves. And all IEP team members who are responsible for implementing IEP goals and reporting progress towards those goals (e.g., general and special education teachers, speech language pathologists) should also be responsible for collecting data and using it to make decisions (Etscheidt, 2006).

The importance of data from multiple sources cannot be overstated. Too often, teams rely on limited data points collected from a small number of settings or activities to make enormously consequential decisions about what to teach and how to teach students. In doing so, teams often make errors that result in lower expectations of students and even more restrictive placements. Supporting all team members to collect data across home, school, and community settings can avoid this. For example, family members may collect and share communication data across home and community settings, while the speech language pathologist shares data collected during speech therapy services, and teachers and paraprofessionals collect and share the same data collected during work and play activities at school. In reviewing all these data, teams are positioned to find patterns, strengths, and support needs that will best assist teams in refining goals or services to facilitate student learning. This process of triangulation allows teams to consider multiple points of data and multiple sources of information to arrive at the most holistic view of student skills in natural settings. Although this type of team approach to data collection may seem self-evident, in reality, too often the data collected and shared by parents or other non-school IEP team members is discounted or devalued (Fish, 2006). To support a full team approach to data collection, a data collection plan should be developed and agreed upon by all IEP team members.

Creating and Sharing a Data Collection Plan

To support teams in distributing the task of collecting data across environments and activities, a data collection plan is created. A data collection plan is a strategy for determining what data to collect, where, how, when, and who will collect data. This plan is prepared for each goal and includes helpful information such as operational definitions and data collection templates. A data collection plan is important for ensuring we are teaching generalizable skills–skills that are useful across settings and activities. A data collection plan will also be useful in guaranteeing data are collected that capture student ability; for example, some activities or settings may be more or less motivating to a student. If data are only collected during times when the student is less motivated, lowered expectations of the student are likely to result. Finally, a data collection plan guarantees data are collected across a variety of natural activities and settings; data collected during contrived activities only (e.g., a speech therapy office) will likely paint a different picture of a student than data collected in natural settings when the skill is needed. Figure 4.1 shows a sample data collection plan. (A full-size, blank, reproducible version of this form is provided as an appendix to this chapter and on the Brookes Download Hub.)

As seen in this example, teams start by clearly defining the skill to be measured. They will also define correct, incorrect, and non-responses in jargon-free, objective language so that all team members will be able to collect data on the same skill and have a consistent understanding of the kind of student responses and how to report them. Next, the type of data to be collected will be reported, and a data collection template will be attached so that all team members are using the same tools to collect data. As an alternative, teams might select an application to use to collect data on their smart phones or tablets; the data collection plan should specify which application will be used and provided to all to ensure all team members are using the same one.

Next, all of the people responsible for collecting data should be identified. All possible data collectors should first be known, and then those with ample opportunities to observe the student or provide instruction on the targeted skill should be selected to be responsible for data collection, whereas those with inadequate opportunities to provide instruction or observation of the skills should be removed from responsibility for collecting data on a particular skill. Then, the types of activities where data should be collected will be identified, with careful consideration to ensure students have enough opportunities to be taught or observed in a variety of natural contexts or activities. Similarly, data should be collected across settings or contexts to be certain student skill is measured in a variety of places. The times at which data will be collected must also be identified, again, ensuring data are collected at varying times so that teams understand how student skill may vary across times of the day or even days of the week. For example, factors such as student medication may impact attentiveness, and if data are collected only when students are tired due to medication, an inaccurate representation of the student from collected data will emerge.

FORM 4A ## Skill Data Collection Plan

Question	Response
Skill definition	
Provide a measurable and objective definition of the skill.	*Jamie will identify the correct picture from a field of 4 to answer questions related to science content, correctly answering 80% of the questions asked per unit, for 6 units of study.*
Define a correct response:	*Jamie points to the picture representing the correct response after receiving a verbal or written cue.*
Define an incorrect response:	*Jamie points to the incorrect picture after receiving a verbal or written cue.*
Define a nonresponse:	*Jamie does not point to any picture within 10 seconds of receiving a verbal or written cue.*

Type of data to be collected			
Duration		Task analytic	
Frequency		Latency	
Interval		Accuracy	✓

Figure 4.1. Sample skill data collection plan.

FORM 4A **Skill Data Collection Plan** *(continued)*

*Attach data collection template or link to data collection application			
Who will collect data?			
General education teacher	✓	Special education teacher	✓
Paraprofessional	✓	Speech therapist	
Family	✓	Student	✓
Occupational therapist		Other:	
During what types of activities will data be collected?			
Free time		Large group	
Small group	✓	Independent work	✓
Other:			
Where will data be collected?			
Home	✓	Noisy setting	
Community		Quiet setting	
School—classroom		School—hallways	
School—cafeteria		School—playground	
School—therapy room		Other:	
When will data be collected on this skill?			
Before school		School—mornings	
School—afternoons	✓	After school	✓
Daily		Twice per week	
Once per week	✓	Monthly	
Quarterly		Other:	

Figure 4.1. *(continued)*

What to Do When Families and Professionals Present Conflicting Data

When multiple team members collect data on a skill across home, school, and community settings, and even across activities within these settings, differences in data are certain to arise. At first, this might be concerning, with team members assuming other team members collected faulty data. More likely, however, differences that emerge in data from multiple sources indicates differences in student skills in relationship to the cues available in different settings, student motivation or preference differences across different settings and activities, and differences in supports available across various settings and activities. As such, differences in data across team members are a powerful finding! This finding enables teams to see how student performance can vary based on these and other factors, and guide teams to identify the supports, cues, or motivating factors that may need to be used in other settings to enhance student learning.

USING DATA TO MAKE DECISIONS

Once the team has collected sufficient data, the data need to be analyzed to identify patterns and make decisions. Graphing data is useful for completing this analysis.

Why Graph Data?

There is an old saying that a picture is worth a thousand words. This saying is especially relevant to understanding student data and progress. By creating a literal picture (i.e., a graph) of progress, the numerical data obtained about a student comes alive and illustrates clearly how the student is making progress, and how that progress is occurring relative to the student's ultimate goal. In the next sections, we discuss how this process of graphing data is completed and how graphed data are used to make timely and accurate instructional decisions.

How to Make Decisions Using Graphed Data

The first step of visually representing data is to transpose numerical data into a linear graph. To do so, the student's raw data points are plotted. In general, the x-axis of the graph represents the date or instructional opportunity, and the y-axis is the range of possible scores a student could achieve (e.g., accuracy). In Figure 4.2, the number of correct words per minute read by Sam are graphed. The x-axis (horizontal) represents instructional probes, and the y-axis (vertical) shows the number of possible words read per minute. As seen in this figure, Sam read 18 correct words per minute on probe 1, 16 correct words per minute on probe 2, 19 correct words per minute on probe 3, 18 correct words per minute on probe 4, and 19 correct words per minute on probe 5.

In addition to plotting student data, teams will also want to include an aim (or goal) line for each skill. The aim line connects the student's baseline data with the criterion data point. The baseline point is created from 3 to 5 data points collected over a short period of time; once these data are collected, the teacher identifies the median score (i.e., the score that falls in the middle when scores are ordered from lowest to highest). The baseline point is where the aim line originates from. Next, the criterion point is the target for the student set in their IEP: In this example, Sam's goal is to read 50 correct words per

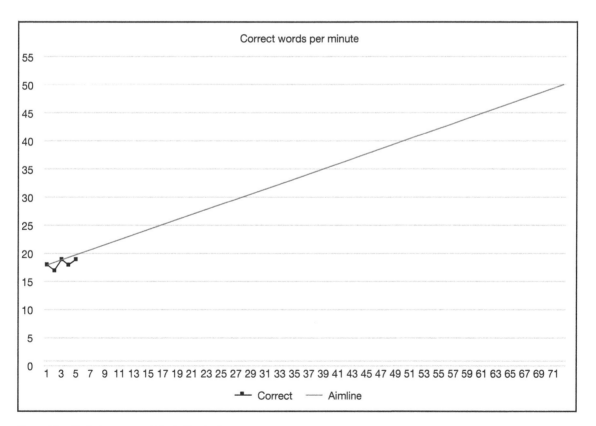

Figure 4.2. Student progress relative to the aim line.

minute, so the aim line begins with probe 1 (when Sam read 18 correct words per minute) and ends at 50 correct words per minute at probe 70 (the criterion level).

Once data have been graphed, teams will apply decision rules to determine student progress. As shown in Figures 4.3 and 4.4, an inspection of graphed data enables teams to draw conclusions, and consequently make decisions, about student progress (Browder et al., 1986; Wakeman, 2010). At least five instructional decisions can be made from graphed data (Browder et al., 1986; Wakeman, 2010). These instructional decisions will be made throughout the year and reported to the full team during progress monitoring periods (e.g., at parent-teacher conferences), and graphed data will be used to set new instructional targets when creating a new IEP.

Skill Mastery   When a student has at least 3 data points at or above the criterion level (i.e., the mastery level of performance specified in the IEP), the student has mastered the skill. In this situation, a new goal should be taught. The current goal would then enter maintenance, meaning teams would take periodic probes (i.e., data collection) to make sure the student can still perform the task at criterion levels. A new goal would be developed that extends the current skill, such as improving fluency (i.e., the speed or accuracy for completing the skill), criteria (i.e., performance level) or focusing on generalization (i.e., ensure student can use the skill in a variety of settings, using a variety of materials, and with different people present).

No Progress   Teams may review graphed data and determine the student has failed to make progress. This occurs when the mean of data for the past 6 data points (Browder et al., 2011) is essentially the same as the baseline performance. In this case, the team would conclude the student is not making sufficient progress and changes in instruction are needed to enable the student to reach the goal. These instructional changes could include simplifying materials or responses, breaking the skill into more discrete steps, incorporating assistive technology, or simply providing more teaching opportunities throughout the day.

Good Progress   Inspection of the graphed data may reveal the student is making adequate progress. In this case, the mean of the data for the last 6 data points is higher than the mean of the previous 6 data points by at least 5%, but is not yet at criterion (i.e., the mastery level specified in the IEP goal). In such a case, the teacher would conclude the student is making adequate progress and should continue instruction without any changes.

Inadequate Progress   A fourth conclusion may be the student is not making adequate progress. In this instance, the data continue to be above baseline, but the overall trend is flat (i.e., the most recent 6 data points have the same mean as the previous 6 data points). As an alternative, the trend of the most recent 6 data points may be accelerating, but the mean of these data points is less than 5% from the previous 6 data points. In both instances, the team would decide to continue instruction, but change instructional practices. These changes could include making more precise prompts, using a more specific prompting hierarchy (e.g., least to most prompting), increasing the wait time before delivering a prompt, or only reinforcing correct responses as opposed to reinforcing effort, for example.

Motivation Concerns   Finally, student performance may be highly variable. In these cases, the student's performance fluctuates, sometimes dramatically. For example, perhaps the student is able to perform the skill at the desired criteria some days yet is unable to perform the task other days. A team has two conclusions to reach here. First, teams must rule out other explanations for the variable data, including changes in medication, health concerns (e.g., tooth ache), or setting factors (e.g., changes at home, including where students live or whom they live with, or factors in the learning environment, including the noise, lighting, materials, and people present). When these factors are ruled out, a team can conclude the student is not adequately motivated to complete the skill and will then focus on improving motivation. Considerations to improve motivation may include completing a reinforcer assessment to determine highly motivating reinforcers, only reinforcing the best performance of the skill, embedding more choices for the student while completing the skill, infusing self-monitoring, or using natural consequences for failing to perform the skill at criterion.

Data Pattern	Sample Graph	Conclusion	Decision
Reached goal criterion (i.e., 30 correct words per minute), with at least 3 data points at the criterion (mastery) level.	Correct words per minute 40 / 35 / 30 / 25 / 20 / 15 / 10 / 5 / 0 1 2 3 4 5 6 7 8 9 10 11 12 13 14 15 16 17 18 19 20 21 22 23 24 25 26 27 28 29 30 Correct — Aimline	Mastery	Goal mastered. This becomes a maintenance goal. Develop a new goal to maintain and extend (i.e., fluency, generalization) skill (e.g., read 50 correct words per minute).
Data is similar to baseline (approximately same mean) with no improvement in student performance.	Correct words per minute 35 / 30 / 25 / 20 / 15 / 10 / 5 / 0 1 2 3 4 5 6 7 8 9 10 11 12 13 14 15 16 17 18 19 20 21 22 23 24 25 26 27 28 29 30 Correct — Aimline	No progress	Skill is too difficult. Change goal or instruction, such as: • Simplify responses or materials • Break skill into more discrete steps • Include AT • Provide more opportunities to practice skill

Figure 4.3. Decision making based on inspection of graphed data.

(continued)

69

Figure 4.3. (continued)

Data Pattern	Sample Graph	Conclusion	Decision
Data is above base-line and is improving by at least 5% every 6 data points. Not yet at criterion (mas-tery) level		Adequate progress	Continue instruction without any changes.
Data is above base-line, but the trend is flat. The mean of the data for the current 2 weeks is the same as the last 6 data points, or higher but by less than 5%		Inadequate progress	Continue instruction. Improve prompts so student can make more independent correct responses. Increase time delay (wait time). Only reinforce correct responses.

Data Pattern	Sample Graph	Conclusion	Decision
Data is variable, showing the student can complete the skill some days, but not other days. There are no other explanations for the variance (e.g., medications, overall health).	 Correct words per minute Legend: Correct, Aimline	Motivation problem	Improve motivation to perform correctly and independently. Only reinforce best performance. Vary reinforcement. Use natural con-sequences, self-monitoring, and/or embed choices.

Data Pattern	Sample Graph	Conclusion	Decision
Reached goal criterion (i.e., 30 correct words per minute), with at least 3 data points at the criterion (mastery) level.	Correct words per minute 40 35 30 25 20 15 10 5 0 1 2 3 4 5 6 7 8 9 10 11 12 13 14 15 16 17 18 19 20 21 22 23 24 25 26 27 28 29 30 Correct Aimline	Mastery	Goal mastered. This becomes a mainte-nance goal. Develop a new goal to maintain and extend (i.e., fluency, generalization) skill (e.g., read 50 correct words per minute).
Data is similar to baseline (approxi-mately same mean) with no improve-ment in student performance.	Correct words per minute 35 30 25 20 15 10 5 0 1 2 3 4 5 6 7 8 9 10 11 12 13 14 15 16 17 18 19 20 21 22 23 24 25 26 27 28 29 30 Correct Aimline	No progress	Skill is too difficult. Change goal or instruc-tion, such as: • Simplify responses or materials • Break skill into more discrete steps • Include AT • Provide more oppor-tunities to practice skill

Data Pattern	Sample Graph	Conclusion	Decision
Data is above baseline and is improving by at least 5% every 6 data points. Not yet at criterion (mastery) level.	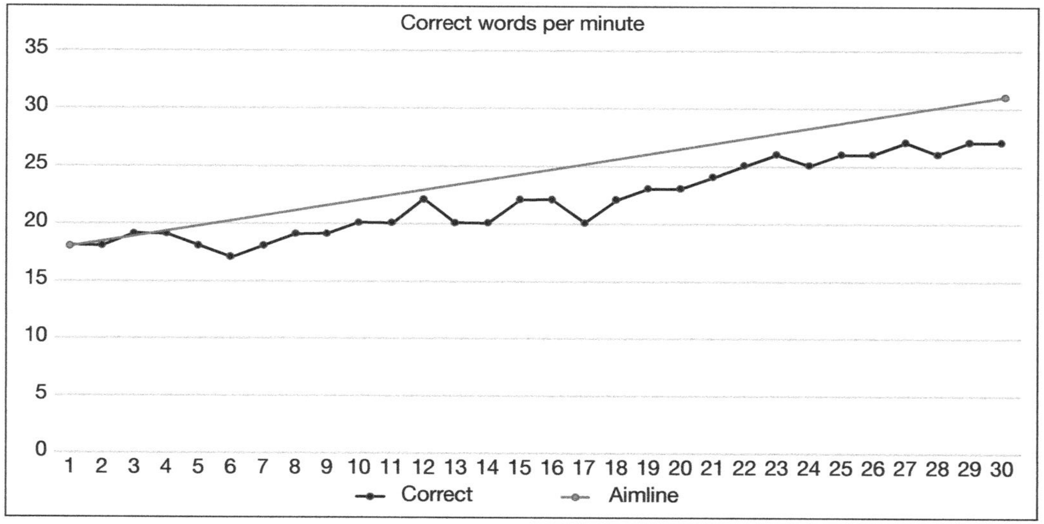 Correct words per minute —●— Correct —○— Aimline	Adequate progress	Continue instruction without any changes.
Data is above baseline, but the trend is flat. The mean of the data for the current 2 weeks is the same as the last 6 data points, or higher but by less than 5%.	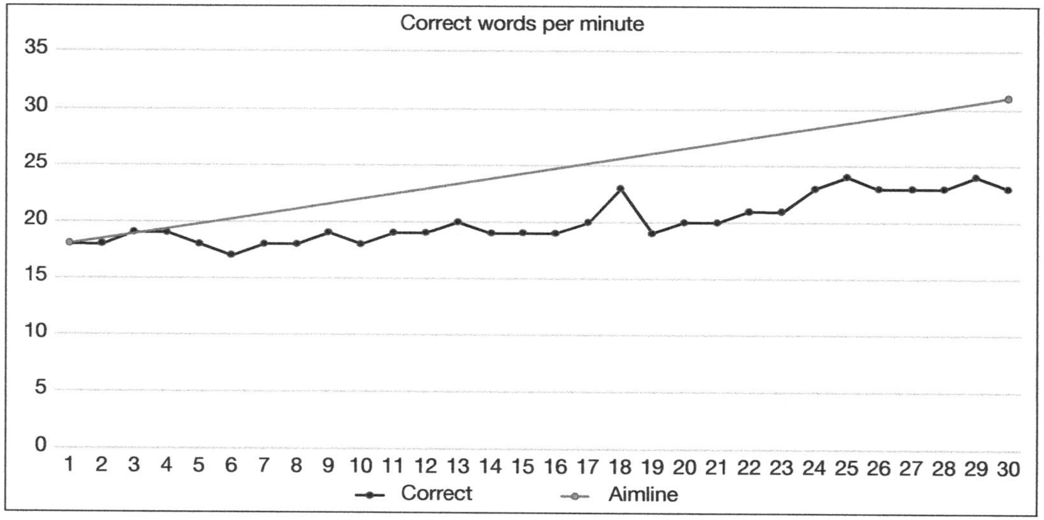 Correct words per minute —●— Correct —○— Aimline	Inadequate progress	Continue instruction. Improve prompts so student can make more independent correct responses. Increase time delay (wait time). Only reinforce correct responses.

(continued)

Figure 4.4. Data-based decisions guidelines. (*Sources:* Browder et al., 1986, and Wakeman, 2010.)

Figure 4.4. *(continued)*

Data Pattern	Sample Graph	Conclusion	Decision
Data is variable, showing the student can complete the skill some days, but not other days. There are no other explanations for the variance (e.g., medications, overall health).	Correct words per minute 	Motivation problem	Improve motivation to perform correctly and independently. Only reinforce best performance. Vary reinforcement. Use natural con-sequences, self-monitoring, and/or embed choices.

Connecting Data to Outcomes

As described throughout this chapter, accurate data collected across natural environments are essential to ensuring teams make instructional decisions and set IEP goals, objectives, and services that maximize student learning and facilitate positive student outcomes. As noted in Chapter 7, progress on IEP goals must be reported to families at the same frequency as progress is reported for students who do not have disabilities. However, teams should communicate their shared data throughout the school year, on a weekly or monthly basis, and review all data thoroughly at IEP meetings to set new goals, objectives, and services for students. The five steps outlined in this chapter, and summarized below, are critical to giving educational teams the information they need to understand student progress and achieve positive student learning outcomes:

- Write measurable goals and objectives

- Develop a data collection system and collect data

- Represent the data visually (usually with a graph)

- Evaluate the data

- Adjust instruction as guided by the data

CONCLUDING THOUGHTS: DATA-BASED DECISION MAKING

Special education teachers have incredibly busy, demanding jobs. Because the ultimate outcome of special education is student progress, it is essential special education teachers have the tools and information to make timely and informed instructional decisions for their students. By determining the best kind of data to collect for each IEP goal, using a team approach to collect data across natural environments, graphing data, and communicating progress, teams can ensure their instructional decisions are timely and support student progress.

REVIEWING THE COMMITMENT: *Making Decisions Based on Data*

This chapter discussed what types of data are used for decision making, how to plan for data collection, and how to analyze data and use it to make decisions.

Recall the student whom you identified at the beginning of the chapter. After reading, what new ideas do you have about any of the following?

- What additional data to collect about this student and why it is needed

- How data is or will be collected (i.e., how often, by whom, when, and where)

- Conflicts or discrepancies between different sources of data (e.g., family report and school)

- How data are shared among team members

- How your team analyzes data

- Data patterns and related decisions

_____

_____

_____

_____

ACTING ON THE COMMITMENT: *Making Decisions Based on Data*

The appendix to this chapter includes a template for creating data collection plans for your students. Use the template, along with your notes above, to create a data collection plan for the student you have identified.

Skill Data Collection Plan

Question	Response
Skill definition	
Provide a measurable and objective definition of the skill.	
Define a correct response:	
Define an incorrect response:	
Define a nonresponse:	
Type of data to be collected	

Duration		Task analytic	
Frequency		Latency	
Interval		Accuracy	

*Attach data collection template or link to data collection application			
Who will collect data?			
General education teacher		Special education teacher	
Paraprofessional		Speech therapist	
Family		Student	
Occupational therapist		Other:	
During what types of activities will data be collected?			
Free time		Large group	
Small group		Independent work	
Other:			
Where will data be collected?			
Home		Noisy setting	
Community		Quiet setting	
School—classroom		School—hallways	
School—cafeteria		School—playground	
School—therapy room		Other:	
When will data be collected on this skill?			
Before school		School—mornings	
School—afternoons		After school	
Daily		Twice per week	
Once per week		Monthly	
Quarterly		Other:	

Developing the IEP

The next part of this book focuses on development of the IEP document. The chapters in this part are in a specific order; this order is based on the order in which an IEP should be developed, given that different sections of the IEP rely on decisions made in other parts of the IEP. This part of the book also depends on the practices described in Section I to ensure a truly equitable partnership is established among all team members, especially including students and families, when developing the IEP document.

Developing the IEP document requires your commitment

- To knowing your student's abilities and needs and describing them in a clear, accurate, strengths-based way

- To planning for special factors and for any options that may benefit your student, such as extended school year and alternate assessment

- To determining a curriculum and goals that provide your student with a fair, appropriate public education

- To removing barriers to general education by identifying supplementary aids and services

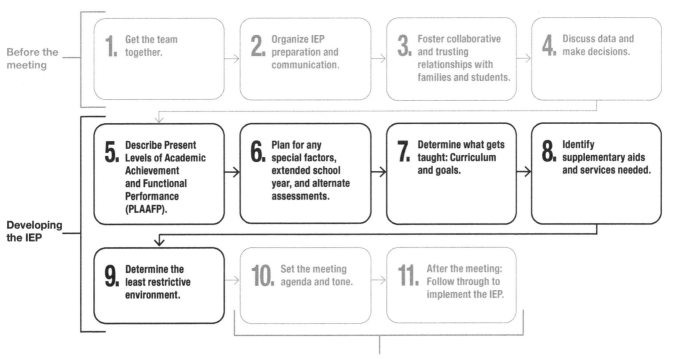

- To determining the least restrictive environment that will maximize your student's participation in general education while meeting their individual needs

Chapters 5–9 explain in detail how to fulfill these commitments as you work with the team to develop the IEP document, section by section.

Describing Present Levels
of Academic Acheivement
and Functional Performance

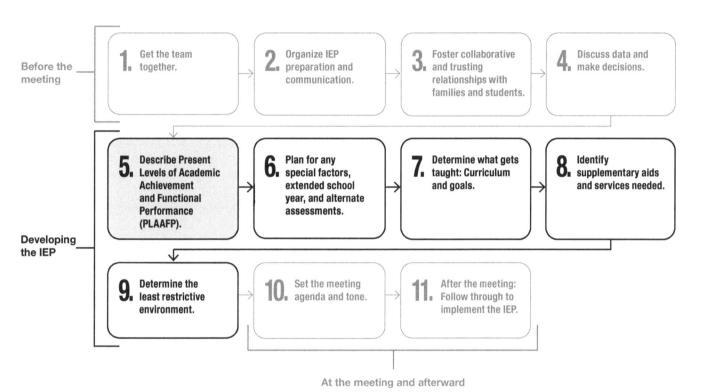

Before the meeting

1. Get the team together.

2. Organize IEP preparation and communication.

3. Foster collaborative and trusting relationships with families and students.

4. Discuss data and make decisions.

Developing the IEP

5. Describe Present Levels of Academic Achievement and Functional Performance (PLAAFP).

6. Plan for any special factors, extended school year, and alternate assessments.

7. Determine what gets taught: Curriculum and goals.

8. Identify supplementary aids and services needed.

9. Determine the least restrictive environment.

10. Set the meeting agenda and tone.

11. After the meeting: Follow through to implement the IEP.

At the meeting and afterward

Imagine you are planning a vacation to an exciting new location: you have packed your bags, found a house sitter, obtained days off from work, and are ready to go and have the time of your life. To get to your vacation spot, you need to plan on how you'll get there. Will you drive? Take a boat? Fly in a plane? To make these decisions, you quite obviously will need to know both where you currently are and where your vacation destination is. The Present Levels of Academic Achievement and Functional Performance (or PLAAFP) section of the IEP functions similarly as that first step in vacation travel planning. The PLAAFP tells IEP teams where the student is currently performing so that IEP teams can map out, in subsequent sections of the IEP, how to arrive at the individualized destination of the student's learning. The PLAAFP, then, is critical in setting the groundwork upon which the IEP team will make the remainder of IEP decisions.

UNDERSTANDING THE COMMITMENT: *Describing Your Student's Abilities and Needs*

The PLAAFP is the foundation upon which other IEP decisions are made, so developing a clear picture of the student's abilities and needs is critical to the success of IEP planning and implementation. The choices you make about what information to present and how to present it will have a lasting impact.

To portray the student's strengths and needs in the PLAAFP, you will need to focus on the student's strengths; provide comprehensive, interdisciplinary data; and connect the PLAAFP to general education settings and standards. Each of these tasks are explained in depth in this chapter. For now, start on your commitment by thinking about a student with whom you work. Brainstorm a list of this student's strengths. These may be academic strengths, such as strong math ability, or other strengths such as perseverance or good social skills.

_____

_____

_____

_____

_____

_____

_____

_____

_____

Next, list a few areas of need related to this student's disability. Again, needs may be connected to specific academic areas such as reading, or they may be related to other areas (e.g., needs support to stay on task, needs support to interact appropriately with peers).

_____

_____

_____

_____

_____

_____

_____

_____

_____

WHAT ARE THE PRESENT LEVELS OF ACADEMIC ACHIEVEMENT AND FUNCTIONAL PERFORMANCE?

Often, the PLAAFP is simply referred to as the "present levels" section of the IEP. IDEA 2004 requires IEP teams to provide "needs-based" services to students with disabilities; "needs- based" simply means that all special education goals and services are individualized to each child's academic and functional learning needs that result from their disability (34 C.F.R. § 300.320). The PLAAFP is where individual student needs resulting from the disability are identified as part of a comprehensive, strengths-based evaluation. By generating this list of individual needs, IEP teams will make all subsequent decisions, including goals, services, and ultimately where students will receive special education services. A key feature of a quality IEP, then, is that there is a clear linkage, or congruence, between what is written in the PLAAFP and all other sections of the IEP (Yell et al., 2016). So, what is the PLAAFP? Simply put, the PLAAFP consists of a series of narrative descriptions that succinctly and accurately describe the student's performance and resulting needs, using objective data to report current (baseline) performance. The PLAAFP is central in forecasting all other IEP components and is at the heart of the IEP document.

WHAT GOES INTO THE PLAAFP?

To meet IDEA requirements, the PLAAFP section of the IEP must provide three key pieces of information: 1) a description of the child's needs in all academic and functional areas affected by their disability; 2) objective and measurable baseline information about the child's current levels of performance in the general education curriculum; and 3) how the student's disability affects their involvement and progress in the general education curriculum. Each of these key components is discussed next.

Description of Individual Student Needs

To begin, individual student needs must be identified in all areas of educational and functional activities affected by the child's disability. Academic areas reference the general education curriculum, including reading, writing, math, and the various skills associated with science and history. A thorough PLAAFP will examine components of these areas. The IEP team must also describe needs in functional areas, which IDEA 2004 defines as nonacademic skills needed to complete routine activities of daily life, such as communication, mobility, behavior, social, and daily living skills (Assistance to States for the Education of Children With Disabilities, 2006, p. 46661). As needed, the PLAAFP must also include statements regarding health, vision, hearing, intelligence, and any other area of suspected student need that results from their disability and could impact student learning.

Baseline Data

To report baseline data, teams should refer to data gathered from informal sources (e.g., teacher analysis of student work samples) and formal assessment sources (e.g., standardized assessments). IEP teams must describe the student's current levels of performance, which will serve as a baseline from which to measure subsequent progress (IDEA 2004, (§1414)(d)(1)(A)(i)(I)). Therefore, the baseline data can be thought of as the starting point for every measurable goal in the student's IEP. Because of this, every goal should use the same measurement method as reported in the PLAAFP. For example, if the IEP team reports in the PLAAFP that Sara currently communicates with a mean length utterance of 3 words, we would also expect the related communication goal to measure mean length utterance. Similarly, if the IEP team reports, "Marta currently attempts to bite to request help three times per hour," the corresponding goal should also report the number of attempted bites per hour. As discussed later in this chapter, person-centered assessment is also an important component of determining baseline data to report in the PLAAFP.

Involvement and Progress in General Education Curriculum

In addition to describing student needs with supporting data, the PLAAFP must also indicate how the student's disability affects their involvement and progress in the general education curriculum. Specifically, this section should describe how the student's disability affects involvement in, access to, and progress in the general education curriculum. The purpose of this is to determine which of the child's needs are the highest priority to be addressed, given the need for all students to have access to and make progress in the general education curriculum. This is particularly important for students with more complex support needs who may have many potential needs identified.

WRITING THE PLAAFP

To write the PLAAFP section of the IEP, it is important to keep the following considerations in mind. First, your description of the student should be strengths-based, not deficit-based. Second, your statements in the PLAAFP should incorporate quality, interdisciplinary data. This means that data should be specific, objective, and measurable and should be collected frequently, across a variety of academic disciplines and other areas. Finally, when you describe the student's levels of performance, your point of reference should be general education settings and the content learning standards used in those settings.

The sections that follow discuss each of these considerations in depth.

Developing a Strengths-Based Description of the Student

To understand why it is so important to write strengths-based descriptions, consider the following two examples, which describe the same student.

Example 1: Matthew is a fourth grader with an educational label of intellectual disability. In the area of reading, Matthew's recall of literal facts is average, but he struggles to dive deeper into the text and definitely has trouble retelling events concisely and accurately. Matthew has not mastered decoding multisyllable words. As a result of these difficulties, Matthew is falling behind his grade-level peers in reading and is not reading books independently.

Example 2: Matthew is a resilient fourth-grade boy who enjoys dinosaurs and monster trucks. He has a good sense of humor and enjoys working with his peers. When faced with obstacles, Matthew maintains a positive attitude and continues to work hard on his assigned tasks. Given his interest in dinosaurs and monster trucks, his comprehension of books on these topics is far higher than books on less interesting topics. When Matthew reads a book to himself written at a first-grade level on topics other than trucks and dinosaurs, he answers who, when, where, and what questions with an average of 67% accuracy. Matthew's disability label of intellectual disability affects his comprehension and memory; supports for these areas are beneficial. Specifically, when he is given graphic organizers to write down essential information from the text with his learning partner, his accuracy improves to an average of 98%. Matthew responds to inferential questions (e.g., why, how) with an average of 49% correct. However, when provided "thinking aloud" summaries of pages as he reads with a partner, as well as visuals or pictures to support the text, Matthew's comprehension of inferential information increases to 72%. When supported to draw picture summaries of key events in the text as he reads them, Matthew's ability to retell a story in correct order averages 75%; without this support, his retell usually omits key information. Reading multisyllabic words is best accomplished by supporting Matthew to look for the vowels in words and to draw a line dividing consonants in a word (e.g., fan/tas/tic). Using this strategy, he can decode multisyllabic words with an average of 68% accuracy.

As you read both reading PLAAFP statements, what are some of the things you noticed about each? How do the different descriptions impact your expectations of the student? How might they affect your approaches to teaching Matthew? Did you notice how Example 1 focuses on what Matthew is not able to do, whereas Example 2 emphasizes what Matthew can do when he uses supports and strategies?

How students are described impacts the resulting goals and services made available to them (Elder et al., 2018). Describing the student in such a way that highlights their capacity and potential is thus critical. Yet, creating a strengths-based narrative about the student is both an art and a science, as word choices can suggest a variety of solutions. In this section, we provide an overview of strengths-based approaches to writing the PLAAFP and describe how a comprehensive and cohesive narrative, guided by data from multiple team members, parents, and the student themselves, can set the stage for a robust educational plan.

Strengths-Based Approaches

As illustrated earlier, the PLAAFP tells the story of the student and sets the stage for the contents of the remainder of the IEP. Providing a story of the student that emphasizes their capacities and potential, in addition to any support needs, is thus much more likely to result in an IEP that promotes high expectations—as opposed to providing a PLAAFP statement that focuses on deficits and weaknesses.

What We Mean by "Strengths-Based"

A strengths-based approach focuses on the positive attributes of a person, seeing them as resourceful and resilient, and able to affect positive changes in their own lives. A strengths-based PLAAFP is *not* focused on hiding or ignoring areas of weakness; instead, it focuses on understanding the demands of an age-appropriate, inclusive environment and what supports a person needs to build on their strengths and maximize their personal growth and participation (Shogren et al., 2017). A strengths-based approach, then, focuses on what the person can do and become, with or without supports. Rather than saying a student "cannot, is unable, or won't," a strengths-based approach identifies what the person can do and does with supports (Weishaar, 2010). Any "deficits" within a student are not problems—they are simply concerns we have not yet found appropriate supports for.

What Are Supports?

Individualized supports refer to resources and strategies designed for a specific person to support them in everyday life, including instruction, pursuing personal interests, and promoting personal well-being (Thompson et al., 2009). Remember, everyone benefits from personal supports. For example, I (Jennifer) require the support of an alarm clock to wake up on time for work. I also require the support of a GPS app on my phone to drive to new locations. And I even prefer the support of sunglasses to keep me comfortable on sunny days. In short, supports are widely available, and each of us personalizes those supports to best match our preferences and needs. For example, we personalize the location, type, or even number of alarm clocks we use each morning, the voice that speaks on our GPS device, and the style of sunglasses we wear. What is important to remember, here, is that each of us uses personal supports, and some people will use different types or numbers of supports than others. Using supports is natural and benefits each of us; having the autonomy to choose which supports we feel most comfortable with and being able to direct those supports is paramount. Certainly, the same is then true for students with disabilities: they need opportunities to learn about different supports and the autonomy to select and direct those supports they prefer.

How Do We Use a Strengths-Based Approach to Develop IEPs and PLAAFPs in Particular?

Weick and colleagues (1989) explain that a strengths perspective involves practitioners supporting people to identify and appreciate their own strengths and resources. IEP teams can then work with and from these strengths, drawing upon them as a basis for developing learning goals and supports. The question to ask is: what does the student do well? To start working towards a strengths-based IEP, teams should first identify student strengths. These might be academic strengths and preferences, but it is also important to consider character strengths. Character strengths include creativity, honesty, curiosity, self-regulation, and perseverance, among others. A strengths finder assessment can help IEP teams learn about a student's abilities, but it also tells students about their own abilities. Completing a strengths finder assessment, such as the VIA Survey (accessible at https://www.viacharacter.org/character-strengths-via) can be one easy and interesting way to identify, and ultimately build on, strengths that help chart a path to student learning. It is important to note that character strengths are relevant to instruction, goals, and activities. Personality traits, on the other hand, tend to center on what other people like about the student, and are not relevant to instruction, goals, or activities.

Refer to the examples of PLAAFPs provided earlier for Matthew. As you read Example 2, ask yourself, what are some *interests* of Matthew's that could be incorporated into instruction? Certainly, an educator could use his interest in monster trucks and dinosaurs to read books with him on these topics to work on emerging reading skills, such as decoding, fluency, and comprehension. Did you notice any of Matthew's *academic strengths* in these PLAAFP statements? It appears he has strengths in answering literal comprehension questions in addition to strengths in using various supports in his learning. Further, these supports were clearly listed, meaning it would be easy enough for another teacher or support provider to implement them with Matthew. Finally, did you notice any of Matthew's *character strengths* that could be incorporated in your planning? The PLAAFP notes he is resilient and persists despite encountering obstacles; it also states he has a good sense of humor and enjoys peer work. These types of character strengths can be readily incorporated into learning activities and used to leverage additional learning opportunities.

Reference to General Education Standards and Activities   In addition to seeking strengths, IEP teams should consider the general education content standards and activities to write a strengths-based PLAAFP statement. Often, PLAAFP statements draw upon data collected while students are completing standardized assessments (e.g., the Wide Range Achievement Test) or assignments and activities in special education settings (e.g., articulation production in speech language therapist offices or completion of worksheets in the self-contained special education classroom). As noted previously, however, a strengths-based approach focuses on understanding the supports a person has, uses, and needs to maximize their growth and participation in age-appropriate, inclusive settings. PLAAFP statements, then, should refer to what this particular student does in relation to general education content standards (e.g., third-grade math standards) and activities (e.g., playing with other third-grade students at recess). This might include, for example, a discussion in the PLAAFP of how a student uses the support of a number line to solve third-grade–level addition problems, or the support of a speech-generating device to communicate with peers at recess. By including reference to the supports students use in the inclusive environment, you can use the PLAAFP to present a picture of a person who has capacity and resourcefulness, rather than a student who is performing well below grade level or a student who is unable to communicate with her peers effectively. Alignment of PLAAFP statements to general education standards and activities will be discussed in more detail later in this chapter.

Table 5.1 provides a list of questions that sometimes guide educators' thinking in drafting the PLAAFP, along with a list of alternative questions to help you draft a strengths-based PLAAFP.

Incorporating Quality, Interdisciplinary Data in PLAAFP Statements

As noted in the previous examples, the data reported in the PLAAFP will vary based on student needs (e.g., frequency of challenging behavior, number of words read correctly in a minute). All data selected and reported must be

Table 5.1.   Questions to consider regarding student ability

Instead of this . . .	Ask this . . .
What do I like about the student?	What does the student do well?
What are the student's deficits and weaknesses?	What are the student's preferences and priorities?
What is the student behind in, or unable to do, currently?	What are student strengths that can be built on to address areas of need?
What can the student do on standardized assessments or in special settings?	What can the student do with specific supports in the inclusive setting?

1. Specific, meaning the behavior or skill being measured is clearly defined

2. Objective, meaning that everyone involved will be able to measure the skill or behavior and come up with the same results

3. Measurable, meaning the skill or behavior can be observed, counted, or otherwise measured

4. Frequent, meaning the skill or behavior can be assessed frequently to allow student progress to be measured in a timely way

5. Strengths-based

These criteria are each discussed next.

Specific   Imagine you are reviewing the behavior PLAAFP section of IEP for an incoming student named Karl, and the team reports "Karl struggles to return to class from recess." As you read this, you immediately have a lot of questions. What is Karl doing instead of returning to class? What is the struggle—is it that he didn't hear the recess bell, or that he heard the bell and chose to continue to play, or something else? How often does this happen—is it every day? Every recess? Or just on some particular days? Finally, you might be wondering, does this struggle even matter? Maybe Karl whines and complains briefly, but still returns to class on time. Altogether, this PLAAFP statement just leaves us with too many questions. To avoid this situation, each PLAAFP statement must be very specific. The skill or behavior should be described clearly enough so that other team members can objectively understand what to expect. There are certainly many ways to rewrite the problematic PLAAFP about Karl's recess behavior. One example of how it could be rewritten is as follows:

> *Karl does not independently respond to the recess bell and continues to play on the bars on average 88% of recesses; in these instances, Karl is late for class. When a peer says, "Karl, I heard the bell. I'll walk in with you," Karl responds to the peer on average 95% of the time and is on-time to class. It is recommended that a peer support Karl to return to class on time.*

Not only does the second statement describe Karl's behavior at recess in more specific, precise language; it also concludes with a recommended support to increase the behavior the team would like to see from Karl.

Objective   As you continue to read Karl's IEP PLAAFP, you come across the following statement: "Karl obtained a standard score of 78 on the Wide Range Achievement Test (WRAT). This indicates his reading skills are in the 'low' range for his age." At first glance, this is clear, objective information. It is encouraging here to have a standard score; this allows us to compare Karl's reading to an average reader Karl's age or grade. However, in doing so, the tester concluded that Karl's reading scores were "low" compared to his same-age peers. This inclusion of a designation of Karl as a "low" reader quite obviously does not highlight what Karl can read, nor does it capture his strengths to build upon to maximize his potential in the area of reading. What's more, this WRAT score leaves us with a whole host of questions. We know how Karl reads in comparison to his peers on a single measure, but we do not know how he performs in a nontesting session. We also do not clearly know how Karl reads best—is he a phonetic reader? Does he read specific sight words? What supports does Karl use to decode or comprehend text? How is his reading fluency? Comprehension? At what grade level is Karl reading? An objective statement would answer these kinds of questions, enabling everyone to be able to measure Karl's reading skills and come up with the same results. Once again, there are many ways this PLAAFP could be written to better reflect Karl's strengths. For example,

> *Karl is able to read 90 high-frequency sight words from the Dolch word list, and on average learns to identify three new content vocabulary words in his fourth-grade content classes (science, language arts, and social studies) per unit of study (e.g., "living" and "universe"). Karl is able to comprehend his fourth-grade level texts when they are provided via audiobook*

with 85% accuracy (who, what, where, when questions). He also benefits from color photographs of key concepts. When reading independently, Karl reads first-grade level materials with a fluency of 33 words per minute with 95% accuracy.

What differences do you notice between the second statement and the first? The first describes what Karl *can score* on a standardized assessment and how that score compares to typical scores of his same-age peers. The second describes exactly what Karl *can do* when he reads. It is richer in detail, as well as being based in his strengths.

Measurable   Karl's PLAAFP statements also report his communication skills. You note the speech language pathologist (SLP) wrote, "Karl has difficulty articulating /l/ and /s/ sounds, making his speech difficult to understand by unfamiliar communication partners." This PLAAFP statement gives us some information to measure: we know to measure his intelligibility with familiar and unfamiliar communication partners when Karl makes /l/ and /s/ sounds. However, it is less clear how and when this skill should be observed, counted, and measured. A clearer PLAAFP might read: "Karl produces /l/ and /s/ sounds correctly in the speech therapy room 90% of the time when given a visual and verbal model from the speech language pathologist but pronounces these sounds correctly in his classroom 42% of observations of small group work, and at recess in 35% of observations." This revised PLAAFP helps the team understand what sounds to measure, as well as where and when to measure them. This revised PLAAFP also helps us understand some factors that might support Karl to improve his articulation.

Frequent   For data to be useful, teams must be able to monitor student progress frequently. For example, the previous reading example noted Karl obtained a standard score of 78 on the WRAT. Norm-referenced, standardized assessments are generally completed annually at most; more frequent administration of these tests can make the results unreliable and invalid because students can remember test items, among other concerns. Therefore, reporting scores from standardized assessments has limited utility in the PLAAFP. If they are reported, other data should always be included as well, enabling the team to take more frequent data on student progress. The previous revised reading PLAAFP would enable teams to collect a variety of data on Karl's decoding, comprehension, fluency, and support use, all of which will support his team in making timely educational decisions as they monitor Karl's progress throughout the school year.

Strengths-Based   As discussed previously in this chapter, strengths-based PLAAFPs are essential for ensuring students are positioned as capable, resourceful, and full of potential. The data we collect can greatly impact whether the student is seen through a strengths-based lens. For example, in your review of Karl's PLAAFP, you read in the behavior section, "Karl attempts to elope from the classroom at a rate of 2 occurrences in 60 minutes; elopement is most likely to occur in unstructured activities (90% of instances) versus structured activities (10% of instances)." In this PLAAFP example, the basic elements of specific, measurable, objective, and frequent are all present, but Karl's skills, capacity, and resourcefulness are not highlighted. To accomplish this, teams must collect data about the supports Karl uses and benefits from. For example, the revised PLAAFP statement might read:

Karl currently elopes at a rate of 2 occurrences per 60 minutes and is more likely to do so during unstructured activities (90% of instances) than structured activities (10% of instances). These data suggest Karl benefits from a structured learning environment. Supports to offer structure that have been used include visual schedules, break cards, and checklists. With these supports in place, Karl's elopement from unstructured activities reduced to a rate of 1 occurrence per 60 minutes in the past month. It is recommended that Karl and his team continue to identify supports to participate in unstructured classroom activities.

Collecting Data That Are Comprehensive and Interdisciplinary

To achieve a comprehensive assessment of student present levels, an interdisciplinary team must work together to assess student performance in all areas of suspected need. Family members, related services providers, teachers, and students themselves will usually be members of these interdisciplinary teams. Together, and independently as appropriate, each team member should collect specific, objective, measurable and frequent data on student progress throughout the year. Then, when the team meets to develop an IEP, data from everyone can be synthesized to develop the PLAAFP.

Note how this approach contrasts with the status quo, in which a single team member drafts each section of the PLAAFP—the special education teacher might draft the academic present levels, the speech therapist drafts the communication section, the occupational therapist drafts the motor section, and so on. The result of this kind of an approach is both disjointed and restricted. The PLAAFP would be *disjointed* because each team member only reports from their perspective. For example, the speech therapist might know how the student performs a skill in the therapy setting but not how the student performs that skill across the school, home, and community setting. The result is a PLAAFP section that is fragmented with no cohesive report of how the student performs a variety of skills in a range of settings with a diverse group of people. It is also vulnerable to being more *restricted* and *shallower* in content for many of the same reasons, and instead of providing a comprehensive and detailed overview of student skills and strengths, this kind of approach to writing a PLAAFP relies on team members to only report the narrow set of data they collected through observations, work samples, or testing.

How might a team shift to writing this kind of comprehensive, integrated PLAAFP? We offer five tips below to set teams on track.

Tips

❑ *Provide data templates to all team members to use throughout the year.* This will ensure all team members are collecting information in the same way on the same set of skills. These templates should include a description of skills or behaviors that are measurable and objective.

❑ *Regularly review data as a team to make conclusions about how the student is performing.* Team members can commit to collecting data once or twice a week, and then reviewing it together monthly in-person, via a virtual meeting, or using collaborative online tools such as Google docs.

❑ *Involve the student in collecting their own data on how they are performing, what supports they prefer, and their personal priorities.* Teaching the student to collect data on their own skills is an important life skill. It enables students to have more autonomy over their own lives, setting and directing their own goals. Tools such as timer apps can be used to remind students to collect or enter data, and data collection apps can be used to support students to accurately and discreetly collect data on skills or behaviors of interest, using their smart phones or tablets.

❑ *Involve families in collecting data on how the student performs skills or behaviors in the home and community settings.* Families can also receive app-based reminders and tools for ongoing data collection. A benefit of these tools is that they are easy to use and can be easily downloaded and integrated with other data sources. Families might also benefit from this participation by identifying opportunities to practice important skills at home and in the community, increasing the chances skills will be acquired and generalized.

❑ *Prepare team members to give reports during the IEP meeting.* Let all team members know what data to share, how to summarize their data, and what they see as student strengths, preferences, and areas of support need. By knowing what is expected of them and how they will participate, more team members will be able to meaningfully participate in developing the IEP.

When teams gather to draft the IEP together, they can share and discuss data. All data are also integrated into one statement, allowing teams to understand how student performance, for example, varies across settings or activities. The example below shows how data can be integrated into a social PLAAFP for a student with complex communication needs.

> *Example: Social PLAAFP: Lisa is well-liked at school, and she enjoys social interactions both inside the classroom and during passing periods. She is also consistently friendly and kind to her classmates both in the classroom and during break times between classes and at lunch. One concern noted by the special education teacher is that Lisa does not respect personal space expectations of her peers and stands very close to them or even leans against them. This happens in 4 out of 5 opportunities, resulting in her peers moving away from Lisa. General education teachers have also observed this occurring, and the family reports Lisa is often reminded to use "personal space." Family members note that giving Lisa a reminder to keep one arms-length distance between herself and her friends is helpful. With this cue, Lisa is more likely to respect personal boundaries.*

Teachers also report Lisa has challenges keeping up with conversations between herself and her peers; they observe Lisa losing track of the topic of conversation and making off-topic comments in 3 out of 5 conversations. The speech language pathologist and family data concur, finding Lisa makes off-topic comments in 4 out of 5 conversations lasting more than 5 minutes. Teachers also note that Lisa tends to use repeated phrases to start a conversation; some of these are socially appropriate (e.g., "How was your weekend?"), whereas others are not (e.g., "You smell; you need some body spray."). Lisa uses appropriate social starters in 2 out of 5 opportunities at school, and inappropriate phrases in 3 out of 5 opportunities. The family shares that Lisa really loves body spray and likes to "smell good," which could explain this particular phrase. The team agrees Lisa could learn a different strategy for incorporating her interest in starting a conversation and her appreciation of body spray, by using a phrase such as "Hi! I have this body spray I like; would you like some too?"

Referencing General Education Settings and Standards in the PLAAFP

At the outset of this chapter, we identified three required components to every PLAAFP: 1) a description of the student's needs in all academic and functional areas affected by their disability; 2) objective and measurable baseline information about the student's current levels of performance in the general education curriculum; and 3) description of how the student's disability affects their involvement and progress in the general education curriculum. In this section, we focus on the final component, how teams describe the impact of the student's disability on their involvement and progress in the general education curriculum.

Unfortunately, many PLAAFP statements give a cursory reference to general education and emphasize student deficits rather than objectively describing the impact of the student's disability on their involvement in general education. As a consequence, this component of the PLAAFP too often refers to general education settings, curricula, and activities as inappropriate for students with disabilities. In fact, a common sentence in PLAAFP statements is something along the lines of, "The student is performing below their grade level peers and needs specially designed instruction in the special education classroom." This type of statement in the PLAAFP may seem adequate at the outset, but it certainly presents many problems. Most importantly, however, it assumes that specialized instruction and support can only occur in the special education classroom. This is simply untrue; research over the past several decades has shown many ways specialized instruction can be provided in the general education classroom, using strategies such as embedded instruction (Jimenez & Kamei, 2015), universal design for learning (Lowrey et al., 2017), and co-teaching (Murawski & Lochner, 2011), among others. This statement is also in direct opposition to the meaning of special education as outlined in IDEA (2004), which defines special education simply as specially designed instruction that should be provided in the general education setting in most circumstances. In other words, any student receiving special education services will need specially designed instruction by definition, and therefore the need for such services cannot be used to justify their exclusion from general education.

Given the lack of accuracy in this statement, another approach is needed. The information presented in this chapter, particularly strengths-based descriptions and data-informed statements, are both things that educators will rely upon when writing a PLAAFP that 1) references general education and 2) clearly and objectively describes how the student's disability affects their involvement in general education. Note that we will use "general education" to refer to the setting, activities, and curriculum. To start our thinking on this topic, consider the following two-sample reading PLAAFPs for Joey. Both refer to reading standards for fifth grade from the Common Core State Standards for English/ Language Arts (National Governors Association Center for Best Practices and Council of Chief State School Officers, 2010):

> *Example 1: Reading Comprehension PLAAFP: Fifth graders are expected to be able to "determine the theme of a story, drama, or poem from details in the text, including how characters in a story or drama respond to challenges or how the speaker in a poem reflects upon a topic; summarize the text." (RL.5.2). However, Joey is performing well below grade level because of his significant cognitive disability and speech language disorder. He is still learning basic reading decoding skills and can read 58 high frequency sight words. He is only able to comprehend basic who, what, and when questions and does not understand point of view.*

> *Example 2: Reading comprehension PLAAFP: Fifth graders are learning to "determine the theme of a story, drama, or poem from details in the text, including how characters in a story or drama respond to challenges or how the speaker in a poem reflects upon a topic; summarize the text." (RL.5.2). Joey has complex communication needs and benefits from a speech generating device with dynamic overlays to participate in the general education lessons. Due to his cognitive disability, he also benefits from memory supports to access materials, such as choices and visuals. Joey is able to use his speech generating device to navigate to the characters page and identify the character speaking in a 5th grade passage read aloud to him with 78% accuracy in 4/5 opportunities. Joey can choose a theme (e.g., honesty, good vs. bad behavior, courage) from a field of 3 color picture icons with 66% accuracy in 4/5 trials. When given two characters or events to compare from a story (e.g., "Which character was nicer?"), Joey can select the correct response with 40% accuracy in 4/5 trials.*

As you read both PLAAFP statements, what are some of the things you noticed about each? How do the different descriptions of Joey's participation in general education impact your understanding of Joey? Did you notice how Joey's deviation from fifth-grade content standards is emphasized in the first example, while the second example highlights how he uses supports to access those same standards? Both examples also reference the grade-level standards, but only Example 2 did so in a way that detailed how Joey accesses these standards, with specific supports. Both also reference Joey's disability, but Example 1 positioned his disability as a problem that results in his inability to participate, whereas Example 2 positioned it as a background for the supports he uses. From these examples, it is clear that word choice makes an impact on how students are portrayed and the resulting decisions teams might make from these portrayals.

As illustrated in the examples, referring to grade-aligned content standards is a key strategy when writing PLAAFP statements. Doing so accomplishes two critical outcomes: 1) It addresses the requirement from Congress that PLAAFP statements describe how the student's disability affects their involvement and progress in the general education curriculum, and 2) It sets the foundation for a grade-aligned IEP. As noted previously, the PLAAFP is the foundation upon which all other IEP components are based. Too often, student IEPs are disconnected from the general curriculum, leaving teams to feel that the IEP is in competition with, or in place of, participation and progress in the general curriculum. This disconnection occurs because goals are not related to general curriculum (e.g., an eighth-grade student has a goal to learn coin values and names, but this is not taught in eighth-grade general education), or services are not inclusive (e.g., students need to be removed from class to receive speech therapy). By writing a PLAAFP that is grounded in general education, educators can avoid these kinds of conflicts. How does one write a PLAAFP that is grounded in general education? See the following tips.

Tips

❏ *Reference grade-aligned standards whenever possible.* When reporting present levels related to academic skills (e.g., reading, writing, math), the team should refer to their state's content standards and describe 1) what is expected of students in the grade, and 2) how the student is performing those tasks, using any individualized supports. Doing so will enable teams to develop a PLAAFP that clearly relates to general education.

❏ *Reference age-respectful activities.* When standards do not exist for a needed skill (e.g., motor, communication, social), reference general education and age-respectful activities.

❏ *Describe the impact of the student's disability from a point of view of strengths.* Using the strategies described earlier in this chapter, the impact of the student's disability on their involvement in general education can be described in a way that emphasizes ability, resourcefulness, and potential. This will include describing how the student participates in general education using supports, what strategies have been used, and potential strategies to try based on input from the team.

PULLING IT ALL TOGETHER

Students receiving special education services will have unique learning profiles, interests, strengths, and support needs. How these are described in the PLAAFP sets the stage for the rest of the IEP: the wording and portrayals of students are fundamental in setting high expectations, focusing on capacity, and facilitating inclusive instruction. Every PLAAFP must contain three components:

1. A strengths-based description of the child's needs in all academic and functional areas affected by their disability

2. Specific, objective, measurable, and frequent baseline information about the child's current levels of performance in the general education curriculum that is collected by the interdisciplinary team and is aligned with general education standards

3. A description of how the student's disability affects their involvement and progress in the general education curriculum, which incorporates the supports and strategies used by students to support their involvement and progress

These three components are depicted in Figure 5.1.

Figure 5.1.   The Present Levels of Academic Achievement and Functional Performance (PLAAFP) formula.

CONCLUDING THOUGHTS: WRITING THE PLAAFP

The PLAAFP section of the IEP sets the groundwork for the remainder of the decisions made during the IEP process. Creating a strengths-based narrative about the student is both an art and a science, as word choices can suggest a variety of solutions. A complete picture of the student provides a holistic view of their strengths and instructional needs. Only a comprehensive and cohesive narrative, guided by data from multiple team members, families, and the student themselves, can set the stage for a robust educational plan that emphasizes strengths and facilitates inclusive education.

REVIEWING THE COMMITMENT: *Describing Your Student's Abilities and Needs*

This chapter provided guidance on how to describe a student's present levels of performance—both academic and functional—in a way that is clear, precise, and based on the student's strengths as well as data about the student's performance. The PLAAFP section of the IEP is the foundation for the rest of the document, so what you say here and how you say it impacts the rest of the decisions your team will make.

Think back to the student you identified at the start of the chapter and the strengths you listed for that student. Next, identify one area of academic or functional skill to focus upon—preferably one where you are very familiar with what the student can do:

_____

_____

Think about the student's present level of performance in this area. Use the following questions to stimulate your thinking:

What does the student do well?

_____

_____

_____

What are the student's preferences and priorities?

_____

_____

_____

What are student strengths that can be built on to address areas of need?

_____

_____

_____

What can the student do with specific supports in the inclusive setting?

_____

_____

_____

What data do you have to support your answers to these questions (e.g., observation, behavioral data collected over time)?

_____

_____

_____

ACTING ON THE COMMITMENT: *Describing Your Student's Abilities and Needs*

Identify another member of the IEP team who would be knowledgeable about the student's performance in the skill area you identified. Plan a time to talk with the team member to gather further information. (For example, if you identified reading as your focus skill area for Janelle, and Janelle's social studies teacher is on her IEP team, discuss how Janelle does with reading in her social studies class.)

Working together, draft a statement for the PLAAFP about your student's abilities and needs in the skill area you identified. Be sure to base your statement on data that are 1) specific, 2) objective, 3 measurable, 4) frequently collected, and 5) focused on strengths.

_____

_____

_____

_____

_____

_____

_____

_____

_____

_____

_____

_____

_____

Planning for Special Factors, Extended School Year, and Alternate Assessment

6

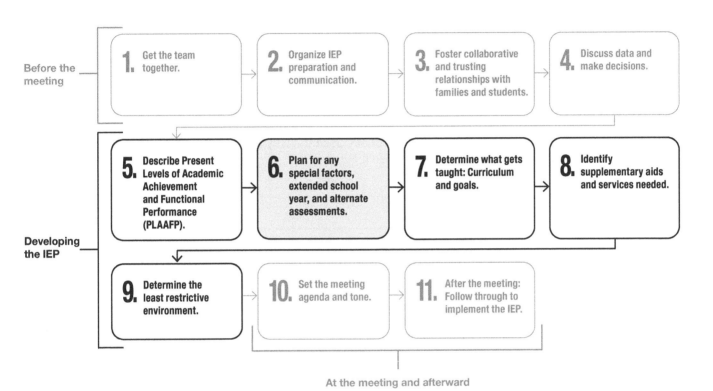

Before the meeting

1. Get the team together.

2. Organize IEP preparation and communication.

3. Foster collaborative and trusting relationships with families and students.

4. Discuss data and make decisions.

Developing the IEP

5. Describe Present Levels of Academic Achievement and Functional Performance (PLAAFP).

6. Plan for any special factors, extended school year, and alternate assessments.

7. Determine what gets taught: Curriculum and goals.

8. Identify supplementary aids and services needed.

9. Determine the least restrictive environment.

10. Set the meeting agenda and tone.

11. After the meeting: Follow through to implement the IEP.

At the meeting and afterward

In addition to the present level of performance, annual goals and objectives, supplementary aids and services, and least restrictive environment, the IEP team must also make a collection of other decisions related to the student's education. IDEA 2004 specifies five special factors that must be considered in IEP development. They are as follows:

- Communication needs/Deafness

- Behavior

- Limited English proficiency

- Blindness or visual impairment

- Assistive technology

In addition, teams must consider if the student is eligible for extended school year (ESY) services. Finally, the team must determine the student's eligibility for alternate assessment. Although many of these factors are unlikely to apply to most students who receive special education services, it is possible that a student with complex support needs will require decision making in all of these areas.

UNDERSTANDING THE COMMITMENT:

Planning for Special Factors and Options That May Benefit Your Student

Considerations related to special factors, extended school year, and alternate assessment will depend on your student's particular abilities and needs.

Think about a student with whom you work. For each of the special factors included in IDEA 2004, determine how relevant it is to this student. Rate each from 1 to 5 (1 = little to no relevance, 5 = very relevant to planning for this student).

- Communication needs/Deafness _____

- Behavior _____

- Limited English proficiency _____

- Blindness or visual impairment _____

- Assistive technology _____

For any special factors you rated at 3 or higher, briefly describe why they are important to consider when planning and writing this student's IEP.

_____

_____

_____

_____

_____

_____

_____

Do you think ESY or alternate assessment will be important factors to plan for in this student's case? Why or why not?

_____

_____

_____

_____

_____

_____

_____

SPECIAL FACTORS

The sections that follow will explain how the special factors listed above are often relevant for students with complex support needs, with reference to IDEA 2004. For each factor, a resource list is included to help you gather more information about how best to meet your student's needs.

Communication Needs/Deafness

It is almost guaranteed that students with complex support needs also will have communication needs. Therefore, every team supporting students with complex support needs should address communication needs in present levels of performance, goals, and supplementary aids and services (including assistive technology, discussed later in this chapter). Communication is recognized as a basic human right in Article 19 of the Universal Declaration of Human Rights (United Nations, n.d.). Therefore, if a student is nonspeaking and does not have another way of communicating, it is the *ethical responsibility* of the IEP team to match the student with an AAC system and begin teaching communication.

The following point cannot be emphasized enough: *Teaching communication should be the Number 1 priority of the IEP team.* Communication should be taught in every activity of every day. Communication devices and systems, such as iPad apps or picture symbols, should be treated as the student's voice. Just as a teacher would never place their hand over a student's mouth to quiet talking, a teacher should never take away a communication system—even if it seems like the student is "just playing with it." *Students should never be without their communication devices, ever.*

IDEA 2004 recognizes that students who are D/deaf or hard of hearing have unique communication needs. Many students who are D/deaf use American Sign Language (ASL) as their primary mode of communication. It is important to remember, however, that ASL is a language and can be inaccessible for students who have other language- and communication-related needs. For example, teams sometimes teach a few simple signs to children who are nonspeaking; however, these isolated signs are unlikely to develop into language unless the child is immersed in an ASL language environment. Many students who have complex communication needs struggle with learning language, and ASL is a language like any other. Therefore, aided communication systems might be needed, with attention paid to both expressive and receptive language.

Resources for Meeting Communication Needs

Online and print resources for meeting students' communication needs include

- Communication Fact Sheets from Parents from the National Technical Assistance Consortium for Children and Young Adults Who Are Deaf-Blind, accessible at https://documents.nationaldb.org/products/communication-a.pdf

- Project CORE's free professional development for teaching communication from the Center for Literacy and Disability Studies, accessible at http://www.project-core.com/

- PrAACtical AAC's tips for supporting students with complex communication needs, accessible at https://praacticalaac.org/

- Resources from the Laurent Clerc National Deaf Education Center at Gallaudet University, accessible at https://clerccenter.gallaudet.edu/national-resources/resources/our-resources/new-to-deaf-education.html

---

Behavior

IDEA 2004 requires that teams must consider Positive Behavior Intervention and Supports when the student's behavior impedes their learning or the learning of others. Specifically, a functional behavioral assessment (FBA) and behavior intervention plan might be needed if the student is engaging in behavior that is limiting their opportunities to learn. FBAs are designed to identify the underlying reasons, or functions, for a challenging behavior. In other words, what purpose does the behavior serve, from the perspective of the student, when they do it? Does it get them something they want, such as physical stimulation or attention from others? Does it help them get out of a task or environment they dislike? FBAs are especially important when working with students who have limited ability to communicate their needs.

The most important points to keep in mind when assessing the behavior of students with complex support needs are as follows:

1. *Use observational data*, such as antecedent-behavior-consequence (ABC) charts and scatterplots, to identify patterns of behavior throughout the day.

2. *Take note of the actual consequence of the behavior* when it occurs. For example, is the student left alone to calm down? Or are they taken out of the classroom on a walk? The consequences that the student experiences are the reasons the behavior continues; in other words, the consequences maintain the behaviors.

3. *Teach a communication replacement to the challenging behavior that matches the function of the challenging behavior.* For example, if a student is exhibiting aggression, and as a result, he leaves the classroom, teach the student a more appropriate way to ask to leave the classroom.

4. *Identify ways to improve the environment in which the behavior is occurring.* If a student is consistently engaging in escape-related behaviors in a particular class setting, consider why the student might be trying to escape that setting. For example, if the setting is unpredictable for the student, or if the student does not understand the directions, try creating a written, visual, or tactile schedule to make the setting more predictable.

Numerous resources are available to assist teams working with students with complex support needs who require behavior supports. A strong behavior support plan for a student with complex support needs is almost certain to include communication supports and a clear plan for teaching communication skills. Some resources are listed in the box.

Positive Behavior Intervention and Support (PBIS) Resources

Online and print resources for planning behavior interventions and supports include

- The website of the Center on PBIS, accessible at https://www.pbis.org/

- The Behavior Suite page on the website of the Center for Parent Information and Resources, accessible at https://www.parentcenterhub.org/behavior/

- The Ohio Center for Autism and Low Incidence (OCALI) autism internet modules, accessible at https://autisminternetmodules.org/

- The website of the Center on Secondary Education for Students with Autism Spectrum Disorders, accessible at https://csesa.fpg.unc.edu/

- *Individualized Supports for Students with Problem Behaviors: Designing Positive Behavior Plans, Second Edition* by Linda Bambara and Lee Kern (2021).

Limited English Proficiency

English proficiency is rarely considered for students with complex support needs, often because students' communication challenges make it difficult to discern the relationship between communication needs and English language needs. Currently, tools designed to measure English language proficiency are in development but are not yet widely available for students with complex support needs. Even though students with complex support needs might require language-related services, they are often thought of as "special education students" and therefore might not receive language-related services (Gholson, 2018).

Karvonen and Clark (2019) explained that "when it is not possible to evaluate a student's English language status because of limited communication, intensive interventions should be prioritized, and their effectiveness evaluated, to remove communication-related barriers to understanding students' language status" (p. 83). That is, if a student is believed to be an English language learner—perhaps because of their recent immigration to the United States, or because of the primary language spoken in their home—intensive communication instruction should immediately be implemented to help uncover language-related barriers. Once again, the answer is communication instruction no matter what the question is! Here are some resources.

Resources for Teaching Students With Limited English Proficiency

Online resources for teaching students with limited English proficiency include

- The Considering a Student's Limited English Proficiency in the IEP page on the website of the Center for Parent Information and Resources, accessible at https://www.parentcenterhub.org /considering-lep/

- The Alternate English Language Learning Assessment project's *Case examples of English learners with significant cognitive disabilities* (ALTELLA Brief No. 6), accessible at https://altella.wceruw .org/pubs/ALTELLA_Brief-06_Case-Examples.pdf

- The document Dear Colleague Letter: English Learner Students and Limited English Proficient Parents, from the U.S. Department of Justice's Civil Rights Division and the U.S. Department of Education's Office for Civil Rights, accessible at https://www2.ed.gov/about/offices/list/ocr /letters/colleague-el-201501.pdf

---

Blindness or Visual Impairment

Two decisions must be made if a student is identified as having a visual impairment. First, IDEA 2004 specifies that a student's "reading and writing skills, needs, and appropriate reading and writing media" must be evaluated to determine if instruction in braille is needed. In addition, the need for supports and instruction, including accessible instructional materials and environments, should also be determined. For students with complex support needs, this is the most common area requiring consideration. Orientation and mobility instruction might be needed; this service can be provided by an itinerant teacher. Materials should be provided in an accessible format; enlarging print, high contrast materials, audio materials, and tactile materials might be necessary.

Cortical visual impairment (CVI) is a particular type of visual impairment that sometimes affects students with complex support needs, particularly those with the physical disability cerebral palsy. CVI is caused by neurological damage to the visual pathways or visual processing areas of the brain. That means that students with CVI have trouble processing what they see. People with CVI describe that the world looks like a "swirling kaleidoscope of color and light," sometimes causing students to avoid looking around because of the meaningless visual information that their brains struggle to understand. Sometimes, students with CVI experience behavior challenges due to challenges with sensory integration or fatigue (Perkins School for the Blind, n.d.). CVI is sometimes overlooked, and it can interfere with literacy instruction if not accounted for. Students with CVI benefit from the support of a careful approach to the use of visual information. A teacher of the blind and visually impaired can teach the student to use their vision more effectively.

Resources for Teaching Students With Blindness or Visual Impairment

Online resources for teaching students with blindness or visual impairment include

- The Considering Blindness and Visual Impairment in the IEP page on the website of the Center for Parent Information and Resources, accessible at https://www.parentcenterhub.org/considering -visual/

- The Perkins School for the Blind website, accessible at https://www.perkins.org/

- CVI resources from Perkins, accessible at https://www.perkins.org/what-is-cvi/

- CVI resources from Teach CVI by B&H The National Institute for the Blind, Visually Impaired and Deafblind in Iceland, accessible at https://www.teachcvi.net/

Assistive Technology

IDEA specifies IEP teams should determine if assistive technology is needed for every student with a disability. However, as of this printing, IDEA has not been reauthorized since 2004. For perspective, in 2004, speech-to-text, text-to-speech, and typing prediction were specialized technologies that were individually loaded onto computers. Smartphones were only yet on the horizon. Today, those features benefit everyone and are widely available. Clearly, the world of technology has expanded exponentially since IDEA was last updated, and today every child in school uses technology. At the same time, assistive technology has advanced considerably and has opened more and more possibilities for students with complex support needs to participate in general education activities. Therefore, teams should not consider *if* a student benefits from technology. Instead, teams should ask, "What kinds of technology could make school more accessible for this student?"

In addition to assistive technology devices, assistive technology services are also required to ensure the device is properly selected, fit, and customized for the student. All team members need to understand the technology and how to support the student's use of the technology throughout the day. The Assistive Technology Act Amendments of 2004 (PL 108-364) require each state to host an Assistive Technology Act Project, or AT Program for short. AT Programs coordinate with families, services, and other agencies to provide access to assistive technology for individuals with disabilities in the state. The AT Programs also provide technical assistance to support the implementation of assistive technology. Some school districts also employ one or more assistive technology specialists. Ultimately, the entire team—the special and general educator, speech-language pathologist, occupational therapist, physical therapist, and any vision or hearing specialists—must coordinate assistive technology assessments and services.

Resources for Assistive Technology

Online resources for helping students use assistive technology include

- Quality Indicators for Assistive Technology Services, accessible at https://qiat.org/

- CAST Online Tools, accessible at https://www.cast.org/products-services/online-tools

- Resources and technical assistance from the National Center on Accessible Educational Materials, accessible at https://aem.cast.org/

- The Assistive Technology Act Information page on the website of the Center for Parent Information and Resources, accessible at https://www.parentcenterhub.org/wp-content/uploads/repo_items /cpir-on-ata.pdf

- The AT3 Center's page to find your state's AT Program: https://www.at3center.net/stateprogram

EXTENDED SCHOOL YEAR

Besides the special factors discussed above, another important planning consideration is whether extended school year services are needed for the student. What these services entail, and how to plan for them, is discussed in the sections that follow.

What Is Extended School Year?

ESY refers to special education supports and services that are provided beyond the regular school year and are necessary for students with disabilities to access a free and appropriate public education. Interestingly, ESY is not mentioned in the IDEA statute, and instead is described in the IDEA regulations. According to the regulations, "Each public agency must ensure that extended school year services are available as necessary to provide FAPE" as determined by the IEP team (section 300.106 of regs; https://sites.ed.gov/idea/regs/b/b/300.106). In addition, a district or other public agency cannot limit ESY services to students with a particular type of disability, and cannot "unilaterally limit the type, amount, or duration" of ESY services.

This brief mention of ESY in the IDEA regulations leaves individual IEP teams with substantial room for discretion when determining ESY eligibility and services. Most states provide guidance about ESY in statutes (see Burke & Decker, 2017, for a detailed list and links to ESY guidance in each state).

Why Extended School Year?

Eligibility for ESY can be determined by taking multiple factors into account; however, the most common criterion is the extent to which the student's progress toward IEP goals might regress over the summer, and thus would require extensive time to recoup those skills during the school year. If started in kindergarten, an additional 3 months of instruction per year can add up to 3 or more additional cumulative years of instruction. For a student with complex support needs, the additional instructional time available during ESY is extremely valuable and should not be wasted.

Because students with complex support needs often require regular practice to maintain learned skills, it is likely that most every student with complex support needs would qualify for ESY based on the regression/recoupment criterion. However, careful data collection is still necessary to identify priorities for instruction during ESY, and other factors—such as the amount of time needed for the student to successfully transition to a new school routine during ESY—should also be considered. Burke and

---

Procedural Note: Regression and Recoupment

As determined in *Reusch v. Fountain* (1994) and reaffirmed in Letter to Given (U.S. Department of Education, 2003), a school can consider a variety of factors when determining student eligibility for ESY, including the following:

- Regression and recoupment

- Degree of progress toward IEP goals

- Emerging skills

- Interfering behaviors

- Severity of disability

- Special circumstances

As Barnard-Brak and colleagues (2018) suggest, IEP teams should understand their own state regulations, recent case law, and student-specific progress monitoring data to determine students' eligibility.

Data collection	Example
Retrospective data	Examine data taken for goals and objectives of the student; for example, did the student regress over past summer breaks? Holiday breaks? Spring breaks? Specific example: Teacher-created data sheets documenting progress or regression in goals and objectives over breaks
Predictive data	Examine evaluations of the student, especially statements suggesting whether the student will need continual supports to retain information, the severity and nature of the disability, and potential medical and behavioral needs. Specific example: Case study and medical evaluations
Quantitative data	Examine quantitative data taken for measurable goals and objectives as well as evaluations; specifically, examine percentages and accuracy of meeting goals and objectives. Specific example: Assessment data documenting the degree of progress or regression toward IEP goals and objectives
Qualitative data	Examine parent, teacher, and other stakeholder comments on past progress reports, IEPs, and evaluations. Specific example: Comments written on progress reports by school personnel and parents
Anecdotal data	Examine parent, teacher, and other stakeholder comments made during informal communication. Specific example: Comments made on parent–teacher logs or therapist notes

Figure 6.1. Five types of data that can be used to make ESY decisions. (From Burke, M. M., & Decker, J. R. [2017]. Extended school year: Legal and practical considerations for educators. *TEACHING Exceptional Children, 49*[5], 339–346. Reprinted by permission of SAGE Publications.)

Decker (2017) identified five types of data that can be used to make ESY decisions: retrospective data, predictive data, quantitative data, qualitative data, and anecdotal data. These types of data are outlined in Figure 6.1. These data can help a team decide if the student might benefit from ESY.

Skill generalization is an important factor for consideration during ESY for students with complex support needs. Often, students with complex support needs have trouble applying learned skills in new situations. ESY provides an opportunity for students to practice skills in new environments, with new teachers, and with different materials. Therefore, ESY can provide an important learning context for students to ensure generalization of skills learned during the school year.

Planning for Extended School Year

When ESY has been identified as potentially beneficial to the student's FAPE, advance planning ensures that these benefits are realized. Barnard-Brak and colleagues (2018) suggest that ESY teachers observe students during the spring to ensure appropriate supports and services are in place during ESY. Transitions to and from ESY can be difficult as students adjust to a new school schedule and expectations. Using materials and routines from the regular school year will help facilitate this transition and support students' progress. Most importantly, a students' augmentative/alternative communication system should always be available and should travel from school to home to ESY and back again.

When planning for ESY instruction, a special educator should identify activities that promote natural opportunities for maintenance and generalization of skills. ESY can be quite challenging to plan when a special educator is assigned to a group of students with a wide range of disabilities for a set amount of time per day. Balancing individual work time with direct instruction can ensure students receive regular skill practice and continue to make progress toward IEP goals.

For transition-age students, summers offer a natural opportunity for employment instruction that does not conflict with general curriculum activities (Carter et al., 2009). Carter and colleagues (2009) note that the three months of summer across four years of high school can result in an additional year or more of cumulative instruction. They suggest early conversations with a variety of stakeholders and the student to identify the student's long- and short-term employment goals and related community-based

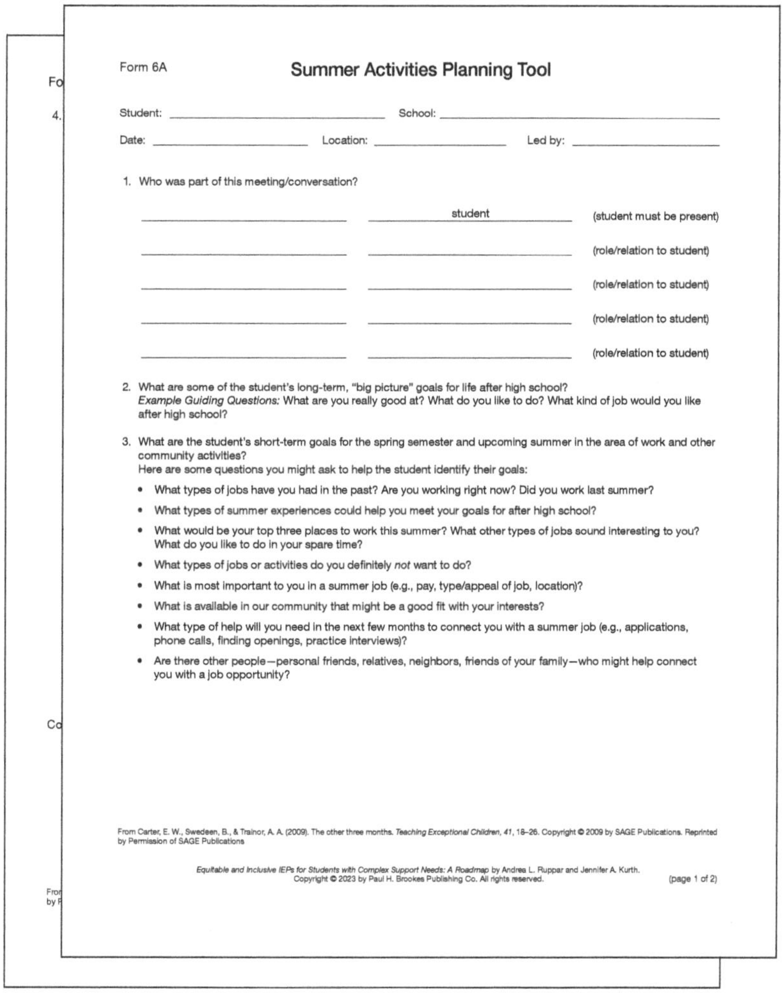
Form 6A

Summer Activities Planning Tool

Student: ______________ School: ______________

Date: ______________ Location: ______________ Led by: ______________

1. Who was part of this meeting/conversation?

______________	student	(student must be present)
______________	______________	(role/relation to student)
______________	______________	(role/relation to student)
______________	______________	(role/relation to student)
______________	______________	(role/relation to student)

2. What are some of the student's long-term, "big picture" goals for life after high school?
   Example Guiding Questions: What are you really good at? What do you like to do? What kind of job would you like after high school?

3. What are the student's short-term goals for the spring semester and upcoming summer in the area of work and other community activities?
   Here are some questions you might ask to help the student identify their goals:
   - What types of jobs have you had in the past? Are you working right now? Did you work last summer?
   - What types of summer experiences could help you meet your goals for after high school?
   - What would be your top three places to work this summer? What other types of jobs sound interesting to you? What do you like to do in your spare time?
   - What types of jobs or activities do you definitely *not* want to do?
   - What is most important to you in a summer job (e.g., pay, type/appeal of job, location)?
   - What is available in our community that might be a good fit with your interests?
   - What type of help will you need in the next few months to connect you with a summer job (e.g., applications, phone calls, finding openings, practice interviews)?
   - Are there other people—personal friends, relatives, neighbors, friends of your family—who might help connect you with a job opportunity?

From Carter, E. W., Swedeen, B., & Trainor, A. A. (2009). The other three months. *Teaching Exceptional Children, 41*, 18–26. Copyright © 2009 by SAGE Publications. Reprinted by Permission of SAGE Publications

 (page 1 of 2)

Figure 6.2. Summer Activities Planning Tool. (From Carter, E. W., Swedeen, B., & Trainor, A. A. [2009]. The other three months. *TEACHING Exceptional Children, 41*, 18–26. Reprinted by permission of SAGE Publications.)

employment activities. See Figure 6.2 for a planning tool designed to match students with disabilities with summer community-based employment opportunities. (A full-size, blank, reproducible version of this form is provided as an appendix to this chapter and on the Brookes Download Hub.)

Overall, ESY experiences should be meaningful and based on students' long-term goals and interests. Like any aspect of the IEP, ESY for students with complex support needs should be individually determined by a team of professionals, in collaboration with the student and their family.

ALTERNATE ASSESSMENT

ESSA (PL 114-95) requires that all students must have instruction based on grade-level academic standards. However, grade-level academic standards are not accessible to all students, particularly students with complex support needs. Therefore, IEP teams must determine whether the student should take the regular assessment with accommodations, or an alternate assessment based on alternate standards. If taking the alternate assessment, the student receives a modified academic curriculum and might not be eligible for a high school diploma. These regulations vary by state. No more than 1% of all students can be tested using an alternate assessment. This accounts for approximately 10% of students with disabilities. Alternate standards are aligned with regular standards but reduced in depth and breadth. All students must receive instruction related to these standards, because these standards are the content of the assessment.

It is important to also recognize that students follow a modified curriculum, NOT an alternate curriculum. Alternate curricula marketed to special educators often do not align with general education content standards. Instead, students with complex support needs should follow the general curriculum of their grade, participating in general education activities alongside peers without disabilities, with intensive, individualized instruction aligned to alternate achievement standards.

Resources for Alternate Assessments

Online resources for learning more about alternate assessments include

- The TIES Center brief titled *Taking the Alternate Assessment Does NOT Mean Education in a Separate Setting*, accessible at https://files.tiescenter.org/files/MdKEf-nTpN/ties-brief-2

- The National Center on Educational Outcomes publication "Start with the End in Mind: Decisions about Student Participation in the Alternate Assessment," accessible at https://nceo.umn.edu/docs/OnlinePubs/Tool7Infographic.pdf

- The TIES Center Tip titled *Academic Standards for Students with Significant Cognitive Disabilities in Inclusive Classrooms*, accessible at https://publications.ici.umn.edu/ties/foundations-of-inclusion-tips/academic-standards-for-students-with-significant-cognitive-disabilities-in-inclusive_classrooms

---

CONCLUDING THOUGHTS: SPECIAL FACTORS, EXTENDED SCHOOL YEAR, AND ALTERNATE ASSESSMENT

When developing an IEP, teams must consider the extent to which special factors might be relevant to student learning, and address these factors through specific goals, supports, or services. Teams must also address student learning needs and the extent to which an extended school year will be necessary. Although these considerations are made for all students, those students with complex support needs are more likely than others to have special factors and needs for ESY, making this section of the IEP uniquely important.

REVIEWING THE COMMITMENT:

Planning for Special Factors and Options That May Benefit Your Student

Revisit the special factors you listed for your student at the beginning of this chapter. After reading the chapter, have your thoughts changed concerning which factors are relevant to your student and why?

_____

_____

_____

_____

_____

Have your thoughts changed concerning whether you need to plan for ESY or alternate assessment for your student?

_____

_____

_____

_____

_____

List the sources of data you will use to help your team plan for special factors, ESY, and/or alternate assessment.

_____

_____

_____

_____

_____

ACTING ON THE COMMITMENT:

Planning for Special Factors and Options That May Benefit Your Student

Whether or not your student needs ESY services, it is important to plan for summer activities that will build on their strengths and help meet their long-term needs.

If your student is in high school, set up a time with the student and family to work through the Summer Activities Planning Tool together.

If your student is in elementary or middle school, share options for summer camps and experiences. Summer is an important time for socialization, so learn about local parks and recreation programs that might be of interest to your student and share the information with parents. Summer travel is also an exciting time for learning, and students should be encouraged to share photos and mementos from important events with their teachers. This is especially important for pre-symbolic or early communicators because they are unable to communicate about events and topics beyond the "here and now." Parents might also benefit from local respite camps run by organizations like the Easter Seals and United Cerebral Palsy.

Summer Activities Planning Tool

Student: _____   School: _____

Date: _____   Location: _____   Led by: _____

1. Who was part of this meeting/conversation?

_____   _____student_____   (student must be present)

_____   _____   (role/relation to student)

_____   _____   (role/relation to student)

_____   _____   (role/relation to student)

_____   _____   (role/relation to student)

2. What are some of the student's long-term, "big picture" goals for life after high school?
   Example Guiding Questions: What are you really good at? What do you like to do? What kind of job would you like after high school?

3. What are the student's short-term goals for the spring semester and upcoming summer in the area of work and other community activities?
   Here are some questions you might ask to help the student identify their goals:

   • What types of jobs have you had in the past? Are you working right now? Did you work last summer?

   • What types of summer experiences could help you meet your goals for after high school?

   • What would be your top three places to work this summer? What other types of jobs sound interesting to you? What do you like to do in your spare time?

   • What types of jobs or activities do you definitely *not* want to do?

   • What is most important to you in a summer job (e.g., pay, type/appeal of job, location)?

   • What is available in our community that might be a good fit with your interests?

   • What type of help will you need in the next few months to connect you with a summer job (e.g., applications, phone calls, finding openings, practice interviews)?

   • Are there other people—personal friends, relatives, neighbors, friends of your family—who might help connect you with a job opportunity?

4. List these short-term goals and needed supports.

Short-term/ Summer goals	What are some possible places in our community that might provide opportunities?	Who do we already know—or need to seek out—who might be able to help?	What supports or resources are needed to make this happen?	Who will take responsibility for following up on this?
1.				
2.				
3.				

Consider some of the following questions when thinking about the supports and resources the student might need:

- Will the student need direct help or support on the job? If so, who could provide that support?
- Will the student need someone to check in with them periodically during the summer?
- Are there transportation issues, scheduling conflicts, family concerns, or other logistical considerations to be addressed?
- Are there skills the student should learn to better prepare them before a job starts?
- What roles will the student, family, teachers, and/or business representatives play in connecting to this job?

Determining What Gets Taught

Curriculum and Goals

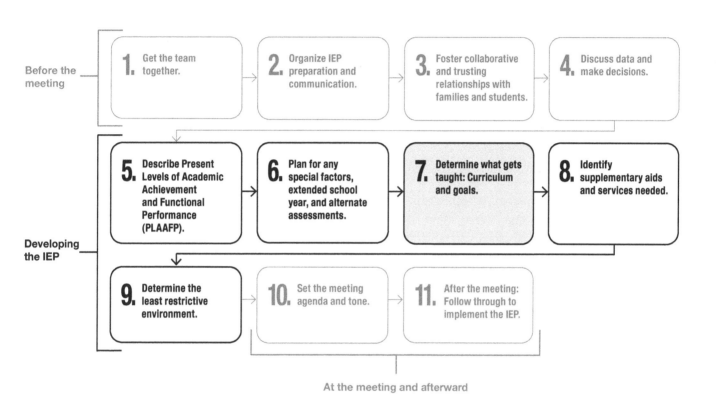

Before the meeting

1. Get the team together.

2. Organize IEP preparation and communication.

3. Foster collaborative and trusting relationships with families and students.

4. Discuss data and make decisions.

Developing the IEP

5. Describe Present Levels of Academic Achievement and Functional Performance (PLAAFP).

6. Plan for any special factors, extended school year, and alternate assessments.

7. Determine what gets taught: Curriculum and goals.

8. Identify supplementary aids and services needed.

9. Determine the least restrictive environment.

10. Set the meeting agenda and tone.

11. After the meeting: Follow through to implement the IEP.

At the meeting and afterward

In Chapter 5, we used the analogy of planning a vacation to describe the PLAAFP as an integral part of mapping and planning. To extend the analogy of vacation planning to IEP development, we need to know where we are (present levels) to figure out how to get where we want to go (IEP goals). We begin by considering what curriculum means for students with complex support needs. We then turn our attention to IEP goals, which describe the IEP team's vision for the student in their upcoming educational year. Student strengths should provide a jumping-off point for goals as well as instructional methods. Although curriculum content can be individualized, it also needs to be grade-aligned and age-appropriate. In addition to academic skill areas such as literacy, social studies, math, and science, additional curriculum areas such as social-emotional, recreation, functional, and self-determination skills can be, and often are, included in the IEP.

UNDERSTANDING THE COMMITMENT:

Providing a Fair and Appropriate Public Education

The goals included in a student's IEP are key determinants of what and how students will be taught for the upcoming year. As such, the choices you make about what goals to create will have a significant impact on what that student learns, or fails to learn, for the next year.

When developing goals, you will need to focus on the student's preferences and priorities, ensuring the goals are personally relevant from the student's perspective. Goals should also be technically adequate to communicate exactly what students will learn, to what criterion, and with what supports. Finally, goals should facilitate students in learning the general education academic, nonacademic, and extracurricular curriculum in the inclusive setting. These will be discussed in depth in this chapter. For now, work on your commitment by thinking about a student with whom you work. Brainstorm goals for the student's academic, nonacademic, and extracurricular learning.

_____

_____

_____

_____

_____

_____

_____

_____

_____

_____

CURRICULUM

To understand how to determine a curriculum for students with complex support needs, it is important to have an in-depth understanding of what is meant by "curriculum." This term encompasses far more than academic content explicitly taught in lessons. The sections that follow will

- Provide a comprehensive explanation of what curriculum includes—not only the *explicit curriculum* but also the *hidden curriculum* and the *null curriculum*, that which is not taught

- Discuss different curriculum areas—academic, nonacademic, extracurricular, and functional—and their relevance to students with complex support needs

- Explain how to use an *ecological framework* to develop a curriculum for a student with complex support needs

Understanding the Types of Curricula

The "curriculum" is often thought of as the formal instruction students receive, such as textbooks, activities, and materials used to learn. In reality, this is only one component of the curriculum, often referred to as the *explicit* or *overt curriculum*. A more complete definition of curriculum refers to what is taught explicitly, what is taught implicitly, and what is not taught (Glatthorn et al., 2016). Curricula for all students, including those with complex support needs, can be any of the following, as seen in Table 7.1.

In this book, we refer to the "general education curriculum" as including each of these components of the curriculum: the *general education curriculum* is the textbooks, handouts, worksheets, lab

Table 7.1. Types of curricula

Type of curriculum	Definition
Explicit/overt curriculum	The explicit curriculum refers to the formal instruction, including textbooks, materials, and experiences used in teaching and learning.
Hidden curriculum	That which is implied by the very nature of schools, much of which revolves around daily or established routines (e.g., competition for grades; how to act during class; timed segments of instruction; annual schedule of schools). This hidden curriculum is not explicitly taught but is learned through repeated interactions with peers, teachers, and administrators.
Null curriculum	The null curriculum refers to that which we do not teach, giving students the message that these elements are not important to their educational experiences or in our society.

Source: Glatthorn, Boschee, Whitehead, & Boschee, 2016.

activities, and experiences that support student learning of specific content. For most students with complex support needs, this formal instruction must be adapted to facilitate their participation and progress in learning academic, nonacademic, and extracurricular content. The general education curriculum also refers to the *hidden curriculum* of the school; students' learning of this hidden curriculum is best accomplished when they are included in general education academic, nonacademic, and extracurricular activities because these are the situations in which *all* students learn the hidden curriculum. For example, students learn to interact with peers and develop friendships through repeated interactions with peers in classrooms, playgrounds, and community settings. Finally, the general education curriculum includes the *null curriculum,* or that which is not taught. For example, the experiences of people with disabilities are often missing from explicit instruction (e.g., textbooks describing Nazi atrocities typically omit the persecution and extermination of people with disabilities). As a result of the null curriculum, critical perspectives and information are simply not taught to students. As another example, some families and politicians insist that topics they consider part of critical race theory should not be included in the curriculum, arguing students should not learn how institutionalized racism, including practices such as redlining, results in a system that relegates people of color to the bottom tiers of society. By not teaching the racist foundations of the United States, that which is not taught (i.e., racist foundations of our society) is the null curriculum. In yet another example, many students with complex support needs are not taught literacy skills beyond reading sight words (Allor et al., 2018); as a result, their ability to comprehend texts, make inferences, and take the perspectives of various characters is never learned.

Making Sense of Curricular Areas

Curricula can also be grouped into academic, nonacademic, extracurricular, and functional areas. The *academic* curriculum is most recognizable and includes content instruction in reading, writing, mathematics, physical education, science, and social studies. The academic curriculum is usually designed based on state educational standards. These standards are the learning goals for what students should know and do at each grade level (Core Standards, 2021b). Schools also offer *nonacademic* and *extracurricular* activities, usually organized and supervised by school personnel. These include clubs, sports teams, lunch, recess, assemblies, pep rallies, field trips, and after-school programs. The IDEA 2004 requires students with complex support needs have an equal opportunity to participate in all academic, nonacademic, and extracurricular activities as students without disabilities (34 CFR § 300.117).

Students with complex support needs are likely to have learning support needs that are *functional.* Functional skills are the proficiencies a person needs to live their everyday life, including communication, mobility, social skills, self-determination, leisure, safety, self-care, and vocational skills. These skills are personally relevant for the student's current and future school and community environments (Hunt et al., 2012). Unfortunately, however, the use of the term "functional skills" has evolved, and now can imply a different curriculum for students with complex support needs, primarily addressing daily living skills, such as cooking, cleaning, counting money, and telling time (Trela & Jimenez, 2013). As Trela and Jimenez note, the unintended consequence of this has been that students with complex support needs receive a different curriculum, taught in a separate setting, rather than an education based on the general education curriculum with SAS provided that enable students to access and make progress in the general education curriculum. (One resource that highlights the importance of teaching both academic and functional skills to this student population, and provides detailed strategies for doing so, is *Systematic Instruction for Students with Moderate and Severe Disabilities, Second Edition* [Collins, 2022].)

Using Ecological Frameworks to Determine Curricular Type and Area

Students with complex support needs will require a personally relevant curriculum (Trela & Jimenez, 2013), meaning that curriculum content meets students' priority needs now and into the future. An *ecological framework* is one way to determine what is personally relevant to individual students; this framework identifies and teaches the routines, activities, and skills students will need to learn and to support their full participation in school, home, and community settings (Hunt et al., 2012). By using an ecological framework for determining the curriculum and goals for students with complex support needs, teams determine priority skills based on the routines and activities in which students participate.

Ecological assessment is a tool used to identify skills within an ecological framework (Downing, 2005; Macfarlane, 1998; Watson et al., 2011). Assessment is conducted through a series of simple observations of typical routines and activities. The observer records the activities and routines in the school environment and then notes the support or instruction that the student needed at each step to be successful. The first four steps are completed during a live or video observation of the student in the natural (inclusive) environment. These steps help the observer identify the demands of a given environment and how the student performs under those demands compared to their peers. The final two steps are completed after the observation. This requires the observer to analyze the information from Steps 1–4 to identify supplementary aids or instruction (services) the student needs to access the environment and plan how those supports and services will be embedded in the observed environment. The following list describes each column and how to complete it.

The process consists of six steps:

1. Break the activity into chunks or steps.

2. Identify environmental cues that support students in doing the task.

3. Determine and record skills needed to do the task.

4. Do a discrepancy analysis to identify any mismatch between the student's skills or capacities and the environment.

5. List the supports and skills you will need to teach.

6. Develop an action plan.

These six steps are explained in detail in Table 7.2.

An example of an ecological assessment appears next, highlighting each of these five steps. In this activity, a first-grade teacher is teaching students how to alphabetize. Students start the activity on the carpet, watching the teacher demonstrate how to complete the activity. The teacher shows students a worksheet with two caterpillars. Each caterpillar has four body parts with sight words written in them (see Figure 7.1). The teacher models underlining the first letter of each sight word and singing the "ABC" song to determine which letters come first in alphabetical order. The teacher then writes the words on lines under the caterpillar in alphabetical order. After this demonstration, the students are to return to their desks and complete this task on their own. When they finish, they can color in their caterpillars.

Next, we see this lesson on the Ecological Assessment form, including the five steps, described earlier (see Figure 7.2; A full-size, blank, reproducible version of this template is provided in the chapter appendix and on the Brookes Download Hub). In this lesson, Sam, a first-grade student with Down syndrome, is observed, and information about her performance is recorded.

Table 7.2. Six steps for completing an ecological assessment

Step	Task	Definition
1	Break the activity into chunks or steps	Note what a competent peer is doing. A competent peer is any peer who appears to be "doing the right thing." Observe and record what that student is doing. If you are interested in exploring student support needs for an entire class session, chunk classroom actvities together in your notes (e.g., getting ready for class, whole group instruction, independent work). If you want to learn more about student support needs during a specific activity such as getting ready for class, you should record each step of the chosen activity in this column (e.g., find and sit in assigned seat, remove needed materials from backpack, place homework on teacher's desk).
2	Identify cues	Record the natural cues in the environment that support students to complete the task. The cues signal to the student what is expected, and could be things that students see, hear, feel, or otherwise sense. Identifying the cues that students without disabilities use in an environment can help a teacher decide how to teach participation and independence in the environment by drawing student attention to natural cues. For example, a bell ringing might be a cue to come inside from recess; a timer might be a cue to transition to another activity.
3	Determine and record skills needed	Record all skills needed for a student to succeed in the observed tasks. Think about each task and the individual skills it may require. For example, writing the date on a paper requires fine motor skills, comprehension of calendar and date structure, and number identification skills.
4	Do a discrepancy analysis	This analysis is intended for the observer to identify the mismatch between the student's skills or capacities and the environment. Record what the student does during the observed time and why you think they responded to the situation or task in that way. In the example in this chapter describing Jake, Jake does not write due to fine motor support needs and limited story comprehension. He currently responds via gestures, object selection, and big-button switches. This information will be used in the following columns to identify supplementary aids and how to provide them.
5	List the supports and skills to teach	After the observation, complete the discrepancy analysis to help identify and record the material, physical, or instructional supports that may help the student better access the content or activity observed. For every discrepancy, list possible supports needed or skills to teach the student to remediate the discrepancy in the future. These may include: physical and accessibility supports (e.g., adapted equipment such as seating or writing utensils, larger text to support vision, amplification to support hearing); instructional supports (e.g., curricular modifications that reduce complexity or provide comprehension supports such as images, access to read-aloud, graphic organizers); behavior supports (e.g., token economy system, increased access to reinforcement); social-communication supports (access to augmentative and alternative communication (AAC) device, planned peer support); and collaborative supports (e.g., increased adult assistance, staff training in communication supports) (Kurth et al., 2018). These data on supports and services should be reported on in the final individualized education program (IEP) document.
6	Develop an action plan	The action plan should describe who among the team members will deliver the supports and services described in Step 5—along with how, and when. This data should be reported in the present level section of the IEP document and used to plan adaptations to the program throughout the school year.

Inspection of this ecological assessment offers some clear ideas for supports to use when teaching Sam, including label makers, alphabet strips, and color overlays. These same supports might be helpful in other activities and routines that are observed as part of ecological assessment of other activities in the first-grade classroom. In doing so, a robust list of supports will be generated and used in determining supplementary aids and services (see Chapter 8). Similarly, examining the skills Sam needs to learn across activities and routines, such as learning the alphabet from memory and writing letters with correct size and formation, might help the team prioritize these skills as IEP goals, assuming these skills are regularly needed and personally relevant to the student. We next discuss developing IEP goals.

IEP GOALS

Once the IEP team has done the initial thinking about developing a curriculum for the student, as described above, the next step is to develop IEP goals. The sections that follow define IEP goals and explain how to write technically adequate goals, using a goal-writing blueprint based on the elements

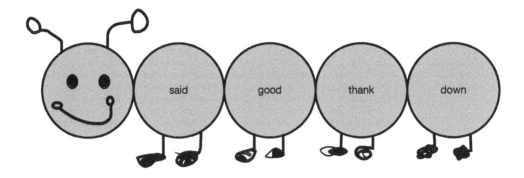

Figure 7.1.   Caterpillar alphabetizing worksheet. (*Source:* TLS Books, n.d.)

of SMART goals. SMART is an acronym formed from the initial letters of the following words: Specific, Measurable, Action-Oriented, Realistic and Relevant, and Time-Limited information (Jung, 2007). We describe tests that educators can apply to ensure the IEP goals they have written are sound.

What Are IEP Goals?

A meaningful IEP is developed based on individual student needs, as described in the student's PLAAFP, with a rich and personally relevant curriculum as the backdrop. As such, the specific details of the type and the number of IEP goals will necessarily vary: IDEA 2004 does not dictate the content of IEP goals. Instead, the student's IEP team determines those details. This gives IEP teams the necessary flexibility to develop appropriate and meaningful goals for an individual student. The goals are the engine of the IEP, driven by the PLAAFP, and are uniquely calculated every year based on the student's current level of performance in areas of need. Importantly, goals should be implemented in multiple settings (e.g., teachers can address a reading goal during social studies or a communication goal during physical education). This encourages generalization and meaningful skill application.

How to Write Technically Adequate Goals

To develop goals that clearly communicate what a student will be working toward over the school year, goals cannot be vague or general. Instead, they need to specify very clearly what the student will learn in measurable, specific terms. In Figure 7.3, we present a goal-writing blueprint that incorporates each element of SMART goals, and we describe each element next. (A full-size, blank, reproducible version of this template is provided in the chapter appendix and on the Brookes Download Hub.)

Conditions   The condition specifies what the student will be provided, or given, to learn and demonstrate their learning of a skill. This could include *materials* (e.g., spelling list of consonant-vowel-consonant [CVC] words, voice output communication device). For example, a condition statement for Sara might read: "Given a typing device such as tablet or computer...." This clearly states that Sara should have access to typing devices to work on and demonstrate mastery of her IEP goal. The condition may also describe *settings* (e.g., crowded hallway) or *people* (e.g., same-age peer). For example, a condition statement for José might read, "Given a recess game with same-age peers...." This condition statement describes that José must be participating in recess (i.e., the setting) with his peers (i.e., the people) to work on and meet the IEP goal. Together, the condition spells out what the student will use, where, or with whom to demonstrate their ability to complete the goal.

Sam's Ecological Assessment for the Caterpillar Activity

FORM 7A   # Ecological Assessment

Peer Inventory/ Task Analysis	Cues	Student Performance	Discrepancy Analysis	Adaptations/ Cues to Teach
Watch teacher describe the lesson	Teacher verbal instructions	Incorrect	Jumping on the side of the classroom, hugging paraprofessionals	Peer asks Sam to sit with her in a chair. The teacher asks Sam a question every 2 minutes.
Walk to desk	Peer models	Incorrect	She goes to the back of the classroom and plays with the pet.	Peer walks Sam to the desk. Sam matches icon on desk.
Get a worksheet and pencil	Teacher verbal instructions	Correct		
Underline s, g, t, d	Teacher verbal instructions	Incorrect	No response	Shine laser pointer on the first letter. Give a choice—is this the first or is this the first?
Sing "ABC" song	Teacher verbal instructions	Incorrect	No response	Use alphabet strip with color overlays over each letter. Learn the ABC song.

Figure 7.2. Sample ecological assessment for Sam.

(continued)

Figure 7.2. *(continued)*

FORM 7A **Ecological Assessment** *(continued)*

Peer Inventory/ Task Analysis	Cues	Student Performance	Discrepancy Analysis	Adaptations/ Cues to Teach
Write "down" on the first line	Teacher verbal instructions	Incorrect	Incorrect word selected	Use label maker. Cut words out for her to tape down. Learn to write words with proper size and letter formation.
Write "good" on the second line	Teacher verbal instructions	Incorrect	Incorrect word selected	Use label maker. Cut words out for her to tape down. Learn to write words with proper size and letter formation.
Write "said" on the third line	Teacher verbal instructions	Incorrect	No response	Use label maker. Cut words out for her to tape down.
Write "thank" on the fourth line	Teacher verbal instructions	Incorrect	Incorrect word selected	Use label maker. Cut words out for her to tape down.
Color in caterpillar	Teacher verbal instructions	Incorrect	Draws outside of lines	Thicken lines with a marker. Use drops of glue to raise lines.

Student   Although it may seem rather obvious who the student is, it is also an important point to consider. Sometimes, teams accidentally write goals for adults (Giangreco et al., 1994). For example, an IEP goal might say, "The paraprofessional will provide Joey a break every 10 minutes. During this break, Joey will engage in an uninterrupted preferred task for no more than 3 minutes every hour." As you read this, part of the goal appears to be written for the paraprofessional (whose goal, presumably, is to offer Joey a break). Goals should never be written for adults, so using this blueprint component is a helpful checkpoint.

Specific Skill   This component of the IEP goal states in exact terms exactly what the student *will do*. It includes a clear description of what will be taught and the student's specific behavior in measurable, objective terms. For example, consider these two goal statements: "Sara will improve her writing" and "Sara will be able to type a paragraph with at least four sentences each containing at least five words with no more than two typographical and no more than three spelling errors." Do you agree that the second example provides much greater detail? The second example is thus more specific: we know what Sara needs to do. It is also measurable; we know how much Sara should write and how many of each type of error she can make and still achieve her goal. Finally, the second example is objective: it is free from bias and potential differences in interpreting what Sara should do and how.

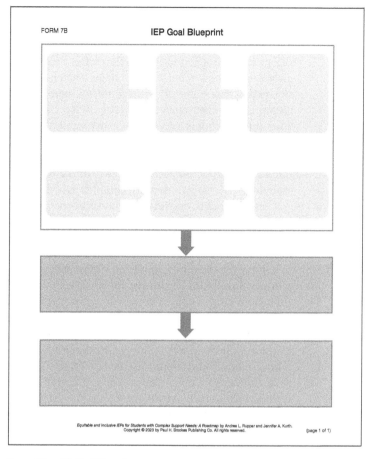

Figure 7.3.   IEP Goal Blueprint.

Criterion   The goal must also state exactly what the expected level of performance will be. In other words, how "well" must a student complete a skill for it to be considered mastered? Usually, this is reported in terms of accuracy, fluency, or latency. For example, a team might require Sara to type using a QWERTY keyboard with 80% accuracy. Other goals will lend themselves toward a fluency measurement. For example, a student might only master putting on a coat when he accomplishes putting on the coat correctly within 2 minutes. And yet other goals might be measured using latency; for example, a student might be taught to respond to a social greeting within 3 seconds.

There are two key considerations to selecting a criterion: The criterion set should 1) align with the type of goal and 2) be reasonable for the goal. Alignment with a goal will be needed to ensure the goal is best measured via accuracy, fluency, or latency. Different types of goals will necessarily lend themselves to different types of measurement. For example, a goal to complete addition and subtraction could have an accuracy criterion if the goal is concerned with completing addition and subtraction correctly. Alternately, the goal might have a fluency criterion if the team is concerned with the student's ability to quickly answer addition and subtraction problems from memory. The second consideration in selecting criteria asks, is this criterion reasonable? Several factors would be considered in this decision. Of most importance, the team must choose an objectively reasonable criterion. For example, crossing the street with 80% accuracy is not objectively reasonable on face value: none of us believe that being unsafe while crossing the road is ever a good idea. This type of goal should have a criterion of 100% simply because the alternative to completing the goal at the specific criterion is not safe.

This is an excellent opportunity to pause and consider criteria in general. In our experience, most IEP goals have selected 80% as the de facto criterion for mastery. How or why 80% has become so ubiquitous is unknown, but it is worth considering the consequences of this criterion. One logical conclusion is that this generally represents low expectations of students with complex support needs, who are presumably never expected to truly master skills but simply perform skills at 80% accuracy. This is quite unlike what is expected of other students, who are expected to read grade-level words with 100% accuracy or calculate long-division with 100% accuracy. Failure to do so on a repeated basis would likely result in remedial instruction or even failing grades. Thus, we suggest teams question their assumptions about expected performance criteria and ensure they reflect reasonably high expectations of all students, including those with complex support needs.

In addition to considering how reasonable the goal is at face value, teams must also consider factors such as how complex the skill is and the student's learning rate of similar tasks when determining criterion. Skill complexity can be estimated by considering Bloom's taxonomy (see Figure 7.4). Learning more complex skills (those toward the top of the pyramid) will likely take longer for most students to master. For example, recalling simple facts, like 2 + 2, is less complex than applying that knowledge to a word problem. Similarly, the ability to write a complete sentence will take less time to master than acquiring the skills needed to write a persuasive essay in which you draw on facts and justify an argument.

Knowing the student's current rate of learning can also be appropriate when selecting IEP goal criterion. The best way to know a student's learning rate is to graph their progress. In doing so, the IEP team can see the student's learning rate, and in turn, project how many days, weeks, or months a student will need to reach the mastery criterion of a goal. More about graphing was presented in Chapter 4. Briefly here, however, we refer you to Figure 7.5. As seen in this figure, the solid line graphs actual student performance, demonstrating the student progressed from reading approximately three words per minute in September and 15 words per minute in March. Using an aim line drawn through the data (dotted line), we can project that in June, the student will be reading approximately 20 words per minute if they maintain the same learning rate.

Considerations   This component of the IEP goal states any final considerations for the student's ultimate performance, including opportunity and support considerations. Opportunity considerations provide flexibility for students and are generally stated as "2 out of 3" or "4 out of 5" learning

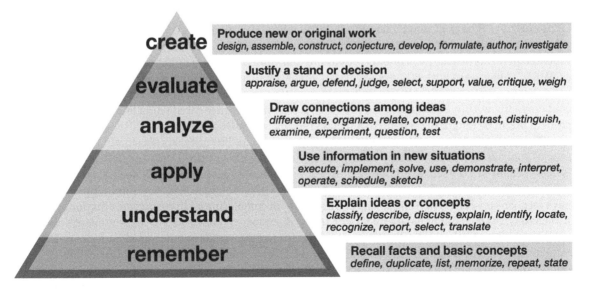

Figure 7.4.   Bloom's taxonomy.

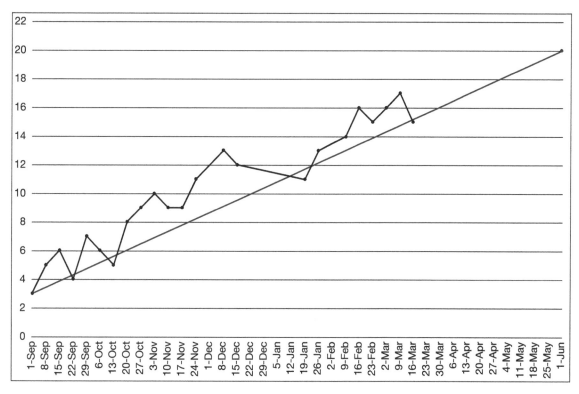

Figure 7.5. Learning rate graph.

opportunities. As we noted, allowing for student performance to vary somewhat allows students to have "off days" and still meet the goal. As with criteria, these opportunities should be reasonable and related to the goal. Other considerations might also be included, such as the provision of prompts. Prompts might consist of verbal, visual, gestural, or any other type of prompt that would be permitted for the students to rely upon and still meet the goal. For example, a goal might state, "Sara will return to the classroom after the recess bell rings with no more than two verbal reminders from her peer." This specifies the consideration that Sara may still achieve her IEP goal of returning to class while receiving up to two verbal prompts.

Date   Finally, the IEP goal must include a date by which the student will meet the goal using the conditions, criteria, and considerations described. This date allows teams to monitor student progress toward goals and make timely decisions. For example, if the team expects a student to read 20 words per minute by June 1, we can measure student progress at regular intervals to ensure the student is on track to accomplish this goal. If the student is not on track to accomplish the goal by the specified date, we can adjust our instruction or supports to ensure the student will make appropriate progress.

Apply Final Tests

To this point, we have described a blueprint for developing SMART goals. However, before finalizing a goal, two final tests must be applied. These are the Stranger Test and Dead Man's Test.

Stranger Test   The Stranger Test requires IEP teams to examine the overall goal and determine, "Would somebody unfamiliar with this student have enough information to know how to implement and measure this goal?" (Carlin et al., 2016). This test is essential because many people are involved in implementing and measuring a student's IEP goal progress, and because IEP team membership tends to change frequently. Often, goals are written with language that is not clear to a wider audience. For example, an IEP goal might refer to a vague condition (e.g., AAC), student skill (e.g., aggression), or criterion (e.g., "Ms. Hansen's social skill rating template.") In the first example, it is unclear what type of AAC the student needs. Is it a voice output device? Paper icons? A static display? For the second example, it is also possible that different team members might interpret the word "aggression" differently. And in the third example, it is not clear what, exactly, Ms. Hansen included on her social skill rating template. Now imagine Ms. Hansen wins the lottery and moves to Jamaica—the team no longer has a way to use her template or measure the goal! This highlights the importance of describing conditions, skills, and criterion in objective terms that even a stranger to the team would understand.

Dead Man's Test   The second test is referred to as the Dead Man's Test. This somewhat morbid-sounding test reminds teams that goals needs to be rewritten or reconsidered if a dead man could achieve the goal (White, 1986). A pop-culture example is the movie *Weekend at Bernie's* (1989), in which Bernie was made to look as if he were behaving in certain ways even though he was dead. For example, a goal that a student "will tolerate hand-over-hand assistance" is a goal a dead man (like Bernie) *could* meet, meaning this goal has not passed the Dead Man's Test. Similarly, a goal for a student to "refrain from hitting peers" would not pass the Dead Man's Test because a dead man is unable to hit peers. How might these goals be reworded? One option would be that a student "will request hand-over-hand assistance to write four letters." A dead man cannot request assistance, so the test is passed. Similarly, a goal to "interact with peers without hitting them" passes the Dead Man's Test because a dead man cannot interact with peers.

Pulling It All Together

At this point, a well-crafted, SMART goal has been developed. The IEP team can now simply transfer the statements developed for conditions, student, specific skill, criterion, considerations, and date boxes into a final goal statement. An example of this is in Figure 7.6.

Goals and Their Objectives

In the reauthorization of IDEA in 2004, Congress specified that all students who complete the alternate assessment must have objectives, also sometimes referred to as benchmarks or short-term goals, aligned with all IEP goals. What is the difference between goals and objectives, and how do they relate? IEP goals are the overall target, stating what a student should be able to do by the next annual IEP meeting. If goals are considered the overall target, objectives are the baby steps, so to speak, needed to accomplish the goal. Objectives support the goals by providing clear steps toward reaching the goal (Hauser, 2017). Well-developed objectives facilitate IEP teams in measuring student progress toward the overall goal, describing the sequence or criterion students will progress through toward meeting the goal. Objectives typically build upon one another, culminating in the goal. There is no set number of objectives required, but three to four are usually provided. Likewise, there is no set time limit specifying when objectives should be mastered, but IEP teams usually select these to correspond with report card timelines or student learning rate.

Some objectives emphasize criteria. For example, the goal might be for a student to solve 2-digit addition problems with 100% accuracy. The first objective might require a student to solve 2-digit addition problems with 60% accuracy in 10 instructional weeks, the second objective with 75% accuracy in 20 instructional weeks, and the third objective with 90% accuracy in 30 instructional weeks. Other objectives might focus on conditions. For example, suppose a student has a goal to write their name on a line with correct spelling and letter formation, but is not yet able to hold a pencil correctly. This student might have the first objective to use a pencil grip to hold a pencil correctly, a second objective to use a pencil grip to write letters of their name, a third objective to use a pencil grip to write letters of their name on a line, and a final objective to use a pencil grip to write letters of their name on a line with proper letter spacing. Finally, some objectives may build toward a goal by adjusting considerations. These objectives might adjust the number of adult-delivered prompts, for example.

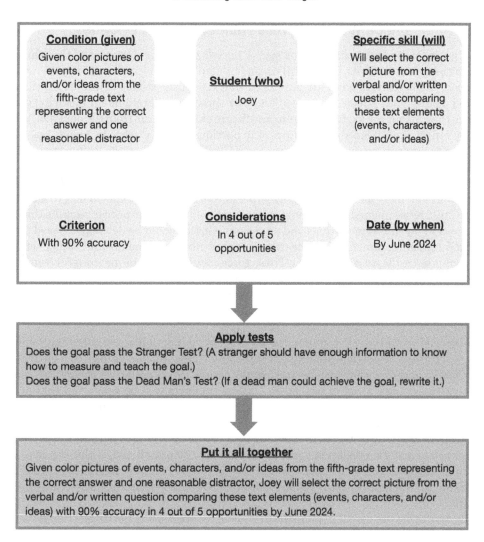

Figure 7.6. IEP Goal Blueprint example.

GOAL CONTENT

Up to this point, we have focused on writing technically adequate IEP goals. Of course, it is crucial to write SMART IEP goals to ensure students have high-quality, measurable, specific goals that facilitate their ongoing learning and development. However, technical adequacy alone is not sufficient to promote positive student outcomes and the development of high-quality, equitable, inclusive IEPs. Teams must also ensure goals 1) address needs identified in the PLAAFP; 2) reflect student preferences and priorities; and 3) are aligned with state standards.

Check Whether Goals Align With PLAAFP

As noted in Chapter 5, a clear linkage is required between the PLAAFP and all other sections of the IEP, including the goals. By reading the PLAAFP, one should be able to predict the content of goals. As also noted in Chapter 5, goals should reflect the highest priority needs reported in the PLAAFP, thus ensuring goals are developed for areas of most importance and relevance to providing student access to and progress in the general education curriculum. Finally, the criterion used to create IEP goals should mirror the type of baseline data reported in the PLAAFP, ensuring consistency between needs identified in the PLAAFP and subsequent IEP goals.

Check Whether Goals Reflect Student Priorities

Developing goals for students with complex support needs requires extensive and thoughtful collaboration among teachers, students, their families, and related service providers. Using this collaborative approach, personally relevant goals are developed that reflect the student's interests, priorities, preferences, and desired post-school outcomes. We offer three considerations for ensuring goals reflect student priorities: 1) they are useful in current and future environments from the perspective of the student; 2) they reflect skills needed for the student to participate in everyday, inclusive, age-appropriate activities; and 3) the goals are useful across contexts (Billingsley et al., 1996; Brown et al., 1976; Brown et al., 1979; Hunt et al., 2012).

As Billingsley and colleagues (1996) explained, educational decisions should increase *membership* in a variety of groups; increase *relationships* with peers; and increase *skills* necessary to maintain membership and build relationships. These considerations should be used to prioritize skills that are generalizable across many different settings and situations. Goals should be developed based on students' current *and future* environments with the overall goal of increasing membership and participation in inclusive communities beyond only school. These goals should further be meaningful from the point of view of the student. By selecting goals that are useful across current and future home, school, and community contexts, the team is more likely to choose meaningful goals. However, each goal should always make sense to the students themselves—they should understand what they are learning and why, and goals should reflect their interests and strengths.

High-priority goals reflect skills needed for students to participate in everyday, inclusive, age-appropriate activities. Ecological assessment of these activities should be used to identify frequently occurring skills necessary for access and participation. By conducting ecological assessments across inclusive settings, a list of needed skills and supports will be generated that are relevant across activities and can become priority areas given their frequency. Some of these most frequent skills include communication and social interaction skills, which also happen to be the highest priority skills for many students with complex support needs. Skills required for participation in grade-appropriate general education contexts should also be prioritized, including academic goals focusing on math, literacy, social studies, and science. Individual characteristics of students should also be considered when prioritizing goals, including the student's mobility, self-determination, and social skills.

Finally, goals that are useful in more than one context should be prioritized (Ruppar et al., 2022). For example, skills that are only useful in one context, such as identifying coins, are less useful to facilitate student learning and participation in a variety of settings. Instead, selecting goals that focus on problem solving and applying knowledge of money in various ways to pay for items or services in everyday contexts, such as using phone apps to send money to friends or credit cards to make purchases in stores, is preferable. In determining which goals are applicable across contexts, teams should once again consult ecological assessments and decide when and where skills are needed in the student's life. If a skill is only infrequently required or used in a limited number of settings, the skill may not become a priority for inclusion in the student's IEP goals.

Align Goals With Standards

Far too often, students with complex support needs are placed in special education classrooms because their IEP goals are unrelated to the standards and activities of the general education classroom. As a result, it appears that IEP goals compete (or even conflict) with general education. Consequently, students are removed from general education for partial or whole days to receive instruction on IEP goals. Other times, IEP goals are written so that they would be taught using flashcards, worksheets, or special education curriculum and materials, essentially dictating placement in more restrictive, segregated classrooms. So how does an IEP team avoid these scenarios? As discussed in Chapter 5, one strategy is to write grade-aligned PLAAFP statements to facilitate the development of a narrative about the student that corresponds to the grade-level content being taught. A second essential strategy is to write IEP goals aligned with general education standards, as described next.

Role of Alternate Assessment   Writing grade-aligned IEPs requires teams to select appropriate grade-level standards to facilitate student access to, and progress in, the general education curriculum (Flowers et al., 2009). Therefore, it is essential IEP teams select standards from the student's current grade level. This point is critical; sometimes, students with complex support needs are learning skills well below their grade level, suggesting that IEP teams would select standards from lower grade levels. For example, an eighth-grade student with an intellectual disability might be reading at a second-grade level, leading the IEP team to erroneously select second-grade standards to develop IEP goals. Instead, the eighth-grade student reading at a second-grade level should have IEP reading goals based on eighth-grade reading standards. This might seem like an impossible feat; after all, the general education curriculum was originally developed for students without disabilities. However, states have developed curriculum extensions that require a different form or complexity, breadth, and depth of content learned but are still based on grade-level standards. These extended standards are the basis of alternate assessments, which states develop to assess the 1% of students with the most significant cognitive disability.

Using this approach, all students with complex support needs are expected to, and can participate in, the general curriculum. IEP team members can locate these extended standards in a variety of ways. The *Dynamic Learning Maps* (DLM) is an alternate assessment consortium that has created Essential Elements, which are statements of knowledge and skills that are linked to the Common Core State Standards (CCSS). The CCSS have been adopted by 41 states and territories, making these resources particularly useful (Common Core State Standards Initiative, 2021a). The DLM offers essential elements in both K-12 reading (DLM, 2013a) and math (DLM, 2013b). Figure 7.7 shows an example of fifth-grade reading standards and corresponding extended standards derived from the DLM Essential Elements. Many other states have created their own extended content standards; as a result, we suggest also investigating the standards developed in your state.

IEP Goals and Inclusion: Potential Obstacles   In writing grade-aligned IEP goals, teams directly facilitate the inclusion of students with complex support needs in general education. Yet, teams are likely to encounter two obstacles: 1) students will often have nonacademic needs requiring IEP goals, and 2) logistical concerns arise when student IEP timelines do not align perfectly with grade-level standards. We turn our attention to these potential obstacles next.

Nonacademic Needs Requiring IEP Goals   Indeed, students with complex support needs will have needs in various domains not traditionally associated with state standards, including communication, social, motor, behavior, and self-care skills. To address this, IEP teams should first review standards to ensure that no reasonably connected standards exist. Many states have adopted social-emotional learning standards, which may form the basis for some nonacademic

Fifth Grade English Language Arts Standards: Reading (Informational Text)	
CCSS Grade-Level Standards	**DLM Essential Elements**
Key Ideas and Details	
RI.5.1. Quote accurately from a text when explaining what the text says explicitly and when drawing inferences from the text.	**EE.RI.5.1.** Identify words in the text to answer a question about explicit information.
RI.5.2. Determine two or more main ideas of a text and explain how they are supported by details; summarize the text.	**EE.RI.5.2.** Identify the main idea of a text when it is not explicitly stated.
RI.5.3. Explain the relationships or interactions between two or more individuals, events, ideas, or concepts in a historical, scientific, or technical text based on specific information in the text.	**EE.RI.5.3.** Compare two individuals, events, or ideas in a text.

Figure 7.7.   Grade standards and aligned extended standards. (From Common Core State Standards © Copyright 2010. National Governors Association Center for Best Practices and Council of Chief State School Officers. All rights reserved.)

goals. Such standards for each U.S. state can be found here on the Positive Action web site: https://www.positiveaction.net/blog/sel-standards. Likewise, goals to address challenging behaviors could be derived from resources such as the Collaborative for Academic, Social, and Emotional Learning (CASEL) (https://www.panoramaed.com/blog/guide-to-core-sel-competencies), and communication goals may be drawn from the American Speech-Language-Hearing Association (ASHA) (https://www.asha.org/practice-portal/clinical-topics/social-communication-disorder/components-of-social-communication/). In other cases, it is appropriate to develop IEP goals that are not tied to standards. For example, a student may need to develop skills to manage and direct their restroom supports. Upon inspection of the standards, the IEP team will likely discover that no reasonably aligned standard exists. In this case, teams will develop goals without a standard linkage. In general, however, and particularly for academic skill areas, state standards should form the basis of IEP goals.

Logistics of Aligning IEP Goals to Grade-Level Standards   Logistical issues can also present obstacles to aligning IEP goals and state standards. For example, a fifth-grade student has an annual IEP meeting in February, leaving the team to wonder, "Should we refer to fifth-grade standards or sixth-grade standards for writing the next annual IEP goals?" This obstacle is likely to be encountered, given that often IEP reviews are held throughout the school year. Table 7.3 offers some practical suggestions for addressing this issue.

Set Functional Goals

Students with complex support needs will also have functional skills needs identified in the PLAAFP. Unlike academic goals, there are usually no state standards with which functional goals can be aligned. Instead, functional skills needs will be highly individual, personally relevant, and age respectful. It is worth noting that many functional skills curricula exist. These curricula tend to focus on skills needed for independent living in homes, schools, and communities and include developing skills such as counting change and reading recipe words. It can be tempting to use these prepared curricula to set IEP goals; however, the skills in these curricula are usually not personally relevant. They do not connect students to their school communities through the development of skills or relationships (Trela & Jimenez, 2013). Instead, students typically leave the school setting, general education curriculum, and peers to practice shopping, counting, cleaning, and hygiene. The use of a completely functional curriculum also risks providing students with a totally separate curriculum, taught in a separate classroom. These curricula also tend to focus on an idealized version of independent functioning. However, it is essential to note that "independence" is rarely an appropriate goal. Instead, teams must acknowledge interdependence and teach skills enabling students to live interdependent lives. For example, many of us do not know how to repair our cars independently but know how to use our skills to shop for repair quotes and communicate the repair needs to a person with special training. Other times, it must be acknowledged

Table 7.3.   Logistical issues in aligning goals to grade-level standards

What if . . .	Possible solution
The individualized education program (IEP) is developed at the beginning of the school year (e.g., the beginning of the student's fifth-grade year)?	You are in luck! Use IEP goals from the current grade level (e.g., standards from fifth grade).
The IEP is developed in the middle of the school year (e.g., in the middle of the student's fifth-grade year)?	Select grade-aligned standards for both years—in our example, some standards are from fifth grade and some from sixth grade.
	Alternately, the team might develop goals that are from the next grade (sixth grade), but objectives leading toward that goal are derived from both fifth and sixth grades.
The IEP is developed at the end of the year (e.g., at the end of the student's fifth-grade year)?	Select grade-aligned goals for the next school year (e.g., standards from sixth grade).

that some students will also rely on others to support their physical needs. For example, a student who has cerebral palsy might always need assistance to dress or use the restroom. In these cases, teaching students skills to direct their own supports would be very appropriate. This might include teaching students to communicate their preference for who provides supports, telling people how to provide supports for them in the most comfortable or dignifying manner, and teaching students how to problem-solve their supports and services.

When developing functional performance goals, teams should consider communication, mobility, social skills, self-determination, leisure, safety, self-care, and vocational skills that are personally relevant to the student. Pivotal skills within these should be selected; pivotal skills support students' capacity to participate in an ever-changing world. Technological developments should also be considered: for example, fewer people use coins and checkbooks today than in the past. Thus, teaching students with complex support needs to count coins and write checks are probably skills that are rapidly becoming obsolete. Instead, teaching students to use money management applications like Venmo might be more meaningful. Similarly, many people now have access to applications that can alert them to take medication or leave for work, making traditional telling time skills less meaningful than managing calendar apps. All told, many changes are occurring that have dramatically altered what it means to "function" as an adult in the 21st century, and IEP goals should reflect this shift. Table 7.4 lists some characteristics to help teams decide if a skill is, in fact, functional for the student and should be considered for an IEP goal.

CONCLUDING THOUGHTS: CURRICULUM AND GOALS

Students with complex support needs must have IEP goals that support their participation in all the academic, nonacademic, and extracurricular components of the general education curriculum. Goals should be written to address needs identified in the PLAAFP that address the academic and functional performance skill needs. Goals reflect the IEP team's vision of the student in their upcoming educational year and should always reflect student strengths, priorities, preferences, and be age- and grade-respectful.

REVIEWING THE COMMITMENT: *Curriculum and Goals*

In this chapter, we described how to develop IEP goals that are technically adequate, reflect student interests and priorities, are congruent with the PLAAFP, and are aligned to the student's grade-level standards. In doing so, an IEP is developed that positions the student to have clear and meaningful learning goals for the upcoming year.

Think back to the student you identified at the start of the chapter and the goal areas you listed for the student. Who would you collaborate with to ensure the goals you develop meet the criteria

Table 7.4. Considerations in functional performance goals

Good candidate for functional skill goal	Poor candidate for functional skill goal
The skill is personally relevant.	The skill does not meet an area of need that is important from the perspective of the student.
It is likely that this particular skill will be needed, given advancing technology, in 20 years and beyond.	The skill will only be needed in the short term or limited settings.
The skill is highly valued by community members, including employers, friends, and family members.	The skill is low status, is not dignifying, or not necessary to employers, friends, and family members.
If the student cannot independently complete a skill, they can instead be taught how to direct others to complete the skill on their behalf.	The skill would not need to be completed by somebody else if the student cannot complete it themselves.
The skill reflects the preferences, interests, and strengths of the student.	The skills are drawn from packaged curriculum and not reflective of the student's routines, activities, and settings.

described in this chapter? How will you ensure the student is a key participant in setting their IEP goals? What information will you need to gather about the curriculum, standards, and student priorities to develop IEP goals?

_____

_____

_____

_____

_____

_____

_____

_____

_____

_____

ACTING ON THE COMMITMENT: *Curriculum and Goals*

Review the resources listed in this chapter, including Common Core State Standards (CCSS), CASEL, and ASHA. With a member of the IEP team, develop a draft IEP goal for your student. Be sure to base your goal on the following: 1) CCSS, CASEL, or ASHA standards; 2) the student's needs as identified in the PLAAFP; and 3) the student's interests and priorities.

_____

_____

_____

_____

_____

_____

Resources for Determining What Gets Taught

1. Ecological Assessment 128
2. IEP Goal Blueprint 130

Ecological Assessment

Peer Inventory/ Task Analysis	Cues	Student Performance	Discrepancy Analysis	Adaptations/ Cues to Teach

Peer Inventory/ Task Analysis	Cues	Student Performance	Discrepancy Analysis	Adaptations/ Cues to Teach

IEP Goal Blueprint

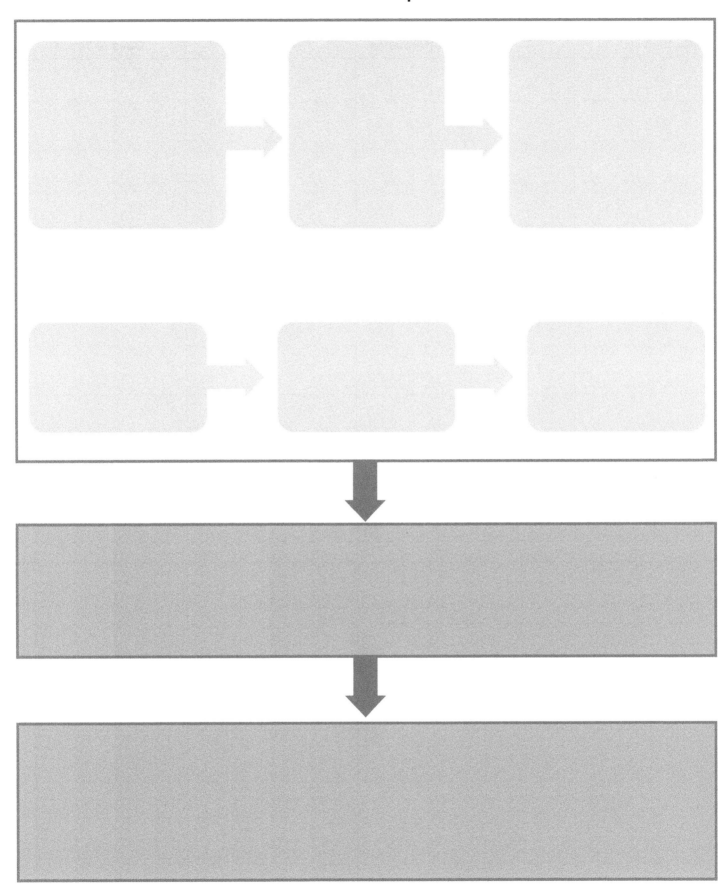

Identifying Supplementary Aids and Services

8

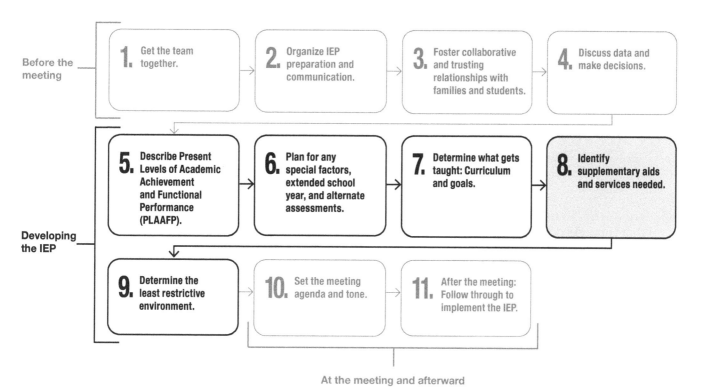

Before the meeting
- 1. Get the team together.
- 2. Organize IEP preparation and communication.
- 3. Foster collaborative and trusting relationships with families and students.
- 4. Discuss data and make decisions.

Developing the IEP
- 5. Describe Present Levels of Academic Achievement and Functional Performance (PLAAFP).
- 6. Plan for any special factors, extended school year, and alternate assessments.
- 7. Determine what gets taught: Curriculum and goals.
- 8. Identify supplementary aids and services needed.
- 9. Determine the least restrictive environment.
- 10. Set the meeting agenda and tone.
- 11. After the meeting: Follow through to implement the IEP.

At the meeting and afterward

Supplementary aids and services (SAS) can be a deceptively simple section of an IEP. Sometimes referred to as "accommodations and modifications," the SAS, together with the IEP goals, make up the heart of the IEP. The primary purpose of SAS is to remove barriers, ensuring equitable physical and cognitive access to school (Turnbull et al., 2016). SAS provide the supports necessary for students with and without disabilities to have access to the same classrooms, curriculum, and everyday school experiences. By removing barriers to general education settings, SAS are the "linchpin" of inclusive education for students with disabilities. Without SAS, involvement and progress of students with disabilities in the general curriculum would be denied. With appropriate SAS, the barriers to involvement and progress in the general curriculum are removed.

UNDERSTANDING THE COMMITMENT: *Removing Barriers to General Education*

Think about a student with whom you work. Consider the specific barriers in general education classes for which your student requires accommodations. Jot down your responses to the following questions.

What supports does the student require for physical access (including fine/gross motor supports)?

_____

_____

_____

_____

What supports does the student require for instruction?

_____

_____

_____

_____

What supports does the student require for behavior?

_____

_____

_____

_____

What social/communication supports does the student require?

_____

_____

_____

_____

In what ways does the instructional team collaborate to provide the above supports?

_____

_____

_____

_____

WHAT ARE SUPPLEMENTARY AIDS AND SERVICES?

Although SAS are determined during IEP meetings every day across the country, surprisingly little guidance is available for IEP teams to make appropriate decisions about them (Etscheidt & Bartlett, 1999). IDEA 2004 defines SAS as "aids, services, and other supports that are provided in regular education classes, other education-related settings, and in extracurricular and nonacademic settings, to enable children with disabilities to be educated with nondisabled children to the maximum extent appropriate" (§300.42). This broad definition gives teams latitude to be creative when determining individualized supports. However, the definition also can cause teams to underutilize this section of the IEP or, conversely, "dump" things that aren't quite a goal, aren't quite a related service, and don't fit under testing accommodations.

What Are Related Services?

Related services are specific services, defined by Congress, that a student might access to enable them to benefit from special education services. Related services have designated duration and frequencies (e.g., twice a week for 20 minutes), and are provided by specific people (e.g., certified physical therapists). The following lists the related services defined in IDEA (2004):

- Speech, language, and audiology services

- Interpreting services

- Psychological services

- Physical and occupational therapy

- Recreation, including therapeutic recreation

- Counseling services, including rehabilitation counseling

- Orientation and mobility services

- Medical services for diagnostic or evaluation purposes

- School health and school nurse services

- Social work

- Parent counseling and training

- Early identification and assessment of disabilities in children

---

Research on SAS is limited, and as a result, research-based recommendations for what constitutes a SAS are difficult to find. Research has revealed five key dimensions of SAS which are commonly included in IEPs for students with complex support needs (Kurth et al., 2018). These include *physical and accessibility supports; instructional supports; behavior supports; social-communication supports;* and *collaborative supports.* Considering each of these dimensions can help teams organize their thinking and decision making. Descriptions of each of these dimensions and some example supports are provided later in this chapter.

Supplementary Aids and Services and Least Restrictive Environment: Finding the Link

IDEA 2004 requires each IEP to contain a statement of SAS, "that will be provided to enable the child . . . to be educated and participate with other children with disabilities and nondisabled children . . ." (§300.320(a)(4)). The IDEA definition suggests that SAS serve the purpose of ensuring that students with disabilities have access to inclusive education. Therefore, SAS are particularly important for LRE decisions. Children can be removed from general education environments only if "education in regular classes *with the use of supplementary aids and services* cannot be achieved satisfactorily" (emphasis added, [Section 612(a)(5)]). Because most students with complex support needs are excluded from general education classes (Kurth et al., 2014), this is especially important. To guard against unnecessary exclusion, decisions about SAS should be based on the needs of the child within the general education classroom. All the activities, environmental features, and demands of the general education classroom should be taken into account when considering the supports and services needed for a child to participate with their peers.

Five Guiding Questions for Making Supplementary Aids and Services Decisions

If SAS are the "linchpin" of inclusion in general education classes, how can educators choose the most appropriate supports? With limited guidance from the research literature, decision making can be difficult. Sometimes, decisions are based more on individual team members' personal experiences, perceptions about what is available, or perceptions about what is feasible, than the law or the student's needs in general education. Lack of clarity about SAS can result in damaging consequences for students with complex support needs. Unclear or poorly defined SAS, leaving too much up to interpretation, can spell the difference between exclusion and inclusion, access to education and days spent in meaningless activities, a high quality of life in school and denial of a student's dignity and access to a free and appropriate public education.

The following are five guiding questions IEP team members can ask while determining SAS for students with complex support needs. These questions can help team members decide if the services and supports are appropriate, clearly written, and reasonable.

   Five Questions About Supplementary Aids and Services

1. Is this a service available to everyone?
2. Could a stranger understand what this means?
3. Could this be defined as specially designed instruction or related services?
4. Could this reasonably be provided in generalized contexts?
5. Will it help the student reach their annual goal or promote independence?

---

1. Is This a Service That Is Available for Everyone?   Sometimes, the routine and typical services available to everyone are written into SAS. SAS should, in fact, be *supplementary*. As such, they should supplement those services that are already universally available and should be accessible to anyone in the school. Examples include access to a locker or water fountain. However, if accommodations are needed for students to access areas that are available for students without disabilities, these accommodations might need to be included in the SAS. For example, if the locker requires a magnetic lock or a particular location to make it accessible, the adaptation would be considered a supplementary aid.

In addition to physical accessibility considerations, the general curriculum should already be available for all students and is not considered a supplementary aid or service. For example, normal teaching activities such as regularly monitoring comprehension or activating background knowledge are not supplementary, because this instruction should be available to anyone in a school. All students' comprehension should be regularly monitored through formative and summative assessments. Although some students do require additional prompts or comprehension checks, it is often the case that mechanisms for prompting students and assessing comprehension are already in place within general education classrooms. If, for example, visual supports were necessary to activate a student's background knowledge, this would be considered a supplementary aid.

To accurately identify needed SAS, the team should conduct an ecological assessment. As described in Chapter 7, ecological assessment is a well-established practice in supporting students with complex support needs (Downing, 2015). Ecological assessments can be used any time a new environment is encountered, including when transferring to a new school or when a new semester starts, or when other changes are made within an environment (e.g., new curriculum is used, changes to instructors have occurred). In an ecological assessment, a task analysis of the steps necessary to complete a classroom routine is created. For each step, the team determines whether a support or instruction is needed to ensure that the student can fully or partially participate. This process would be repeated across settings or activities, generating a robust set of needed supports. Ultimately, the supports that are identified in this assessment can be listed as SAS in the IEP. See Figure 8.1 for a sample ecological assessment.

2. Could a Stranger Understand What This Means?

SAS, like all parts of an IEP, should be written in observable and measurable terms that could be easily understood by someone who was not present at the meeting. You might recall the Stranger Test described in Chapter 7: Could a stranger read this and know how to implement it? In a practical example, would a substitute teacher understand what the student needs when his teacher is out sick?

Some common signal phrases use vague language and should be avoided. One of the most prevalent phrases in SAS is "as needed" (Kurth et al., 2018). The location and duration of SAS must be specified in IEPs; indicating that a support or service would be provided "as needed" does not provide clarity about the length of time or appropriate frequency for the service. The lack of specificity in supplementary aid and service descriptions such as "a quiet place to calm down as needed" may result in the overuse of segregated environments and removal from academic activities. Similarly, indicating a service would be provided "as appropriate" leaves much to interpretation. An alternative is to embed a time limit (e.g., 20 minutes per day) and a system for determining appropriate use of the aid or service (e.g., 2-minute preferred break when the student has filled their token economy behavior support system, not to exceed 14 minutes per school day).

Phrases to Avoid in IEPs

✓ As needed
✓ As necessary
✓ When appropriate
✓ When possible
✓ Approximately
✓ About
✓ With support
✓ X% of the time (ask, *of what time?*)
✓ When prompted
✓ With minimal assistance
✓ Will tolerate
✓ Will understand
✓ Will try
✓ Will learn
✓ Will know
✓ Will remain on task
✓ Goal to "not do" something
✓ Anything in the passive voice

FORM 8A

Ecological Assessment with Supplementary Aids and Services

Student: _Peter_					
Activity: _Transition into classroom_					
Grade: _1_					

List each step in the activity	Cues	Skill(s) needed	Discrepancy	Supplementary aid and service needed	Action plan (what to teach)
Move to locker	Bell rings	Mobility through school	Peter uses a wheelchair, and he cannot move it himself.	Peer or adult to assist with mobility—steering and operating wheelchair.	Peter should learn how to move his own wheelchair. In the meantime, he needs assistance to push his chair.
Take off coat	Other students are taking off their coats, hanging them on hooks.	Remove coat and hang up	Peter cannot take off his own coat or reach to hang it up.	Assistance with removing and putting on clothing, including sleeves, buttons, and zippers	Peter can work on taking off his own coat this year. It will be targeted as a goal.
Take needed items out of backpack	Other students are retrieving needed school materials from their backpacks.	Remove needed items from backpack	Peter cannot take items out of his backpack independently.	Peer or adult assistance managing books, writing utensils, or other school materials	Peter will partially participate in taking his items out of his backpack by holding the backpack on his lap and communicating which items should be taken out and where they should be placed.
Move to desk	Other students move toward classroom.	Mobility to desk	Peter cannot move to the desk independently.	Peer or adult to assist with mobility—steering and operating wheelchair.	Peter will request assistance from a peer or adult to remove any physical barriers in his path and assist him in moving to his desk.

Figure 8.1. Sample ecological assessment for Peter with supplementary aids and services.

3. Could This Be Defined as Specially Designed Instruction or Related Services?

Specially designed instruction includes any goals, including those related to motor, communication, or social needs, which might be carried out, at least in part, by a teacher or related service provider. As defined in IDEA 2004, specially designed instruction refers to the adaptation of content, methodology, or delivery of instruction. SAS might be necessary to allow the student to access specially designed instruction. But on their own, SAS do not constitute instruction. For example, prompting is an instructional strategy that should be outlined as part of a communication goal and would not be listed as a supplementary aid or service. The use of a voice output communication device, however, would be considered a supplementary aid. Help with eating and bathroom use could be supplementary service, but if a student had IEP goals related to eating and bathroom use, these could also fall under nursing or occupational therapy as a related service. Stretching could be a physical therapy service, but it might not be a goal. However, the use of various positioning equipment across the day would be considered a supplementary aid. Teams should be careful to distinguish among SAS, goals, and related services.

4. Could This Reasonably Be Provided or Available in Generalized Contexts?

When determining SAS, it's natural to think of one's own school. Teams base decisions on what's available and possible within the unspoken constraints and resources of their own context. However, this can become problematic—and not just because students might change schools. When considering SAS, teams should carefully examine the supports which could be provided in everyday contexts. The use of personnel supports such as a dedicated paraprofessional is one area where teams might rely on a support that is not natural or available in everyday contexts. Do most people have a person following them around in the grocery store, helping them to make healthy dinner choices? No (even though most of us could use one!). Instead, look at the ecological assessments and identify supports that are necessary in the current environment along with skills that are needed. If a skill could be taught, the student might not need an SAS but rather an IEP goal. And if the service is extraordinary—like speaking in a soft tone of voice all the time—it's not likely to be available in everyday contexts and therefore not an appropriate SAS. Instead, SAS should reflect the routine activities and demands of current and future environments to best prepare students to live inclusive lives now and in the future.

5. Will This Supplementary Aid or Service Help the Student Reach Their Annual Goal and Support Independence?

All sections of an IEP—including the goals, present levels of performance, and SAS—must be aligned. Because SAS are meant to supplement specially designed instruction and related services (Turnbull et al., 2016), they should be directly related to specific goals, which are related to specific present levels of performance. When a school has access to a special feature (e.g., warm water pool, sensory room) or has historically provided a special service (e.g., community-based instruction every day), the team might be tempted to include these in a student's IEP. However, just because a particular service might be available in a school, it might not be appropriate or necessary for all students. A district-provided "bank" of SAS, provided in a drop-down menu on the IEP form, makes avoiding this pitfall even more difficult (Cheatham et al., 2012). Even if the IEP form has a drop-down menu, it's always possible to add individualized SAS—even if it means adding the service to the "notes" section of the IEP. Adding potentially unnecessary SAS could result in an unnecessarily restrictive educational program.

WHAT KINDS OF SUPPLEMENTARY AIDS AND SERVICES DO STUDENTS WITH COMPLEX SUPPORT NEEDS USE? THE SUPPORT DOMAINS FRAMEWORK

Similar to IEP goals, the range of possible SAS that can be used by a student with complex support needs is limited only by the imaginations of the team members. Designing creative solutions to tricky problems and eliminating barriers to education is one thing that makes supporting students with complex support needs fun and challenging. Team members should think expansively about the types of supports that might benefit a student's access to their education and consider ways that services and supports can be provided before dismissing new ideas.

Also, like goals, SAS decisions should be supported by data. Keeping track of the length and frequency of sensory room visits, for example, will help the team understand their impact on the student's access to the general curriculum. Likewise, monitoring a student's on-task behavior while using a particular type of seating might help the team determine if the seating is effective. Overall, collecting data on the student's SAS can help the team decide if the seating SAS is serving its intended purpose.

A final guide to keep in mind when considering SAS is that they should only be as special as necessary. As Janney and Snell (2013) note, supports provided should not be so special as to isolate or stigmatize students. Rather, supports should be natural as much as possible. This means using the materials, tools, learning arrangements, and people already available in a setting, rather than creating different materials or using different tools as much as possible. Universal design for learning (UDL) strategies implemented in general education classes can support the accessibility of the materials, tools, learning arrangements, and people in the setting.

Next, we provide a framework for considering SAS based on items commonly included in IEPs (Kurth et al., 2018). While the following examples provide a useful starting point, there is no exhaustive definition of SAS. Teams should imagine creative ways to support students' access beyond the status quo or even the suggestions below. See Figure 8.2 for a visual representation of the framework. Five dimensions of SAS will be discussed: physical/accessibility, instructional, behavior, social-communication, and collaborative.

Physical/Accessibility Dimension

SAS in this dimension ensure students' gross and fine motor needs are supported, and materials and spaces are physically accessible. The *physical/accessibility* dimension includes environmental supports; vision, hearing, and sensory supports; health and safety supports; assistive technology; and medical supports.

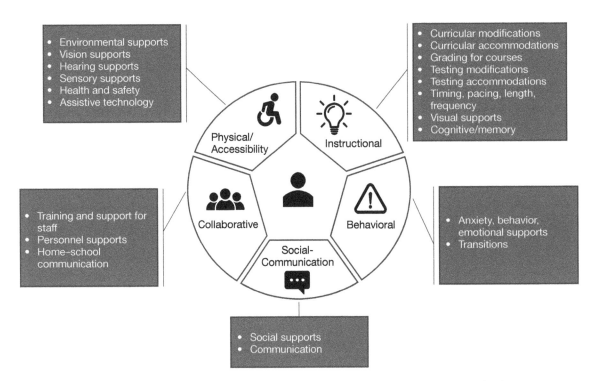

Figure 8.2. A framework for considering supplementary aids and services based on items commonly available in the classroom.

Environmental Supports   *Environmental supports* include alterations to the setting of instruction and can take a variety of forms to serve many different functions. Seating is an example of an environmental support which can be necessary for students to physically access the classroom. A wheelchair-adjustable desk, an adapted chair, or a seat near the door or teacher can all support students' physical access. The environment of the classroom can also be adjusted to accommodate students' needs. For example, students might require filtered lighting or an air-conditioned room. The location of testing and working can also be changed to support students' access; for example, a study carrel or defined work area can reduce distractions, or students might be given alternative locations to complete individual work.

Vision Supports   Vision supports are designed to make visual information or text accessible for students with visual impairments. Examples include large text, braille, screen readers, variations in color or font, or closed-circuit television (CCTV).

Hearing Supports   Hearing supports make auditory information accessible to students with hearing impairments. Examples include frequency modulation (FM) systems, preferential seating to improve hearing, ASL translation, or hearing aids.

Sensory Supports   Sensory supports provide a means for students to regulate their sensory needs and make challenging sensory situations more accessible for students. Examples include fidgets or other sensory tools provided in the general education classroom, ear plugs, or flexible transitions between classes to allow students to avoid crowded hallways.

Health and Safety Supports   Health supports ensure medical needs, personal needs, and nutrition needs are met, allowing the student to access their educational environment. Examples of health supports include tube feeding, toileting, various dietary needs such as a blended diet, adapted utensils, plates and cups, suctioning, and other nursing services. Safety supports ensure the student is physically safe at school, and can include supports such as adult proximity, medical alert bracelets, or extra passing time between classes.

Assistive Technology   Assistive technology (AT) can be used for a variety of purposes and should be considered a necessity for students with disabilities to access their education. As discussed in Chapter 6, nearly all students with complex support needs will use some form of AT. Rather than asking, "Does the student use assistive technology?" a team should ask, "What technology does the student need to access their education?" Many comprehensive guides to assistive technology are available elsewhere. As a starting point, teams should consider how assistive technology can support students' writing, posture, motor skills, emotional regulation, transitions, and academic skills. AAC can include assistive technology and are covered under the *social-communication* dimension.

Medical Supports   Some students will require medical devices or supports to facilitate their learning in school. For example, a student who experiences frequent or unpredictable seizures may wear a helmet to prevent injury. Medical supports and services should be considered in these situations and developed in close collaboration with the child's family and, if appropriate, medical doctors.

Instructional Dimension

Instructional SAS address the needs of students to learn general education curriculum or other prioritized content and make the processes and products of the general accessible (Janney & Snell, 2013). Instructional SAS can take the form of accommodations and modifications to curriculum and testing, as seen in Table 8.1. In this section, we define various types of instructional dimension SAS that include accommodations and modifications. It is important to remember some students may need modifications

Assistive Technology Resources

The following websites provide information and resources about using assistive technology:

- AbleData, https://www.naric.com/sites/default/files/AbleData_brochure_slim.pdf
- Disabilities, Opportunities, Internetworking, and Technology (Do-IT), https://www.washington.edu/doit
- Center on Disability and Technology, https://www.air.org/project/center-technology-and-disability
- The Early Childhood Technical Assistance Center's page "Assistive Technology" http://ectacenter.org/topics/atech/atech.asp
- Quality Indicators for Assistive Technology Services, https://qiat.org
- Closing the Gap, https://closingthegap.com
- SET-BC, https://www.setbc.org
- Assistive Technology Internet Modules from the Ohio Center for Autism and Low Incidence (OCALI), https://atinternetmodules.org
- National Center on Accessible Educational Materials, https://aem.cast.org/navigating/assistive-technology-resources.html#.XJErby2ZN0s

for some content instruction, accommodations for other content instruction, and no extra supports for yet other content instruction. Besides curriculum modifications and accommodations, other SAS in the instructional dimension include modifications to grading or testing; testing accommodations; supports for the timing, pacing, length, or frequency of tasks; general visual supports; and cognitive/memory supports.

Reflecting on student learning data and completing ecological analyses will help IEP teams make the decisions about what types of supports students will need, and when.

Curricular Modifications   Curricular modifications can make curricular content more understandable and meaningful for students who follow curricula aligned with alternate state standards. Examples include a change in reading level, use of alternate assignments, alternate curriculum-based assessments, alternate materials, or alternate content. (For more information

Table 8.1.   Accommodations and modifications

	Accommodations	Modifications
Snapshot definition	To provide access	To make meaning
Key elements	Do not fundamentally alter or change expectations or standards in instructional level, content, or performance criteria	Do alter or change expectations or standards in instructional level, content, or performance criteria
Why they are used	Changes are made to provide equal access to learning and equal opportunity to demonstrate what is known.	Changes are made to provide student meaningful and productive learning experiences based on individualized needs and instructional priorities.
Examples	• Same text provided in braille • Extra time to complete same worksheet • Take same test in a quiet location • Complete fewer problems in same homework assignment • Receive reminders to stay on task or turn in assignments.	• Same text rewritten at a lower reading level • Complete a long-division worksheet using a calculator • Take a test that contains prioritized learning content only • Write an essay using speech-to-text software and pictures
Implications for postsecondary education	• None	• Courses taken with modified learning content may not count towards college admissions criteria

about curricular modifications and accommodations, see works by Diane Browder and by June Downing, among others.)

Curricular Accommodations   Curricular accommodations provide access to grade-level curricular content. Examples include audio books, text enhancements such as color coding or highlighting, typing, using a word bank, graphic organizers, note taking supports (e.g., copy of notes, cloze notes, recorded lectures), calculators, manipulatives, charts, scribes, and having text read aloud. Sometimes curricular accommodations include assistive technology, such as voice-to-text or screen readers. Supports can also increase general accessibility throughout the school day for organization and self-management, including color-coding materials, assistance maintaining materials, and providing additional materials for student.

Grading for Courses   Modifications to grading criteria can be negotiated depending on students' priorities and needs. Grading supports may include assigning grades based on progress toward meeting IEP goals, improvement over past performance, performance on prioritized work, and improvement in learning process (Kurth et al., 2012). For example, students might receive a pass/fail grade in lieu of a letter or numeric grade or be graded according to a modified scale or using modified weights. Teams should create personalized plans specifying how students will be graded; this assists all team members in being consistent and accurate in their grading of products and courses (Munk & Bursuck, 2001).

Testing Modifications   Testing modifications refer to changes in the criteria or content of a text. For example, a test might include a fewer number of items in a multiple-choice question, use open- or close-ended questions, or use an adjusted format such as a scribe. The test delivery might also be altered, or the means of assessment can be modified entirely (e.g., performance-based vs. pencil and paper).

Testing Accommodations   Testing accommodations allow the content of the test to be accessible without changing the content or difficulty. Examples include shorter tests, changes in the presentation format such as font size or spacing of items, the use of a scribe or bubbler, an alternate testing location, or having the text materials read aloud to the student.

Timing, Pacing, Length, Frequency   Many students with disabilities experience cognitive and/or motor processing delays, making it challenging to complete tasks within small windows of time. To accommodate this, teams may identify supports that facilitate a student's participation in activities. Supports for timing include providing additional time for completing assignments or processing information. As noted elsewhere, timing supports should also be specific. For example, stating a student will have "extra time" is much less informative than a statement noting the student must have twice as much time as their typically developing peers have to complete in-class worksheets. Supports for pacing include chunking information into smaller amounts or breaking assignments into smaller sections. Supports for length include shortening the length of required assignments or responses. Again, this should be specific, noting what types of assignments should be reduced and by how much. Supports for frequency include repeated practice and review opportunities, such as ensuring a student has additional opportunities to review spelling words before testing.

General Visual Supports   Visual supports can be provided for a range of purposes, and the specific types of visual supports, including when and where they are provided, should be clearly delineated in the IEP. These supports can also span a variety of other dimensions, such as curricular accommodations and modifications, environmental supports, communication supports, cognitive supports and supports for transitions. Visual supports generally include supports such as visual schedules, visual checklists and picture modeling for routines, visual timers, and other types of visual response and stimulus prompts, as well as video supports such as video modeling. It is important to specify the type of visual support (e.g., written, line drawings, photos) and how they will be used (e.g., for classroom routines, for text support) is important.

Cognitive/Memory Supports   Students with complex support needs usually require significant supports for cognitive processing and memory; however, these supports are rarely considered in the SAS (Kurth et al., 2018). Supports for students to access the cognitive and memory demands of school include processing time, repeated instructions, reminders, and the use of task analyses. Although these are commonly used strategies, including these cognitive and memory supports in the IEP document will provide clarity about the specific ways they should be applied with individual students.

Behavior Dimension

SAS in this dimension relate to the social-emotional needs of the student throughout the school day, particularly those whose behavior interferes with their learning. The *behavior dimension* includes supports for anxiety, emotional, or behavior-related needs as well as for transitions during the school day.

Anxiety, Behavior, and Emotional Supports   Students who experience emotional and behavioral challenges can benefit from supports to ensure their needs do not act as a barrier to their education. Anxiety about transitions, social situations, specific activities, or new experiences can also exacerbate emotional and behavioral challenges. Examples of supports in this category include frequent positive feedback, reinforcement, support for self-monitoring, the use of timers or stopwatches, token economy system, opportunities to request breaks, and the use of a schedule for these needs. Many more resources are available to help support students with anxiety, emotional, or behavior-related needs.

Behavior Support Resources

The following websites provide information and resources for using positive behavior supports:

- Positive Behavior Supports OSEP Technical Assistance Center, https://www.pbis.org/ (search for "severe disabilities")
- National Center for Pyramid Model Innovations, https://challengingbehavior.cbcs.usf.edu/about/index.html
- "Evidence-Based Practices for Improving Challenging Behaviors of Students With Severe Disabilities" (Westing, 2015) https://ceedar.education.ufl.edu/wp-content/uploads/2015/11/EBPs-for-improving-challenging -behavior-of-SWD.pdf
- Association for Positive Behavior Supports, https://www.apbs.org/

Supports for Transitions   Many students with complex support needs experience challenges in the area of transitioning between activities in school. Schedules, advance warnings, and timers are a few examples of common supports for transitions.

Social-Communication Dimension

SAS in the *social-communication* dimension relate to the needs the student has for socializing and communicating effectively with others.

Social Supports   Supporting students' socialization and development of social skills is a key component of effective inclusive education for students with complex needs. For example, supports to develop friendships, such as "peer buddies"; supports to teach social skills, such as social groups; the use of cooperative learning or peer tutors; and the use of social narratives, such as social stories, are commonly used to support students' social development.

Communication Supports   For students with complex support needs, communication is often a central concern. AAC, including high- and low-tech systems, is a basic need for students whose oral language is limited. Even for students who have some verbal ability, supports for increasing the effectiveness of communication through multiple means are essential.

Communication Support Resources

The following websites provide information and resources about communication supports:

- American Speech-Language-Hearing Association (ASHA), https://www.asha.org/public/speech/disorders/aac/
- International Association for Augmentative and Alternative Communication (ISAAC), https://isaac-online.org/english/home/
- PrAACtical AAC, https://praacticalaac.org
- Rehabilitation Engineering Research Center on AAC, https://rerc-aac.psu.edu
- AAC Intervention, http://www.aacintervention.com
- The website of Linda Burkhart, Technology, Communication. and Education Integration Specialist, http://www.Lburkhart.com

---

Collaborative Dimension

SAS in the *collaborative dimension* include training and support for staff, personnel supports, and home–school communications.

Training and Support for Staff   This category covers the range of training and collaborative time staff will need to effectively support the student through the use of evidence-based practices. This might include support for staff to learn how to use assistive technology or program AAC devices, or how to implement instruction pursuant to the child's IEP. Time for co-planning and provision of co-teaching should also be defined here. Finally, any consultations or student observations should be noted.

Personnel Supports   Research has consistently found that personnel supports–specifically the use of paraprofessionals–is the most over-used category of SAS (Giangreco & Broer, 2007; Kurth et al., 2018). The decision to use personnel supports such as a one-to-one paraprofessional should be used with caution. Some forms of adult support are less intrusive but can provide benefits comparable to the benefits provided by using a paraprofessional. For example, frequent adult check-ins can be provided by a variety of staff and allow the student to practice independence. Students who require frequent redirection should have a behavior support plan emphasizing antecedent supports, peer supports, and other and natural supports—such as a reminder on a phone, which could replace an adult in some situations.

Home–School Communication   Home–school communication is essential for facilitating collaborative relationships with families of students with complex support needs (Ruppar et al., 2016). Communication plans should be defined in the IEP and might include daily notes or emails, texting or instant messaging as needed, and regular team meetings throughout the year.

CONCLUDING THOUGHTS: SUPPLEMENTARY AIDS AND SERVICES

SAS are essential to ensuring students with disabilities have access to, and make progress in, the general curriculum in their least restrictive environment. Yet, determining appropriate SAS can be tricky, especially because there is very little guidance for teams in this area. Using the five guiding questions and the support dimensions framework, teams can ensure that the SAS chosen will maintain placement in the least restrictive environment, will be appropriately supportive and not unnecessarily restrictive, and clear to all current and future team members.

REVIEWING THE COMMITMENT: *Removing Barriers to General Education*

After reading this chapter, what additional supports might you consider for your student with complex disabilities? Do you have any new, innovative ideas for supporting your student throughout the day?

_____

_____

_____

_____

_____

_____

_____

_____

ACTING ON THE COMMITMENT: *Removing Barriers to General Education*

This chapter included a sample ecological assessment for a first-grade student named Peter that identified his needs related to the different steps of transitioning into the classroom. A blank ecological assessment form is included in the appendix to this chapter and is available with the downloads for this book.

Think about the student whom you identified at the beginning of the chapter. Identify one activity this student does regularly. Then, conduct an ecological assessment. Use the form to break the activity down into discrete steps and identify related cues, any discrepancies between the necessary skills and your student's abilities, SAS, and an action plan for instruction.

Ecological Assessment with
Supplementary Aids and Services

Student: _____

Activity: _____

Grade: _____

List each step in the activity	Cues	Skill(s) needed	Discrepancy	Supplementary aid and service needed	Action plan (what to teach)

Student: _____

Activity: _____

Grade: _____

List each step in the activity	Cues	Skill(s) needed	Discrepancy	Supplementary aid and service needed	Action plan (what to teach)

Determining the Least Restrictive Environment

9

With Katie M. McCabe

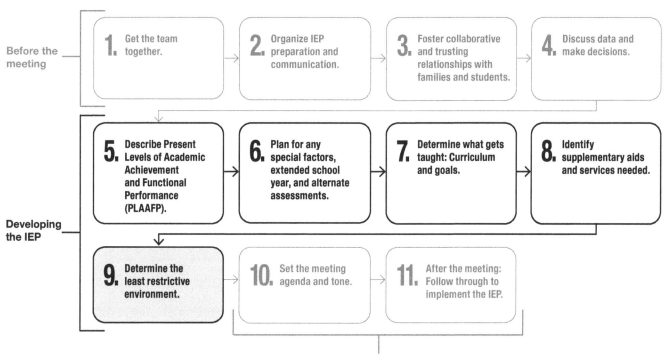

Before the meeting

1. Get the team together.
2. Organize IEP preparation and communication.
3. Foster collaborative and trusting relationships with families and students.
4. Discuss data and make decisions.

Developing the IEP

5. Describe Present Levels of Academic Achievement and Functional Performance (PLAAFP).
6. Plan for any special factors, extended school year, and alternate assessments.
7. Determine what gets taught: Curriculum and goals.
8. Identify supplementary aids and services needed.

9. Determine the least restrictive environment.
10. Set the meeting agenda and tone.
11. After the meeting: Follow through to implement the IEP.

At the meeting and afterward

Students who receive special education services are first and foremost general education students; they simply receive individually designed special education services *in addition to* their general education. Thus, it is critical to recognize special education is a service; it is not a place (e.g., a special education classroom), it is not a teacher (e.g., a special education teacher), and it is not a type of student (e.g., a special education student). So, what are special education services? IDEA 2004 defines special education services as specially designed instruction (SDI) that is reasonably calculated to allow the student to benefit from instruction, and includes

> adapting, as appropriate to the needs of an eligible child . . . the content, methodology or delivery of instruction (i) to address the unique needs of the child that result from the child's disability; and (ii) ensure access of the child to the general curriculum, so that the child can meet the educational standards within the jurisdiction of the public agency that apply to all children. (34 CFR Sec. 300.39(b)(3))

As the final step in developing an IEP, the team must decide the environment where those special education services and specially designed instruction will be provided for each part of the school day. In this chapter, we discuss the issue of placement in context of making a least restrictive environment decision and justifying the rationale for this decision.

UNDERSTANDING THE COMMITMENT:

Maximizing Participation While Meeting Individual Needs

Decisions about where a student receives their special education services not only have a profound impact on their life at the immediate moment, but also impact their lifelong outcomes and relationships. To make this kind of decision, then, IEP teams must carefully consider a variety of factors, including what the student needs, the harms and benefits of each placement option, and what the team will do to support the student to be taught in the general education setting. As we begin this chapter, put yourself in the place of a person whose educational placement restrictiveness is being decided. Respond to the following questions.

1. What does it mean to be "restricted?"

   _____

   _____

   _____

2. Who should decide the degree to which your options are restricted, such as what you eat, who you live with, where you work, and what you do for fun?

   _____

   _____

   _____

3. What factors would you want to have considered when a team of people were determining your fate?

   _____

   _____

   _____

WHAT IS THE LEAST RESTRICTIVE ENVIRONMENT?

With the understanding that special education services are intended to supplement general education through the provision of specially designed instruction, it is clear that the intent of Congress when developing IDEA is that students with disabilities are taught the general education curriculum in the general education setting with their general education peers. In making a least restrictive environment (LRE) decision, teams must balance this intent of IDEA (special education is a service that is offered to eligible students with disabilities) with the unique needs and priorities of an individual student. Teams must decide where special education services are provided, and what steps teams must take before removing a student from general education to receive their special education services.

What Is the IDEA Definition of Least Restrictive Environment?

The LRE section of IDEA 2004 reads as follows:

> Each public agency must ensure that (i) To the maximum extent <u>appropriate</u>, children with disabilities, including children in public or private institutions or other care facilities, are educated with children who are nondisabled; and (ii) Special classes, separate schooling, or other removal of children with disabilities from the <u>regular educational environment</u> occurs only if the nature or severity of the disability is such that education in regular classes with the use of <u>supplementary aids and services</u> cannot be <u>achieved satisfactorily</u>. (§300.114(a))

This statement is very important to developing an IEP; several key terms and phrases have been underlined in the above definition and are necessary to define to best interpret the LRE requirements.

What Is "Appropriate?"
The word "appropriate" appears many times in the IDEA, and it simply means what is right, fitting, or suitable for a student given their specific needs, strengths, goals, and the supports and services that will be provided to help the student reach those goals. Therefore, an "appropriate" education is different for every child; it is individually determined by the student's IEP team.

What Is the "Regular Educational Environment?"
The U.S. Department of Education defines the "regular educational environment" as all classrooms and other settings in schools (e.g., lunchrooms and playgrounds) in which children without disabilities participate (71 Fed. Reg. 46585). In other words, all settings in a school where children without disabilities participate are considered part of the "regular educational environment" (20 USC 1412(5)(B)). In addition, the regular classroom is the school the student would attend if the student was not disabled; this is the first placement option considered for each student.

What Are Supplementary Aids and Services?
As defined in Chapter 8, SAS are any aid, service, and other support provided in regular education, extracurricular, and nonacademic settings to enable the student to be educated with nondisabled peers. As described in Chapter 8, these aids and services can vary significantly based on the individual needs of the student, and can include supports for the student, modifications to the environment, and trainings for educators, among others.

What Is "Satisfactorily Educated?"
There is no specific standard or benchmark within IDEA 2004 for determining what it means for the student to receive a satisfactory education. Instead, each student's IEP is the measuring tool. The IEP team determines if a student's education is appropriate and if it is being achieved satisfactorily through progress monitoring and reporting (see Chapter 4). If a team believes the student is not receiving a satisfactory education, the IEP may be reviewed and revised to make necessary and appropriate adjustments or modifications. These adjustments may be related to the type of SAS provided to support the student's education in a regular classroom setting, their goals, and their related services.

Who Decides the Student's Least Restrictive Environment?

According to IDEA 2004, each student's LRE is determined at least annually based on the student's IEP. Each student's placement decision must be made by the IEP team, including people who know the student well (e.g., families and teachers) and a person who has knowledge about how to interpret evaluation data and placement options. The team is tasked with making decisions grounded in the understanding that special education is a service that is available to eligible students; the team must make decisions that recognize special education as a service and not a place.

What Is the Relationship Between
Least Restrictive Environment and Placement?

Teams must determine the place where students with disabilities receive their special education services in the LRE. As such, the terms "LRE" and "placement" are often used interchangeably, although LRE is broader than placement, as it includes the supports and services students will receive in the placement. And, as noted previously, IDEA contains a clear preference for students with disabilities (who are first general education students and who also receive special education services) to receive those supports and services in regular education settings. However, the IDEA regulations acknowledge that the regular class placement may not be appropriate for every single student. As a result, school districts are required to make available a range of placement options to provide alternate placements in which students might receive their free and appropriate public education in the LRE.

Continuum of Placement Options Placement options are typically considered along a continuum from the least restrictive (i.e., a general education class 100% of the day with individualized supports and services) to highly restrictive placements, such as self-contained classes and special education schools. The options on this continuum must include "the alternative placements listed in the definition of special education under Section 300.17 (i.e., instruction in regular classes, special classes, special schools, home instruction, and instruction in hospitals and institutions)" (34 CFR 300.551(b)(1)). These placement options must be available to the extent necessary to implement the IEP of each disabled student, and IEP teams must select the option along the continuum that is needed for a particular student's IEP to be implemented. In the case that an IEP team selects a placement that is outside of the regular educational environment, teams must maximize opportunities for the student to interact with nondisabled peers. Figure 9.1 shows the continuum of special education placements in order of restrictiveness, including for each the ranges for percentage of time spent in the general education setting.

WHAT ARE PATTERNS IN LEAST RESTRICTIVE ENVIRONMENT?

To this point, we have defined the LRE and discussed that teams must make a placement decision that is the least restrictive for a student and guarantees them maximum opportunities to interact and learn

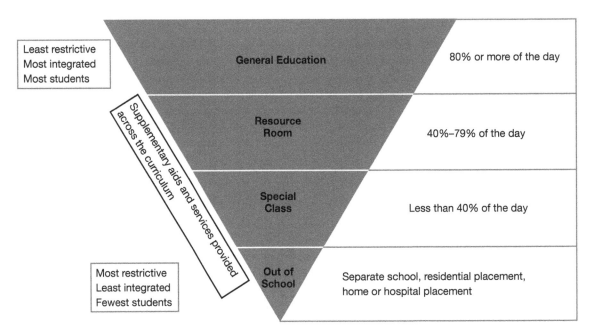

Figure 9.1. Least restrictive environment continuum.

with nondisabled peers. The LRE language of IDEA also asserts that most students should be educated in general education settings, with few students taught outside of general education for the least amount of time possible. To ensure states make progress towards educating fewer students in more restrictive settings, Congress requires states to submit a six-year plan to the U.S. Department of Education, Office of Special Education Programs (OSEP) that sets rigorous and measurable annual targets for improving outcomes for students with disabilities on each of 17 indicators. These State Performance Plans include Indicator 5, in which states report the number of students taught 80% or more of the day in general education, less than 40% of the school day in general education, and in separate schools, home, and hospital settings. Progress on this and all other indicators are sent to Congress every year in an Annual Performance Report. How well are these goals of IDEA realized?

Historically, most students with disabilities who require complex supports and services have been educated in segregated settings (Brock, 2018). Only 17.4% of students with intellectual disability, 39.7% of students with autism, 25.7% of students with deaf-blindness, and 14.3% of students with multiple disabilities are taught in general education classes for more than 80% of the day (U.S. Department of Education, 2021). These data, illustrated in Figure 9.2, show students with disabilities who typically require complex support needs are underrepresented in general education or inclusive placements.

The data presented to Congress examine placement by disability label. As noted above, these data suggest limited access to general education classrooms for many students. However, the extent of segregation was made clear in a review of national placement data of nearly 40,000 students who complete the alternate assessment. In this study, Kleinert and colleagues (2015) found that 93% of students who take the alternate assessment were taught primarily in self-contained special education classrooms, separate schools, or home and hospital settings. Only 7% of students who take the alternate assessment, then, spend 80% or more of the school day in resource or general education classrooms. Because students with complex support needs take the alternate assessment, this study highlights the extent to which students with complex support needs remain segregated from their peers and the general education setting with limited access to the academic, nonacademic, and extracurricular curriculum.

Does placement in general education even matter for students with complex support needs? To this point, decades of research have investigated the role of placement in student outcomes. Students who are taught in segregated settings experience less rigorous instruction (Bacon et al., 2016) and have less rigorous IEP goals compared to students with disabilities taught in inclusive settings (Kurth & Mastergeorge, 2010). Arguments in favor of educating students in segregated settings often focus on the student's need to access specialized curriculum, but students in segregated settings actually receive less individualized or specialized instruction (Causton-Theoharis et al., 2011), are less engaged

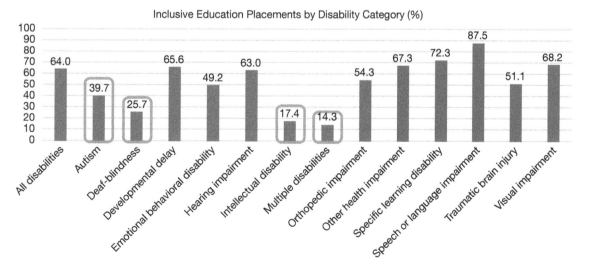

Figure 9.2. Inclusive placement by disability category. (*Note:* Educational environment data can be found in the *Forty-second Annual Report to Congress on Implementation of the Individuals with Disabilities Education Act* [United States Department of Education, 2021].)

in learning (Pennington & Courtade, 2015), and have limited access to highly qualified instructors or effective communication and learning partners (Kurth et al., 2016). In contrast, instruction in the general education or inclusive settings increases students' access to general education curriculum, grade-level standards (Soukup et al., 2007), highly qualified instructors (Mason-Williams et al., 2017), and opportunities for positive social outcomes (Carter & Hughes, 2005). Additionally, students with complex support needs show more progress in their goals when educated in general education settings (Gee et al., 2020).

Who Should Be Restricted?

At this point, it is worth considering the very idea of restrictiveness of environments. A basic right enjoyed by Americans is freedom: our rights and privileges are not restricted without due process. In fact, only two populations have restricted environments: prisoners and children, especially children with disabilities. And the degree to which prisoners are restricted is a matter of the courts, yet the consequential decision of how much to restrict a child with a disability is handled much more casually in too many instances. The decision to remove a child from general education for part or all of a school day must be weighed carefully; outcomes and opportunities vary significantly based on placement as noted previously, and most of the time, once a child is placed in a specific setting, they never leave it (White et al., 2007). Given the importance of the placement decision, what factors should, and should not, be considered? We examine these next.

Factors to Consider When Deciding Least Restrictive Environment   Teams should consider five factors when determining the LRE for an individual student: 1) the student's abilities and needs, 2) the educational benefits available to the student in each possible placement when it is supplemented with appropriate aids and services, 3) the potential harms of each placement, 4) the effects on peers in each setting—including peers with and without disabilities, and 5) the supports the student will receive in that setting. These factors are discussed below (see also Table 9.1).

Individual Abilities and Needs   The overriding rule when deciding placement is that each student's placement is individually determined by the student's IEP team based on their abilities and needs. The IEP is always the basis for the placement decision. The first factor to consider, then, is whether the placement is individualized based on the student's needs, goals, family, and student preferences.

Potential Benefits   The second factor to consider is the educational benefits available to the student in each placement when the placement is supplemented with appropriate aids and services. These benefits must be objectively and carefully weighed, and not simply reflect the observations, ideas, and preferences of the IEP team, but be based on research. In fact, IDEA asserts IEP teams must use scientifically based research to make decisions over 50 times! Today, decades of research have demonstrated positive outcomes for students with disabilities who are educated in general education classrooms across academic, social, communication, and behavior outcomes (SWIFT Center, 2017). Just as importantly, there is no research demonstrating positive outcomes of separate classrooms or schools

Table 9.1.   Factors in the least restrictive environment decision making

Factors to consider	Factors to not consider
✓ Individual student needs, goals, family, and student preferences	✗ Disability label or category
	✗ Severity of disability
✓ Educational benefits of each placement	✗ Available placement options
✓ Educational harms of each placement	✗ Available services
✓ Effects on peers	✗ Existing spaces, materials
✓ Array of special education, related, and supplementary aids and services provided in each placement	✗ Convenience of administrators
	✗ Need for specific teaching arrangements
✓ Scientifically based research	✗ Need for specially designed instruction
✓ Portability	

	Benefits of the general education class	Benefits of the special education class
Academic		
English language arts		
Math		
Science		
Social studies		
Physical education		
Nonacademic		
Communication		
Social		
Behavior		
Extracurricular		
Recess		
Clubs		
Sports		
Assemblies		
Pep rallies		
After school activities (e.g., dances)		
Field trips		

Figure 9.3. Consider the benefits of each placement.

for students with complex support needs. Thus, teams must review research and consider the student's individual needs and identify the potential benefits of all placements being considered. A table, like the one in Figure 9.3, can help teams weigh these benefits with science.

Potential Harms   The third factor for teams to consider is the potential harms of each placement. Again, both peer-reviewed research and the needs of the student should drive these considerations versus the preferences or individual knowledge of the IEP team members. As noted in Chapter 7, students with disabilities must access and make progress in the general education curriculum, which includes academic, nonacademic, and extracurricular learning. This includes the explicit curriculum, including the content that is taught, the materials used, and the conversations and activities engaged in. There is no way to actually replicate the explicit curriculum in a special education classroom, and so the harms of missing the explicit curriculum must be explored. So too must the potential harms of missing the hidden curriculum taught in general education, including the ways students learn to socialize, communicate, play, build relationships, and gain membership to community. IEP teams must consider what hidden curriculum is taught in general education, and how missing this by being removed from general education will potentially harm a student. Finally, teams must consider the null curriculum, or what is not taught. Watered down curricula are associated with special education classrooms, meaning students with disabilities will not have the simple opportunity to learn the breadth and scope of what other children are taught. Congregating students in a special education classroom also limits the availability of skilled communication partners to learn to communicate with, and this must be considered for students who have complex communication needs. These harms must be fully explored as well across all

	Harmful effects of the general education class	Harmful effects of the special education class
Academic		
English language arts		
Math		
Science		
Social studies		
Physical education		
Nonacademic		
Communication		
Social		
Behavior		
Extracurricular		
Recess		
Clubs		
Sports		
Assemblies		
Pep rallies		
After school activities (e.g., dances)		
Field trips		

Figure 9.4. Consider the harmful effects of each placement.

academic, nonacademic, and extracurricular settings. A table to consider the potential harms of each placement is shown in Figure 9.4.

Effects on Peers   The effects on peers in each setting is the fourth factor IEP teams should consider. Specifically, teams must consider the extent to which the student with a disability might distract their peers or disrupt the learning environment. Too often, only peers who do not receive special education services are considered, when in fact the impact of all peers should be noted. Similarly, the impact of peers on the student with disability should also be considered. If the student is easily distracted, placement in a special education classroom might be detrimental to the student given these classrooms are more likely to experience interruptions and distractions than general education classrooms (e.g., Causton-Theoharis et al., 2011). Once again, teams should not only rely on their own observational knowledge, experiences, and preferences, but must refer to research when making these decisions. Just as outcomes of placement on student learning have been widely researched, so has the impact of students with disabilities on the learning of students who do not have disabilities. This research overwhelmingly documents the positive impact of students with disabilities on their peers who do not have disabilities (Dessemontet & Bless, 2013; Kalambouka et al., 2007; Ruijs & Peetsma, 2009), such as improved social, academic, and communication skills.

Supports the Student Will Receive   A fifth factor to consider when IEP teams are determining a student's LRE is the supports a student will receive. The array of SAS, instructional supports, training for teachers and staff, modifications, and accommodations provided to the student must be identified with the team determining how these will be used to support student progress. Given that the first placement considered is always general education with SAS, teams may only consider other placements if they are not able to identify an array of SAS that support student learning. This means teams must attempt different SAS, in different configurations, before even considering a more restrictive placement. The team must therefore think creatively and with an eye towards finding ways to keep the student in the general education classroom using SAS.

Finally, teams must guard against assuming supports and services are tied to a particular placement. The Roncker portability test (*Roncker v. Walter*, 1983) requires teams to determine the extent to which SAS can be provided in different placements. Specifically, can the services and supports provided in the separate setting be provided in the general education setting? If so, placement in the separate setting is inappropriate. For example, if a team determines a student needs access to a sensory item, and the student benefits from using this sensory item in the special education classroom, is there any reason why it could not be used just as successfully in the general education classroom? Too often, restrictiveness of setting is conflated with intensity of services, with a belief that more intensive and specialized services are only available in special settings. However, when honestly considered, there is almost never a device, activity, tool, or strategy that can truly be used only in the special setting. Services that are only provided in special settings lead to students who have been taught to be reliant on supports that are not widely available and will therefore limit their future.

Factors That Should Not Be Considered When Deciding Least Restrictive Environment   It is also worth mentioning that some factors should not be considered when making LRE decisions. As noted earlier, the overriding rule when deciding placement is individualization. However, when teams refer to student disability label, the severity of the student's disability (e.g., the difference between the student's academic performance and their grade level), or the available placement options and services, they risk making predetermined decisions. As noted in Chapter 3, *predetermination* is a serious procedural violation of IDEA that occurs when teams make decisions for students based on current configurations of supports and fail to individualize decisions for students. Therefore, student disability category, severity of disability, the configuration of placements available, and the availability of educational or related services should never be considered when making LRE decisions. Similarly, the availability of things like space, materials, or the convenience of the school district are not appropriate factors to consider when making placement decisions.

Teams should not consider factors such as student need for small group or individualized instruction when making LRE decisions. These supports and teaching arrangements can be provided in all placements. The need for specially designed instruction is also not an appropriate factor to consider. As noted in IDEA (2004), specially designed instruction is special education services. The fact that a student needs special education services is not a rationale for removing them from general education (Kurth, McQueston, et al., 2019). Specially designed instruction (i.e., adapting the content, methodology, or delivery of instruction) is not synonymous with separate classrooms, pull-out, or pull-aside instruction. Like small group and individualized instruction, specially designed instruction occurs in all placements.

MAKING LEAST RESTRICTIVE ENVIRONMENT DECISIONS

One of the most impactful statements from the *Endrew v. Douglas County* (2017) U.S. Supreme Court decision was Chief Justice John Roberts's assertion that *the IEP is not a form*. The development of an IEP should not be treated as a form to complete or a box to check; instead, it needs to be carefully individualized and considered based on the unique needs, circumstances, and priorities of the student. The LRE decisions as part of the IEP should therefore be treated in such a manner: it is not a box to check to indicate placement, but the result of a detailed, careful consideration among all team members who determine the most appropriate placement for an individual student. LRE is not limited to a physical place. Rather, LRE is the constellation of special education, related services, and SAS provided to students in a place.

Before Deciding Placement: Initial Decisions

As noted in IDEA, students with disabilities should be removed from the general education setting or be placed in a separate educational setting *only* when the use of SAS is not successful in meeting the needs of students within the general education setting. In other words, "least restrictive" means an environment where a student is provided with the required SAS for the student to learn and work toward goals in the general education environment for the most amount of time.

Every LRE decision should be dependent on the student's needs, goals, and the supplementary aids and services necessary to keep the student in the general education setting. Too often, biased decision-making results in subjective, and inequitable, segregated placement decisions. To keep decisions collaborative and based on information about the student, teams should consider the general education classroom first and then must consider all components of the IEP (i.e., PLAAFP, goals, and SAS) to decide what an appropriate individualized LRE is for each student.

Considering Present Levels of Performance When Making Least Restrictive Environment Decisions   Information from the PLAAFP allow teams to develop appropriate goals and identify SAS that are required for the student (see Chapter 8 for more about this section of the IEP). PLAAFP are important in LRE decision making because the data reported will inform the LRE decision. Teams should write PLAAFP that consider a student's progress within general education curriculum, to build a foundation for creating goals that students can work on in general education settings. For example, a speech/language pathologist can note a student's ability to use their communication device during conversations with peers in the general education classroom. As another example, a PLAAFP that references grade-level standards (see Chapter 5) facilitates the team's understanding of the supports students use to access and make progress on those standards in the general education classroom.

Considering Goals and Objectives in Least Restrictive Environment Decisions
Since general education should be considered first in LRE decision making, teams should write goals for students within the context of the general education curriculum. For example, a student who is learning to identify vocabulary words in each science or social studies unit must be present in science or social studies class to meet this goal. General and special teachers use modified assessments to monitor progress on students' progress in the general curriculum. And no specialized assessment is needed if assessments are universally designed to be accessible to all learners. Clear and measurable goals can help identify the required SAS to support the student in the general education setting.

Considering Supplementary Aids and Services in Least Restrictive Environment Decisions   Based on the student's needs and goals, team members should identify the SAS that are required to support the student in meeting their goals in general education classes. SAS should facilitate equitable access to LRE if they are offered outside of the general education classroom only when necessary. For example, specialized curriculum access can be provided by making adaptations to the general education curriculum. Likewise, related service providers should support students in the general education classroom unless a separate location is needed to maintain privacy or dignity for the student. Teams should also consider the least restrictive provision of SAS. For example, a one-to-one paraprofessional should not be considered before other options, such as natural peer supports, co-teaching, and assistive technology, have been explored.

An LRE Planning Matrix (see Table 9.2) can help teams to identify where a student will work on goals and where SAS will be provided to the student. The LRE Planning Matrix also allows teams to see exactly how much time is being spent outside of the general education environment and prompts teams to make a clear justification for removal from the general education environment.

Making the Placement Decision

The placement decision is always the *last* step at an IEP meeting. A flowchart for making this decision is shown in Figure 9.5; a full-size, blank, reproducible version of this flowchart is provided in the

Table 9.2 Least restrictive environment planning matrix

	Identified need from PLAAFP				
	Improve communication	Improve reading comprehension	Improve social skills	Improve math computation	Vestibular sensory input for regulation
Is this need addressed by a goal? (If so, where will the goal be taught?)	Yes, fifth-grade general education classroom	Yes, fifth-grade general education classroom	Yes, recess, cafeteria, general education classrooms	Yes, fifth-grade general education classroom	No
Is this need addressed by a SAS? If so, where will the SAS be used?	Yes, AAC in all settings	Yes, text-to-speech software	No	Yes	Yes, in the sensory room

Key: AAC, augmentative and alternative communication; PLAAFP, Present Levels of Academic Achievement and Functional Performance; SAS, supplementary aids and services.

appendix to this chapter and on the Brookes Download Hub. The chart includes the following steps. First, teams evaluate and identify all individual student needs and report them in the PLAAFP (see Chapter 5). Next, teams develop goals to address all areas of need identified in the PLAAFP (see Chapter 7). For each goal, services and supports are identified that support the student to learn the goal in the general education setting; sometimes, additional needs from the PLAAFP are also developed as SAS (see Chapter 8). The team must then determine the placement to teach each goal. This requires the team to ask, "Can the student acquire this goal with special education, related services, and SAS in the general education setting?" Teams need to respond to this question using real data, not simply conjecture, and must try a different array of supports and services first before considering removal from general education. If the team determines the student cannot make satisfactory progress on IEP goals with special education, related services, and SAS in the general education setting, they should continue to consider other placements along the continuum of alternative placements. Teams must also recognize the potential harmful impacts of these more restrictive placements, as well as the potential benefits very clearly. The team will continue to consider each placement until a suitable placement is selected.

Rationale for Removal   The default placement for all students with disabilities is the general education setting. Most students with disabilities should spend most, if not all, of their day in general education settings. This is also true for students with complex support needs. Therefore, if an IEP team decides the student must be removed from the general education setting for any part of the school day, the team must provide a clear rationale for this decision. This rationale must include at least two components: the specific SAS that have been considered and deemed not appropriate, and what content students will be removed from and why.

Teams must document the specific special education, related services, and SAS they have implemented in support of the student's annual goals and describe why those were not appropriate to meet the student's learning needs in general education. To accomplish this, teams should use data to demonstrate how various supports and services were provided individually and in combination, and provide data to demonstrate that, even after attempting multiple combinations of supports and services, the student was not successful and why the support and service individually or in combination was rejected.

Second, teams must identify each academic, nonacademic, and extracurricular area the student will be removed from and justify why this removal is needed, considering the harms and benefits of each placement. The LRE matrix is a useful tool for this process and should be used in combination with a discussion of the potential benefits and harms of each needed skill in each placement being considered. When removal is justified, teams must then develop a plan to return the student to general education as soon as possible. This is an important time to remind teams that students with disabilities

158

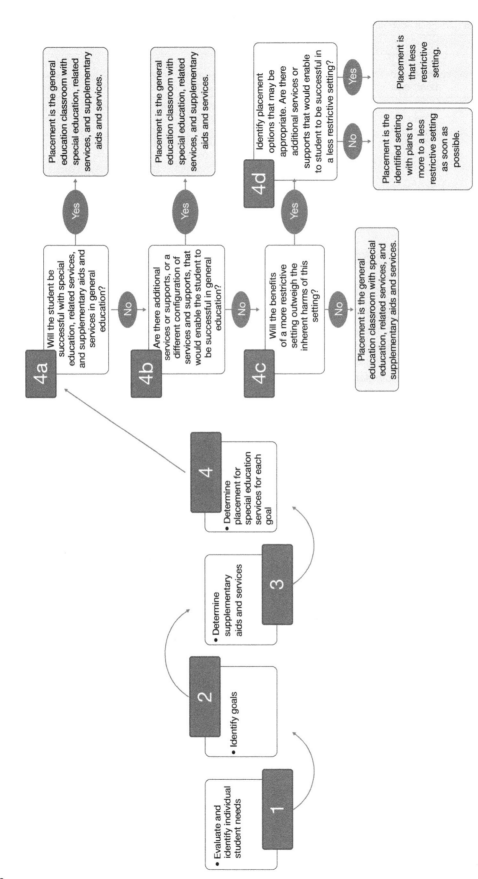

Figure 9.5. LRE Decision Flowchart. (From Kansas State Department of Education. [2013]. Kansas Special Education Process Handbook. [p. 127]; adapted by permission.)

do not have to earn their way into a general education setting; it is the goal and responsibility of the IEP to provide the appropriate supports and services to students, so they are successful in their LRE.

Percentage of Time Removed From General Education   Finally, in addition to providing a rationale for removal, the IEP team must clearly communicate when the student will be removed and for how much time on a typical school day. This is usually reported as a percentage of time. Failure to document when a student is removed and for how long can result in denial of FAPE in the LRE and can also result in individual team members (e.g., paraprofessionals, other teachers) making moment-by-moment decisions that are not in alignment with the decisions of the IEP team. The time removed from general education is reported as a percent; the percent of time inside the general education classroom is calculated by dividing the number of hours the student spends inside the general education classroom by the total number of hours in the school day (including lunch, recess, and study periods); this is then multiplied by 100 (U.S. Department of Education, 2020). For example, Jason is a second-grade student who is usually in school from 8:30 A.M. to 2:30 P.M., representing 6 hours. Over a typical week, Jason is therefore in school 30 hours (6 hours per day, 5 days per week). Jason receives speech and language therapy in the general education classroom as part of general education instruction (e.g., at recess); because this service occurs "inside" the general education setting, the time does not count as removal from general education. However, Jason receives physical therapy twice a week for 20 minutes in the therapy office, these 40 minutes of removal would count as time outside of the regular education setting. Jason also leaves school 10 minutes early each day to get on the special education bus, meaning he misses another 50 minutes per week just to get on the bus. Altogether then, Jason is outside of general education 1.5 hours per week. Of his 30 hours in a school week, this is 5% of his time outside of general education (i.e., 1.5 hours/30 hours times 100).

WRITING THE LEAST RESTRICTIVE ENVIRONMENT STATEMENT

The final content of the LRE statement must reflect the information considered throughout this chapter. The statement must promote an inclusive education with special education, related services, and SAS needed to facilitate the student's learning of the general curriculum and IEP goals. If the team determines that some amount of removal from general education is necessary even with these supports and services, this removal must be justified, and the harms and benefits of each placement must be considered and documented. The LRE statement must also indicate what placements the team considered, which were rejected and why, and which was selected and why. Finally, the statement must include clear, measurable, and objective information about where the student will receive their special education, related services, and SAS with a report of the percent of time the student is removed from general education for any of these supports and services clearly documented. Each of these components of an accurate LRE statement is listed in Table 9.3.

Table 9.3.   Least restrictive environment (LRE) content checklist

LRE component	Objectively documented?	
	Yes	No
1. What supplementary aids and services were considered for use in general education?		
2. What supplementary aids and services were rejected, and why?		
a. Are the supports and services the student requires portable (i.e., useable in the general education setting)?		
3. What placements were considered?		
4. What are the potential harms and benefits of each placement considered?		
5. What placements were rejected and why?		
6. What placement was selected and why?		
7. What percent of time and with what supplementary aids and services will the student be taught in the general education setting?		

Table 9.4. Least restrictive environment (LRE) content checklist completed for Maggie

LRE component	Objectively documented?	
	Yes	No
1. What supplementary aids and services were considered for use in general education?		✗
2. What supplementary aids and services were rejected, and why?		✗
a. Are the supports and services the student requires portable (i.e., useable in the general education setting)?		✗
3. What placements were considered?		✗
4. What are the potential harms and benefits of each placement considered?		✗
5. What placements were rejected and why?		✗
6. What placement was selected and why?		✗
7. What percent of time and with what supplementary aids and services will the student be taught in the general education setting?		✗

Knowing that these are the required components of an LRE statement, let us consider some LRE statements.

> *Example 1: Maggie requires specialized instruction and support not available in the general education classes.*

In Table 9.4, we examine this statement with our 7 points. Next, to improve Maggie's LRE statement, the team writes the following:

> *Example 2: Maggie uses the following supplementary aids and services in the general education setting: curricular modifications focused on the extended content standards (i.e., big ideas), a keyboard and tablet to type her responses, peer-supported learning, a speech-generating communication device, co-teaching of core academic areas, access to a sensory room, and access to a sensory item to help her focus. Maggie receives specially designed instruction in all academic areas as well as in communication and social skills. The use of a weighted pencil as a supplementary aid and services was rejected as the team determined typing was more efficient for Maggie. The students without disabilities do not use the sensory room, and therefore the team determined Maggie should use items from the sensory room as required or access the sensory room with a peer for up to 10 minutes per day. The team considered the following placements with these listed supplementary aids and supports; the second-grade general education classroom, pull-out to a resource room for instruction in reading, math, and speech, and a special classroom for students with autism. By leaving the general education classroom to receive instruction in academics and communication, Maggie will miss opportunities to communicate with competent peers, will miss instructional time as she travels between classroom settings, and will not receive the same rigor or content of instruction as provided in the general education setting. By remaining in the general education classroom, Maggie will have opportunities to learn the curriculum and have supports provided, including co-teaching and peer-supported learning. Due to potential harms, the separate classroom was rejected. The general education classroom with pull-out for academic instruction was rejected because Maggie can receive a modified curriculum with co-teaching from special educators. Pull-out instruction for speech therapy was accepted despite the harms (missed instructional time, lack of communication partners) for a trial period of 3 months while Maggie receives aided language input training on her new speech-generating device. Data on Maggie's language acquisition in the speech room will be evaluated in three months. Maggie will be removed from general education twice a week for 20 minutes for speech therapy; she will remain in general education 98% of the time (1760 minutes of the 1800 minutes per week).*

Certainly, the corrected LRE statement is much longer and much more detailed. However, this level of detail is needed to ensure teams develop an accurate LRE statement. As noted in the *Endrew F. v Douglas County* case (2017), the IEP is not a form; however, the actual IEP form can play a major role in how information such as the student's LRE is communicated. In a review of LRE statements, Kurth, Ruppar, and colleagues (2019) noted some IEPs in their review had no LRE section of the IEP, or the LRE section was a question (e.g., "Can the student receive their special education and services in general education?"). In cases in which the IEP form limits development of a quality LRE statement, we suggest adding a notes page to the IEP to fully document the LRE decision and justification.

CONCLUDING THOUGHTS: DETERMINING THE LEAST RESTRICTIVE ENVIRONMENT

The LRE decision and rationale are the final decisions made during the IEP meeting and must clearly align with all other components of the IEP developed. That is, the LRE justification must describe where the goals, services, and supports developed for the student are to be implemented and how these result in the most benefit and least harm to the student. The LRE decision is therefore one of the most impactful decisions made during the meeting and must be clearly described and justified.

REVIEWING THE COMMITMENT:

Maximizing Participation While Meeting Individual Needs

This chapter discussed the process teams must follow when making the consequential LRE decision, including factors that should and should not be considered.

Recall the thought exercise at the start of the chapter, in which you imagined how a team might meet to decide your degree of restrictiveness to everyday activities. After reading this chapter, how do you think this thought activity relates to the idea of making decisions about how the everyday activities of a child with disabilities is impacted by the LRE decision? Respond to the following questions.

- How should student abilities and needs be considered?

  _____

  _____

  _____

- How would you objectively determine the harms and benefits of different placement options?

  _____

  _____

  _____

- How might you assess the impact on peers of the team's placement decision?

  _____

  _____

  _____

- What constellation of supports and services might you try, and how would you document them, to ensure the student remains in the least restrictive environment?

_____

_____

_____

ACTING ON THE COMMITMENT:

Maximizing Participation While Meeting Individual Needs

This chapter includes a 7-point checklist for writing an LRE statement. Use the checklist, and your reflections on the answers above, to write a comprehensive LRE statement for yourself or a student you know who has a disability.

_____

_____

_____

_____

_____

_____

_____

_____

_____

_____

_____

_____

_____

Determining the Least Restrictive Environment (LRE) Decision Flowchart

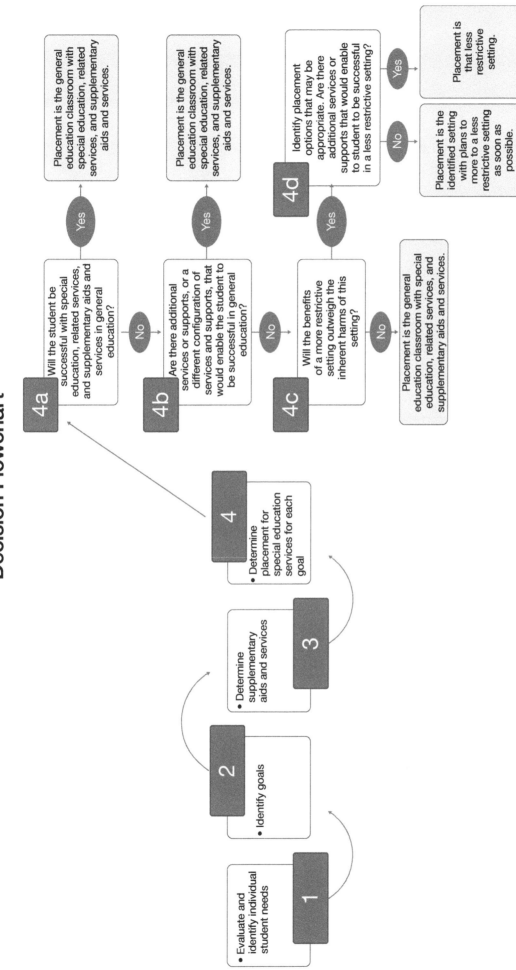

From Kansas State Department of Education. (2013). Kansas Special Education Process Handbook. (p. 127); adapted by permission.

Equitable and Inclusive IEPs for Students with Complex Support Needs: A Roadmap by Andrea L. Ruppar and Jennifer A. Kurth. Copyright © 2023 by Paul H. Brookes Publishing Co. All rights reserved.

At the Meeting and Afterward

In the first section of this book, we offered tips and strategies to prepare for the IEP meeting, including strategies to ensure equitable partnerships and high-quality collaboration. In Section II, we discussed strategies to develop the IEP document, focusing on how to create an inclusive, equitable IEP. In this final section of the book, we discuss strategies to use during and after the IEP meeting to ensure that the collaborative decisions reached before the meeting and during the development of the IEP document can be discussed in an effective meeting and implemented with fidelity after the meeting. A successful IEP process will depend on your commitment to:

- Ensuring the meeting is positive and productive

- Following through with the student, family, and team

Chapters 10 and 11 discuss how to meet these commitments so the IEP the team has worked hard to develop becomes the cornerstone of a meaningful, equitable education for your student.

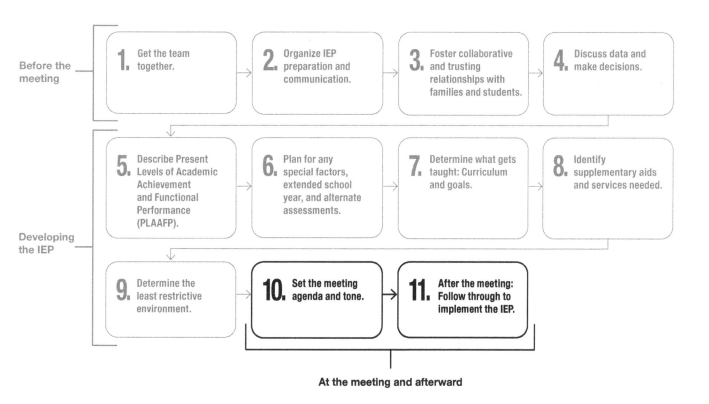

Setting an Agenda and Setting the Tone

Communication During the IEP Meeting

With Lingyu Li, Sarah Bubash, and Yuewn-lann Radeen Yang

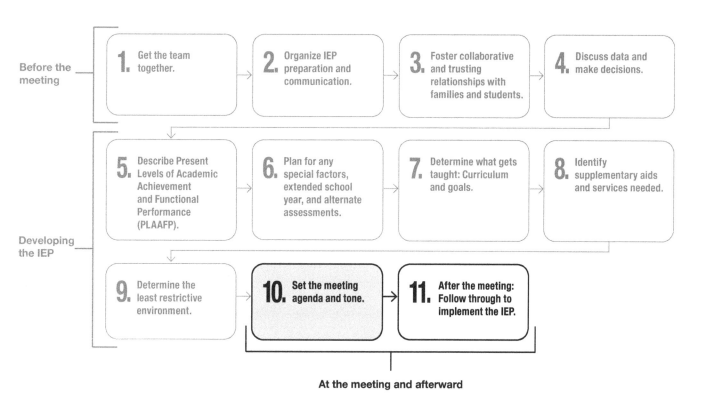

Before the meeting

1. Get the team together.
2. Organize IEP preparation and communication.
3. Foster collaborative and trusting relationships with families and students.
4. Discuss data and make decisions.

Developing the IEP

5. Describe Present Levels of Academic Achievement and Functional Performance (PLAAFP).
6. Plan for any special factors, extended school year, and alternate assessments.
7. Determine what gets taught: Curriculum and goals.
8. Identify supplementary aids and services needed.
9. Determine the least restrictive environment.
10. Set the meeting agenda and tone.
11. After the meeting: Follow through to implement the IEP.

At the meeting and afterward

So far in this book, we have focused on the content of the IEP. We now address strategies for use during the IEP meeting. IEP meetings are often a source of stress for school team members as well as families. Tight deadlines, strong emotions, and competing interests can lead to tense conversations, and school team members might feel pressure to align with each other to keep the peace and save face at work. Meanwhile, families can feel like outsiders who need to fight for everything (Erwin & Soodak, 1995). IEP meetings for students with complex support needs are often lengthy due to the many different services and supports the student might require. Some aspects of the meeting are explicitly outlined on the IEP form. However, communication among team members during the meeting is filled with implicit agreements and nuances. From exploring your identities and the identities of your teammates, to meaningfully involving students and families in the collaborative process, a lot goes on during the IEP meeting conversation.

UNDERSTANDING THE COMMITMENT: *Ensuring the Meeting Is Positive and Productive*

Think about a time you have worked with a team of others. This could be on a sports team when you were younger, as a member of a group project at school, or many other times when your ability to collaborate with others to achieve a common goal was needed. As a member of this team, how did you or a team leader

1. Signal respect and a commitment to the success of each individual member of the team?

     _____

     _____

     _____

2. Ensure every team member had a chance to share their ideas and strengths and build on the ideas and strengths of others?

     _____

     _____

     _____

3. Create a trusting partnership where disagreements are managed respectfully and proactively?

     _____

     _____

     _____

As a current or future member of IEP teams for students with complex support needs, these skills are going to be called upon regularly. As you start reading this chapter, think about your personal goals in each of these three areas (respect, equity, and trusting relationships). Use your reflections on your previous team experiences to set your goals as an IEP team member.

EDUCATORS' IDENTITIES

When preparing to meet with families and other professionals regarding educational planning for students with complex support needs, educators need to examine and understand their own identities in relation to their colleagues and family members of their students with disabilities. Most special educators are white females, and although data are not available about the disability status of teachers, most are likely to be nondisabled (National Center for Education Statistics [NCES], 2017). Regardless of their backgrounds, special educators must examine their own identities in relation to their students and their students' families.

Most important to understand is the different assumptions people hold about disability, which can inform the ways they make decisions and communicate about students. In general, people see disability as either a deficiency in the person, a deficiency in the social environment, or somewhere in between (Smart, 2009). In schools, the social environment includes the people, places, and activities that make up a child's educational experience. As Skrtic (1991) pointed out, a school can be a disabling factor in a student's life by creating barriers to learning, socialization, and physical access. Understanding disability in terms of environmental and social barriers is sometimes known as a *social model* of disability.

This viewpoint recognizes that students bring assets to school that should be built upon, and barriers to learning need to be removed.

The social model contrasts with a *deficit model*, in which disability is understood as a problem in the individual. This perspective fails to acknowledge the ways that schools might influence the expression of disability and the access barriers students face. In addition to deficit-based perceptions about people with disabilities, educators may hold unintentional deficit views of families with low socioeconomic status (SES) or from minoritized communities. Additional identities (e.g., as a parent or not, as the resident of a particular neighborhood, etc.) can also influence teachers' social interactions with parents and students. Understanding your own identity will help you to understand other people.

Your perspectives about students, families, and individuals with disabilities can influence power relationships. As Rossetti and colleagues (2021) explained:

> In the context of special education, parents of children with disabilities risk marginalization due to *discrimination by proxy* in which they may be viewed as lesser by school professionals due to being parents (versus professionals) and, specifically, parents of children with (versus without) disabilities. Though parents might not have disabilities themselves, school professionals who hold a deficit orientation toward disability may generalize that to parents, and this may result in a deficit view of families, especially CLD [culturally and linguistically diverse] families. [emphasis added]

This resulting power difference, in turn, influences the educational decisions that are made. Therefore, you should continually ask yourself about your own positions, and your implicit power (or lack of power) relative to the other professionals and teachers.

STARTING OFF RIGHT: REMINDERS FOR PRACTICES PRIOR TO THE MEETING

As discussed in Chapter 3, a variety of practices held before the meeting will likely lead to a positive IEP team meeting the day of. As you recall from that chapter, these included being aware of family culture, knowing the priorities of the family and strengths and interests of the student, and supporting families to co-construct a draft meeting agenda and IEP document ahead of the meeting. We briefly revisit these here, but also encourage you to review Chapter 3 for more detail.

Seek Out Family Input Before the Meeting

As discussed in Chapter 3, family input should be obtained and interwoven throughout the IEP process. Accessibility is key to maximizing family input and should be prioritized in the planning phase of the IEP meeting. Teachers should ask what the family's preferred language is, which may differ from their primary language, to determine whether interpretation or translation is needed (during the meeting and for documents). Families will have varying background knowledge regarding the IEP process and meeting and should have access to the necessary information to understand what their role is and how to engage in it. If additional support is needed in preparation, teachers can communicate with families to understand what would be most helpful. For example, some families might benefit from resource documents, while other families might request a pre-meeting to go over information, allowing them to be more prepared for the meeting. In addition, families should be invited to share pictures, videos, and stories about their child's growth over the past year.

Co-construct the Meeting Agenda and Draft IEP

Working with families to create a draft agenda, review data, and draft proposed IEP goals and services will also pay off during the actual IEP meeting. As discussed in Chapter 3, an agenda can help ensure that the team focuses on the outcome of the meeting as an achievable action plan for instruction. Very often, IEP teams use the IEP document as the agenda for the meeting; however, the document alone does not constitute the entirety of the steps of an IEP meeting. Moreover, following the document as a de facto agenda reinforces a sense of the process as a bureaucratic set of procedures rather than a genuine conversation among team members (Ruppar & Gaffney, 2011).

Setting the agenda collaboratively can support families to speak up at the outset and ensure that the topics of importance to them are thoroughly addressed (Martin, 2005). Parents are disempowered at school-based meetings where most team members work every day within the same organizational system. Parents are outsiders to this system, and therefore might be less prepared to participate in the procedures of an IEP meeting or any educational decision-making process. Moreover, the school-based team members may hold latent perceptions about their own positions of power as professionals in this situation. School-based team members have positions within the organizational hierarchy of the school, and in relation to the family members. Family members are usually not seen as professionals and are situated adjacent to the professional hierarchy, or at the bottom of the professional hierarchy. While families hold some political power in the IEP process, as the IDEA 2004 allows through due process, the reality is that families require enormous resources to engage in a protracted due process case, and rarely even win due process cases (Richman, 2019). To ensure meaningful family participation, careful attention to communication before, during, and after the meeting can support positive, trusting, and nonadversarial relationships with families.

Keep the Agenda Available Throughout the Meeting

The finalized agenda should be displayed at the IEP meeting and made accessible to all members. Keeping the agenda in a consistent format will help team members quickly understand the key components of the meeting. At the same time, team members should acknowledge that the agenda can be adapted or changed as needed. The team should take a moment to look over the agenda and make any necessary changes or additions prior to beginning the meeting. Referring to the agenda throughout the meeting will help maintain structure by guiding dialogue and keeping team members focused on the topic at hand.

STRATEGIES TO USE DURING THE MEETING

The strategies discussed in Chapter 3 and briefly revisited here are proactive strategies to set the stage for a productive, collaborative, and supportive IEP meeting. The goal is to build on this foundation, by continuing to engage in practices that signal partnership, collaboration, and respect. In the remainder of this chapter, we turn our attention to strategies to use during the IEP meeting that will continue to build on the collaborative strategies started beforehand. The following strategies help ensure the meeting is positive and productive:

- Welcome everyone on the team and begin with introductions.

- Ensure student participation and preferences in the meeting, whether they attend or not.

- Have a conversation—not monologues or overly structured turn-taking.

- Plan for how you will handle difficult situations such as disagreements among team members (including both professionals and family).

- Understand the feelings the family may bring to the meeting.

- Focus on effective communication.

- Manage your time.

Welcome Everyone to the Meeting

A welcoming atmosphere helps everyone feel like valued members of the team. The physical meeting space and the ambiance of the meeting both contribute to creating a welcoming atmosphere. The meeting room should have enough space to accommodate everyone, and meeting materials should be accessible to everyone. If possible, the meeting should be conducted in a private room/space to protect student confidentiality and to create a space that allows members to be vulnerable. As a reminder from Chapter 3, the IEP meeting can also occur in nonschool settings, such as the family home, a hotel conference room, a public library, or another place that is convenient for the family and will support their attendance; meetings can also be conducted online. It is important, however, to make sure the location is mutually agreed upon, private, and free from too many distractions. The location should also be comfortable, with enough chairs and space for all team members to comfortably attend and see one another.

Meetings can be made universally accessible by checking to make sure that everyone has what they need to participate in the meeting. This can be as simple as pointing out where the closest restroom is and by taking regular breaks. Other strategies for making the meeting accessible for everyone include:

- Post the agenda and invite edits prior to the start of the meeting.

- Use individual name cards that specify roles (e.g., Judy Wegman, speech-language pathologist; Joe Trader, Adaptive PE) or, if the meeting is held virtually, screen names that include job titles or roles.

- Remind team members to avoid jargon and to speak in plain language.

- Provide a "cheat sheet" with typical jargon defined, and encourage members to request assistance in understanding jargon as it arises.

- Designate a note taker.

- Have resources or information sheets available about different services and the purposes of the services.

- Have water, tissues, and light snacks available (e.g., bags of pretzels, protein bars, Jolly Ranchers).

Once all team members have arrived, take a moment to recognize the time and contributions of the team members. Remind the team of their shared objective: to collectively develop an IEP, to celebrate growth, and to determine how to best support the student's learning.

Begin With Introductions

Making the time for introductions during a meeting honors each person's role and contribution and gives everyone a sense that they are one team. Everyone should be addressed by their preferred name and their role should be clearly stated. Name cards are a great tool to support this practice. If it is an initial IEP meeting, or if a new member has recently joined the team, more elaborate introductions may be necessary. For example, if families are unfamiliar with what a speech-language pathologist does, the service provider might say, "I support this student by doing X." If outside service providers, a family advocate, or support personnel are present, it will also be important to provide an opportunity for them to introduce themselves.

Ensure Student Participation and Preferences

Student preferences and input should not be overlooked during the IEP meeting, as their involvement can lead to developing future skills for self-advocacy and meaningful participation throughout the IEP process. As discussed in Chapter 2, it is preferable for students to attend their meeting and be involved in it. However, even if a student does not attend their IEP meeting in-person, their input should be gathered. Students can express preferences about their goals, supports, and services, and can also describe their own strengths and interests. Listening to students' perspectives—even if they are expressed through body language or behavior—is the key to developing a meaningful IEP. Rather than only focusing on what they think the student *should* learn, the team needs to also consider what the student *wants* to learn. Consider this example, taking the student's behavioral communication into perspective.

Student Perspective: Rosita's Story

The team at Metcalfe Senior High School was having difficulty teaching Rosita to greet her peers in the cafeteria. Each day, they prompted Rosita to approach a peer and choose a greeting from four choices on a communication device. A 16-year-old student, Rosita resisted this activity and routinely walked away or refused to participate.

What does Rosita's behavior tell the school team about the priority of this goal from Rosita's perspective? Clearly, she does not want to greet her peers in this way. Perhaps she does not want to greet her peers at all, which is perfectly fine. There is no rule book that says all high school students must greet their peers, and especially not in this robotic fashion. Taking Rosita's perspective, it's entirely possible that she is embarrassed by this interaction, as any 16-year-old might be. Simply observing a student's behavior during instruction and using this information to develop, alter, or abandon a plan can ensure the student's needs and interests are centered in the IEP.

There are many ways to involve students in their own IEP meetings if they and their families choose. The simplest way is to support the student to create a presentation, using pictures and videos from the past year to highlight their successes and their aspirations. Students who do not communicate orally can select pictures to include and write short captions using picture symbols. Students can also prerecord their input to play during the meeting if the meeting format is inaccessible to the student. Simply having the student in the room can change the tone of the conversation to be more positive and student-centered. An excellent resource for involving students in IEP meetings is the book *Getting the Most out of IEP Meetings: An Educator's Guide to the Student-Directed Approach* (2010) by Colleen Thoma and Paul Wehman.

Have a Conversation: Avoid "Monologues" and Structured Turn Taking

A common practice at IEP meetings is for each team member to share information in turn. However, this practice has been demonstrated to limit conversation during the meeting, hindering the collaborative process (Ruppar & Gaffney, 2011). Team members and service providers should be encouraged to share how their support overlaps with that of other providers and across environments. For example, if reading progress is being discussed, all team members who support reading (regardless of context) should have an opportunity to provide their input. A team can become adept at "passing the mic" to each other in order to highlight the ways that each team member can support the work of others. In addition, it creates space for parents to interject and ask questions. Lengthy monologues in which team members read reports and share goal ideas should be avoided.

Resources for Meeting Planning

One way to facilitate an IEP meeting that is focused, but conversational, is to use a **slide deck** to organize discussion points ahead of time. We have created a sample IEP Conversation Planning slide deck, available from the Brookes Download Hub with the other online resources for this book.

IEP meetings should be structured to encourage student, family, and professional team members to collaborate through authentic turn-taking and maintaining a focus on the student's needs and environmental barriers. When the IEP meeting is led using only the IEP documents as a guide, it's easy to forget to invite questions or comments as team members rush to go over all the information as quickly as they can. Thus, it is common for families and students to feel that they are not equal team members, but mere information receivers. Intentional invitations of questions and concerns are essential to avoid "monologues" from the special education teacher and/or general education teacher. Using a structured slide deck to guide the IEP meeting can facilitate authentic turn-takings among all IEP team members.

The sample slide deck available on the Brookes Download Hub includes the following features:

- Introductions, beginning with the student and their family to highlight their important role and create a welcoming meeting atmosphere.

- Yellow boxes prompt specific team members to offer input, cueing team members that it's time to slow down and ask for everyone's thoughts.

- Red boxes prompt teams to pause to solicit questions or concerns from the team.

- Off-topic conversations can be placed in the "parking lot" slide to temporarily put aside these conversations.

- The meeting will end with a debriefing to reflect on the process and to plan for the next steps.

This slide deck can be shared with every team member before the meeting, and team members should add information to the slides ahead of the meeting. During the meeting, a notetaker can input information into each slide. Having all the IEP information available and visible will allow the team to collectively review and approve decisions.

Families can continue to have access to the slides if they need to refer to them after the meeting. Importantly, translation features in web browsers (e.g., Google Translate) can automatically translate the IEP information into another language for the family in real time. If they prefer the paper version, the slides can be printed out with translations attached.

Plan How to Handle Difficult Situations

From time to time, interactions among professionals, or between professionals and families, become contentious. Difficulty during collaboration can arise from differing visions for the student or competing interests among individuals. The large number of team members present on IEP teams of students with complex support needs, who have different areas of expertise and priorities, can make differences in opinion more common.

Differing Opinions Among Professionals

Differing opinions among professionals can lead to a lack of alignment in teaching strategies, negatively affecting the student. It is important that all team members align when agreeing on instructional approaches, arrangements, and supports. This does not mean that every team member must teach in the same way, but instruction and supports need to intricately align for the student to be included and supported throughout general education classes and activities.

One area in which all team members *must* unequivocally reach agreement is the least restrictive environment. When team members differ in their opinions about the extent to which inclusion in general education classes and activities is a priority, exclusionary decisions are made "on the fly" and might not align with the child's least restrictive environment. Research shows that LRE decisions are often made in the moment and are not well defined in IEPs (Kurth, McQueston, et al., 2019; McCabe et al., 2020). All team members must agree about the specific circumstances, if any, under which a student might be briefly excluded from the general education classroom and activities. The specific length of time the team can exclude the student from general education activities must also be noted. This prevents unnecessary exclusion.

Differing Opinions Between Families and School Teams

Families are an integral part of the IEP team, and their viewpoints need to be taken seriously. Research shows that IEPs for students with complex support needs do not include more than a passing mention of parents' concerns (e.g., Kurth, McQueston, et al., 2019). As a result, families can feel devalued by professionals because they see that their input is not being taken seriously. Families offer valuable information about their children and need to be supported with the necessary information to make a meaningful contribution to their child's IEP team.

On the other hand, family requests do not need to be met on demand, and sometimes teams are faced with a family member who requests a service that is not supported by research and could even be damaging to the child. In these situations, the team is not required to implement a strategy based on a family request. For instance, consider the following example of Sarina.

Handling Disagreement: Sarina's Family

Sarina's family has a contentious relationship with her school team because of a difference of opinion about the use of rapid prompting, a facilitated communication technique without research support.

Sarina has employed a rapid prompting facilitator and insists that the team honor this method of communication despite the school team's repeated explanations about the lack of evidence for this approach, and the potential damage it can cause. While the family is certainly allowed to make their own decisions at home, the school team recognizes the requirement in IDEA to use research- and scientifically-based practices. A team might handle this with phrasing such as, "You can of course support Sarina however you wish at home, but because we are required to use research- and scientifically based practices, we're not able to commit resources to an approach not supported by the research evidence." This sort of response communicates the team's support of the family while also communicating a commitment to implement research-based practices as mandated by IDEA 2004.

Understand Family Feelings

Family members of students with disabilities can experience a range of emotions and responses to the IEP process, and to their child's education in general. Sometimes, a family member might become upset during the meeting. Taking the family's point of view, it's easy to understand why the IEP experience might be emotional. Parents might blame themselves for their child's disability. The IEP process is complex, and sometimes a family might feel confused and overwhelmed. Some parents might feel anxious about coordinating their child's services, taking an overly controlling approach to the IEP process. These are all normal responses to the highly stressful IEP meeting environment. School team members have a responsibility to ensure that families are comfortable and should recognize that the family might be under a great deal of stress.

One common reason why families might feel overwhelmed during the IEP process is because of the amount of information about their child's deficits that the IEP process invokes. Consider the following scenario.

Discussing Challenges: Gregory's Family

Gregory's parents thought they were ready to hear about Gregory's recent behavioral challenges in school. After all, the special education teacher had been in contact with them for weeks about it, culminating in this meeting. However, Gregory's parents were not prepared when his kindergarten teacher, who had known him since the beginning of the school year, started her description of Gregory's challenges at school.

The general education teacher described Gregory as "wandering the room, barricading himself off in a corner, ignoring adults, taking things off the shelves, trying to get attention from peers by tapping them on the head, rolling in the center of the rug, grabbing students, kicking at students, and when they say stop—his behavior escalates." She went on, "Gregory will shout no, scream over the teacher's voice, take materials off the shelf, push children's work off the table, throw or rip up his own paper, erase whiteboards, run from the classroom, exit the building, write on the tables and rug, crawl on the rug, throw items, throw and flip chairs." She took a breath. "In addition, Gregory has been observed hitting and punching peers and teachers, threatening, and using inappropriate words like stupid, penis, and the f-word, directed toward peers and adults." She went on to explain that this disruptive behavior makes it difficult for her to teach, that peers need to be relocated during behavioral outbursts, that students avoid him or mimic him, and other parents have voiced concerns. She concluded by saying that Gregory is "a child who thinks the rules are optional and that participating in his education is just not a requirement for him."

It was this last piece of information that finally broke Gregory's mother, who could be seen wiping away tears. The thought that he was harming other children, that other parents were unhappy with her, and that he might become even more socially isolated, combined with the statement that Gregory has no regard for rules, caused her to blame herself for Gregory's behavior. The special education teacher was flabbergasted at the general education teacher's tirade. She suggested a 5-minute break and pulled Gregory's mother aside to comfort her.

In the scenario, consider the ways that team members could have avoided this situation. The excessive use of deficit-based and blaming language further isolated Gregory's mother from the school team and made her feel that she needed to be on the defensive for the rest of the meeting. Instead, teams should emphasize strengths and skills that the student has that can be built on in any academic, social, or behavioral situation.

Focus on Effective Communication

Even though there are seven million or more IEP meetings held every year in the United States (U.S. Department of Education, 2021), surprisingly little research has been conducted about how people communicate during IEP meetings, and how their communication can influence meeting outcomes. Sociological research about organizations and meetings suggests that interactions among individuals, collectively, create and carry out institutional rules that are reproduced over time. Therefore, thinking carefully about how to effectively communicate during an IEP meeting, over time, can help teachers and teams shape and reshape educational structures and rules that lead to increasingly positive and inclusive outcomes.

And even though everyone on an IEP team is working within the structure of a local (district, school) special education system, each individual team member brings a particular point of view and expertise on any topic of discussion. Interpersonal communication skills are necessary to effectively collaborate and achieve positive student outcomes. In addition, every IEP team member has competing interests on their time, energy, and focus. If every team member worked around the clock to create the materials, adaptations, and supports needed by a student with complex support needs, there would still be an infinite number of tasks left to complete. Therefore, teams need a shared vision for what a good educational experience looks like for each individual student.

Think Creatively—and Realistically   The range of options for supporting and teaching students with complex support needs is like a universe: endless and limited only by our own creativity. Unfortunately, this can be a blessing and a curse. Teachers are often very creative thinkers. Good special educators must be able to think very divergently about problems they encounter because each student and teaching situation is unique. Team brainstorming can uncover a variety of potential solutions, and an active IEP team should be able to generate many strategies to support the student. However, IEP documents should not resemble the result of a brainstorming activity but should be narrowed to a small and cohesive set of plans that can be reasonably carried out by the individuals at the IEP meeting table. Too often, IEP accommodations and modifications reflect an overwhelming list of strategies that cannot reasonably be carried out by the IEP team members. They also often lack specificity regarding when and where the accommodations, modifications, and instruction will take place. This is why a team needs to be careful to transition out of "brainstorm mode" and into action planning before closing up an IEP or other planning meeting.

Listen Actively to the Family   Clear communication is also an important strategy for developing relationships; therefore, team members should make note of how important active listening is during communication. Professional team members need to shift their focus from thinking about whether they are listening to families to whether families felt heard and valued. In other words, how can teachers show families they are listening? Teachers and service providers should strive to listen for understanding during meetings and not to make a response. The goal, after all, is not to say something, but instead, to learn from other team members when developing the IEP.

To support active listening, families could provide input beforehand and the team can reintroduce it at the meeting. This shows families that their input was not only received but is an active contribution to what is being discussed and planned. When families are talking during the meeting, someone should be documenting family input, so the team can align goals, supports, and services with the family's vision for their student. The facilitator could also work on clarifying what families say by restating or paraphrasing to ensure family input was understood correctly. While it might feel awkward, asking for clarification shows other members of the IEP team are actively listening and want to learn from the unique contributions families make. In addition to verbal listening strategies, nonverbal body language also plays a role in active listening. This is especially true if a translator is present during the meeting. When the family is speaking, IEP team members should direct their bodies towards the person speaking and look at the speaker as a cue that the speaker has the team's undivided attention.

Manage Your Time

In many ways, effective communication during a meeting relies on time management. This is because team members who do not have their needs or priorities discussed or have enough time allocated for their main concerns will likely feel frustrated and disenfranchised. Developing the agenda ahead of the meeting will be useful in ensuring that all team members have a chance to speak and listen and that all necessary content is discussed. However, a team may still run out of time as conversations unfold; in this situation, a follow-up meeting can be scheduled.

When allocating time, it is also wise to reserve a few minutes at the end of each meeting to summarize decisions made and each team member's commitments regarding their responsibilities. This action communicates the importance of consensus and offers an opportunity to clear up any misunderstandings about the implementation of the IEP. Teams should also review the documents and check for completion and correct any errors. If the team agrees the IEP is correct and thorough, each team member will then sign the document and copies will be distributed. However, some families might prefer to have a little time to review the IEP on their own; it is perfectly fine for families to take the complete draft of the IEP home to review for a few days and sign it after they have had an opportunity to review it more closely.

CONCLUDING THOUGHTS:
MANAGING COMMUNICATION AT THE IEP MEETING

Creating an equitable, inclusive IEP requires care and attention from all team members before, during, and after the IEP meeting. In this chapter, we reviewed some strategies to engage in prior to the meeting to set the stage for a collaborative and effective team meeting, and we then noted additional strategies to build on this foundation of collaboration during the meeting. Effective communication, perspective taking, and ensuring a welcoming environment are all critical tasks. Staying mindful of these strategies should help maintain and sustain truly collaborative IEP team relationships.

REVIEWING THE COMMITMENT: *Ensuring the Meeting Is Positive and Productive*

This chapter discussed strategies and tips for creating trusting, collaborative relationships among team members to ensure a respectful, equitable, and problem-solving approach to IEP team meetings. We also emphasized the importance of conversations rather than monologues. At the start of this chapter, you reflected on your previous team member experiences and set goals for yourself as an IEP team member.

1. As an IEP team member, how do you plan to signal respect and a commitment to the success of each individual member of the team? How will you know if your goal has been accomplished?

_____

_____

_____

2. As an IEP team member, how do you plan to ensure every team member has a chance to share their ideas and strengths and build on the ideas and strengths of others? How will you know if your goal has been accomplished?

_____

_____

_____

3. As an IEP team member, how do you plan to create a trusting partnership where disagreements are managed respectfully and proactively? How will you know if your goal has been accomplished?

_____

_____

_____

ACTING ON THE COMMITMENT: *Ensuring the Meeting Is Positive and Productive*

This chapter mentioned a sample slide deck for planning the IEP meeting discussion. Download the slide deck from the Brookes Download Hub (see the front matter of this book for instructions to access the downloads) and use it, along with your notes above, to begin planning the IEP meeting discussion for the student with whom you are working.

After the Meeting

Implementing the IEP

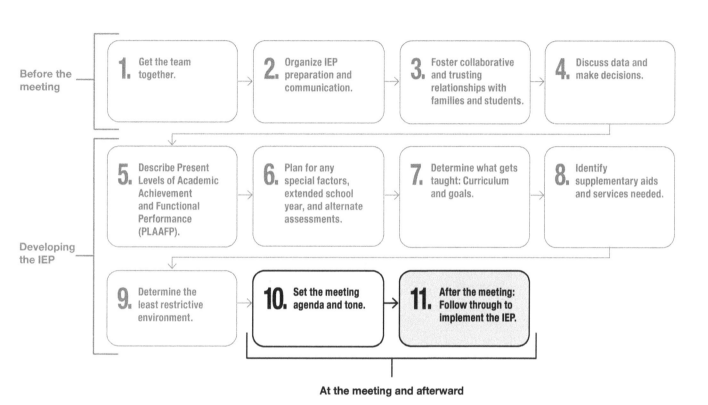

Before the meeting

1. Get the team together.

2. Organize IEP preparation and communication.

3. Foster collaborative and trusting relationships with families and students.

4. Discuss data and make decisions.

Developing the IEP

5. Describe Present Levels of Academic Achievement and Functional Performance (PLAAFP).

6. Plan for any special factors, extended school year, and alternate assessments.

7. Determine what gets taught: Curriculum and goals.

8. Identify supplementary aids and services needed.

9. Determine the least restrictive environment.

10. Set the meeting agenda and tone.

11. After the meeting: Follow through to implement the IEP.

At the meeting and afterward

The IEP meeting is only the beginning of a child's education program for the year. Following the meeting, team members should follow up with each other, including the parents, to communicate progress or necessary changes to the IEP. To do this, team members need clear communication systems in place, as well as systems for collecting data. This chapter provides suggestions for keeping communication open throughout the year, ensuring ongoing collaboration among team members, and sample data collection and communication tools.

UNDERSTANDING THE COMMITMENT:

Following Through With the Student, Family, and Team

What does it mean to be accountable to your students? An IEP document represents an agreement among adults about the services that will be provided to ensure a student with a disability has an accessible, rigorous, and individualized education. Following the meeting, an educational team agrees to implement the IEP, making good on their promise to the student that their education will be accessible and meaningful.

What are some ways you make sure that you follow through with important tasks? What supports do you use to follow through with your responsibilities?

_____

_____

_____

_____

"I'M EXHAUSTED!": FIRST STEPS AFTER THE MEETING

During an IEP meeting many decisions are made, and if some of the decisions were difficult, emotions may take a toll on members of the team. So, it is normal to feel exhausted after an IEP meeting. This is especially true if you were the individual facilitating the decision making during the meeting. IEP meetings can be especially emotional for family members and students who participate in the meeting, so following up with families and students is an essential step. It is important to have some time to organize your thoughts after the meeting and make sure there is a plan for communication with team members to implement the agreed-upon IEP. This is especially important if some items were unresolved, and some decisions still need to be made.

What to Do Before You Go Home

Before you head home after a meeting, make sure you have all your meeting notes in one place. Take a moment to organize them and highlight anything that needs immediate attention. Put those tasks on your to-do list for first thing on the following day. You can also use your notes to organize a task list and show who would be responsible for completing each task. Figure 11.1 shows a sample task list; a full-size, reproducible version is provided at the end of this chapter and with the downloadable resources for this book available on the Brookes Download Hub. Putting these responsibilities in a task list as a shared document, such as Google Docs, will facilitate the timely completion of tasks. This shared document can be updated throughout the year to designate changes in responsibilities, tasks that need to be completed before the IEP is implemented, and to designate tasks and responsibilities once the components of the IEP are put in place.

The After the Meeting Task and Responsibility List is helpful to organize tasks and responsibilities established from the IEP meeting, but oftentimes other follow-up is required after an annual review. Below are two checklists of items that will help ensure proper follow-up immediately following the meeting. Each is also available with the downloadable resources for this book.

FORM 11A   **After the Meeting Task and Responsibility List**

Task or Action Item	Implemented		Team Member(s) Responsible	Other Notes
	Before IEP	During IEP		

Figure 11.1.   After the Meeting Task and Responsibility List.

Checklist: IEP Follow-Up With Families and Students

☐ Make a phone call or email family members. Make sure they shared everything they wanted to during the meeting. Let them know you are available to answer any questions and can make sure all their concerns are addressed before the IEP is finalized. Provide the family with resources to clarify any questions they may have. Although using acronyms (e.g., SAS, OT, PT, SLP, ESY) is not recommended, a quick guide with acronyms that are sometimes used would be helpful for families when digesting all of the information from the meeting.

☐ Be sure to include the student in the conversation with their family members. Make sure that the student was able to voice all their concerns, and provide time to answer their questions.

☐ Provide students and families with a summary of IEP decisions. This summary could include things like a list of services, goals, and a sample schedule so they can understand how much time will be spent in the general education classroom and when the student will be receiving all the recommended services.

☐ Remind families and students of the next steps toward IEP implementation. Let them know that the team will be creating a schedule and determining who will be responsible for providing supplementary aids and services and monitoring goals throughout the student's educational environment. Continue keeping families informed between the meeting and the IEP implementation and make sure you are listening to their concerns and answering any questions.

☐ Develop a communication flowchart to share with families. This way, they know which member of the IEP team they should contact about different aspects of the IEP. This will help both families and providers to streamline communication most effectively. The flowchart creates set boundaries about communication and responsibilities between school-based IEP team members and families.

Checklist: IEP Follow-Up With Other Team Members

☐ Follow up with all team members about the meeting. Make sure there are no changes that need to be made to the present levels, goals, or supplementary aids and services. Send a copy of the completed IEP to the families once it is finalized.

☐ Share the task list with all team members and allow them to mark the document with highlights or check marks once the task has been completed.

☐ Provide all school-based members of the IEP team a copy of the summary of the IEP that you also provided to the family. This will help prepare the school-based team when it is time to create a schedule and manage the implementation of the entire IEP.

☐ Sometimes some IEP decisions may require an outside consultant, or perhaps a request for services needs to be completed. For example, if the student requires a communication device, you may need to submit an AT request through the district. With each of these requests, make sure you are designating roles appropriately. For example, the speech-language pathologist may be the most appropriate person to facilitate the process of obtaining a communication device.

NEXT STEPS: PLANNING IEP IMPLEMENTATION

All decisions have been made, but the task of getting the IEP written is only just beginning. Organizing all components of the IEP into an IEP Matrix will assist in organizing where and when services will be provided to the student, and where goals will be monitored for progress. The LRE Planning Matrix discussed in Chapter 9 assists teams in organizing the location of instruction, and the supplementary aids and services that need to be in place.

Consider Scheduling an IEP Team Follow-Up Meeting

It may be helpful to have a follow-up meeting with the school team, especially if there was a significant amount of time between the meeting and when the IEP is set to begin. For example, an annual review may be held in March that discusses the IEP that is not implemented until the start of the following school year in August or September. A follow up meeting would be an ideal time to use information from the LRE Planning Matrix to complete the IEP Matrix (see Figure 11.2) with the entire

FORM 11B   **IEP Matrix**

CLASS/ PERIOD GOALS	Period 1 *English 10*	Period 2 *U.S. History*	Period 3 *Algebra I*	Period 4 *PE*	Period 5 *Biology*	Period 6 *Computers*
Goal 1 Learn 20 sight words from the core curriculum	Identify high-frequency curriculum words from English novels	Identify high-frequency curriculum words from text (e.g., because, also)	Identify high-frequency curriculum words used in math (e.g., add, less)	Use picture schedule with words to follow PE routine	Identify high-frequency curriculum words from text (e.g., because, also)	Identify high-frequency curriculum words from class (e.g., log-on, user name)
Goal 2 Participate in academic units/ learn 3 facts or vocabulary words per unit	For each novel: 1. Read a modified version of the novel 2. Listen to lecture and participate by answering factual questions, watch videos along with class. 3. For each novel identify the main character(s), identify 3 events from each chapter, sequence the events. 4. Learn 3 new vocabulary words. 5. Present to class.	For each unit of study Jamie will: 1. Identify 3 major figures and their country or state (if the U.S.) of origin. 2. Identify 3 events and the order in which they occurred. 3. Learn 3 new vocabulary words and use them. Jamie will also: Study a region of the U.S. and identify the states in that region and 1 fact about each state.	1. Work on math IEP goals. 2. Do word problems. 3. Identify numbers on a graph. 4. Basic operations with and without a calculator.	Participate in each unit. Use correct name for each activity (e.g., push-up, chin-up).	For each unit of study: 1. Identify 3 facts. 2. Identify and use 3 vocabulary words. 3. Participate in fieldwork.	Type on keyboard. Type words/sentences using a word processing program.
Goal 3 Initiate and respond to 3 social interactions with same aged peers appropriately	Request peer to read with her during shared reading experiences.	Work with peers on projects, read with peers	Greet peers, work with peers on problems	Find and work out with peer buddy	Work with peers in labs, study partner	Work with peers on projects, read with peers
Goal 4 Use a calculator to solve multiplication, addition, division, and subtraction problems and record the answer correctly	n/a	Sequence dates in historical timelines using a calculator	Solve algebraic questions using a calculator	Count materials for class (e.g., number of laps ran)	Use calculator or math problem skills to weigh and measure items in class	Calculate words typed per minute using calculator
Supplementary aids and services	Visual supports for all materials Audio-textbook Speech-to-text software	Visual supports for all materials Audio-textbook Speech-to-text software	Calculator Visual supports and step-by-step directions for solving problems.	Key lock for locker	Calculator, visual representations of all materials, audio-textbook	Visual supports for log on (user name and password); colored overlay for computer keyboard
Data collection procedures (Who will collect data? What data will be collected?)	Paraprofessional will collect data	Special educator	Paraprofessional	Jamie and paraprofessional	Special educator and general educator	Jamie and paraprofessional

Figure 11.2. Sample IEP Matrix for Jamie, a 10th grader with intellectual disability.

team and set a plan for implementing the IEP. A meeting after the annual review may also be necessary because some decisions may not have been finalized. A follow-up meeting may also be useful if there are collaborative planning efforts that need to take place for certain interventions or transdisciplinary goals. (A full-size, blank, reproducible version of the IEP Planning Matrix is provided in the appendix to this chapter and with the downloadable resources for this book available on the Brookes Download Hub.)

Plan Transdisciplinary Interventions

Collaboration is not only an important aspect of developing an IEP; it is also necessary for IEP implementation. Some goals may require interdisciplinary supports and services for the student to make progress. For example, a literacy goal may require the student to be assessed using text-prediction software. In this case, the occupational therapist may need to provide training on the software to paraprofessionals, the general education teacher, and the special education teacher.

Specific goals and supplementary aids and services are the sole responsibility of individual members of the IEP team. In fact, having goals that require collaboration makes providing services in inclusive settings easier. If a goal is monitored only by a special education teacher, the opportunities and environments in which the student can work on the goal are limited. In contrast, a goal that is collaboratively monitored is easier to implement in a variety of settings and will support the student to make progress more quickly. Generalization (i.e., application) of skills will also only be achieved when multiple team members support the student to use the skill in multiple locations. We provide ideas for cross-training and distributing work among team members later in this chapter.

Plan When and Where to Teach

Figure 11.2 provides an example of an IEP Matrix. The first step in completing the IEP Matrix is to outline the student's daily schedule(s). Then, list all the student's goals. Using the LRE Planning Matrix (see Chapter 9), the team identifies the parts of the day when the student should be working on goals. Remember, goals can be monitored at multiple times during the student's schedule. The IEP Matrix provides a space where team members can identify the supplementary aids and services that the student requires during certain parts of the day. There is also a space for team members to list supplementary aids and services that should be available throughout the day. For example, a communication device should be with the student at all times. Lastly, the team should list the method and frequency of data collection (more is always better!) and note who will be responsible for collecting data on the goal.

GETTING READY FOR NEXT TIME: MAKING A PLAN TO COLLECT DATA

The IEP Matrix will help the team determine where and when students will be working on their specific goals. This will also assist in a plan to determine how to collect data. Teams will want to decide who will collect data—it does not always have to be the special education teacher—and how often data will need to be collected on each goal. Progress monitoring for goals will likely come from multiple sources, and the more individuals are involved with progress monitoring, the more likely that the student is working on their goals across inclusive environments. It is important to be organized and train others in how to collect data.

Train Others to Collect Data

Mutual responsibility for data collection is key. Here are some ideas to spread responsibility of collecting data throughout the entry of the IEP Matrix:

- Provide individuals who work in the lunchroom with a clipboard and chart. They can check yes or no if the student uses their communication device to order their lunch.

- Set up a Google Form so a general education teacher can input a student's grade on a weekly vocabulary quiz. Ask them to provide work samples monthly.

- A student can complete a self-evaluation at the end of each week.

- Related service providers can provide data once a month from their sessions on a shared Google Sheet.

- Provide paraprofessionals with goal sheets they can record data on when in the general education environment.

Keep Data Organized

The special education teacher will typically be the one who organizes all the data and reports on student progress in the quarterly reports that are shared with families. Therefore, the special education teacher will be responsible for compiling all the data for each goal and benchmark. Data for student progress will most likely come from multiple environments and be recorded from multiple individuals, so an organization system is important to maintain clear records of students' progress. Special education teachers may want to consider scheduling a monthly or weekly time to gather all student data. The IEP Matrix can help identify all the sources of data. Data can be compiled using various tools (e.g., clipboards, Google Forms, weekly quizzes). The special education teacher can track the data from all the combined sources and methods and report it back to the team in one location. It may be helpful to set up a shared document where the combined data organization is presented. Teams could set up a shared Google folder for each of their students with spreadsheets that organize all the data collected. Putting this information in one location is important because team members, including parents and students, can routinely check progress without waiting for quarterly reports.

When a Student Is Not Making Progress

As discussed in Chapter 4, tracking progress throughout the year is important because teams will be able to identify if a student is not on track to meet a goal. If a student is not making progress, there are two things to consider. First, consider how the instruction could be changed in order to enhance student progress. In this step, critical reflection is extremely important. Team members should collaborate and support each other, and also be ready to consider if the current approach to instruction is not working. For example, a student might fail to make progress on a goal that is not meaningful from their perspective. Or the materials or information might not be accessible for the student—for example, the student might be able to follow a schedule with line drawings rather than photographs because the line drawings are more visually simple. Contextual factors *always* affect how a student progresses—or not.

Second, consider if the goal is appropriate for the student. Students can appear to fail to make progress toward a goal if it is a skill that they already have mastered. Seeing no need to continue demonstrating skills they already know, students often engage in escape-related behavior, such as shutting down or becoming aggressive. Understanding how your student sees the world is the most important skill in teaching, and teachers always need to consider the student's point of view. Sometimes, that requires taking a hard look at how things have always been done—and making a change for the better. Carefully and collaboratively identifying goals in the first place, considering family and student input, can guard against these issues from occurring.

CONCLUDING THOUGHTS: IMPLEMENTING THE IEP

The real work of supporting students occurs after the meeting ends. The IEP needs to be frequently reviewed after it is developed to ensure the full team is following the plan of the IEP with fidelity. By taking steps such as following up on to-do items quickly after the meeting, planning for goal and services implementation across the school day, and carefully collecting and reviewing progress monitoring data, the IEP can support an equitable, inclusive education for students with complex support needs.

REVIEWING THE COMMITMENT: *Following Through With the Student, Family, and Team*

An IEP is a document that reflects a mutual commitment of educators to provide a meaningful, accessible education for a student with a disability. What are your personal commitments to students as you carry out their IEPs?

_____

_____

_____

_____

_____

ACTING THE COMMITMENT: *Following Through With the Student, Family, and Team*

This chapter includes several resources designed to help you follow through with the team to implement your student's IEP:

- After Meeting Task and Responsibility List

- Checklists for following up with the student/family and with other team members

- An IEP Matrix for planning and tracking services and goals across the student's daily class schedule and collecting data throughout the day

Use these resources in planning IEP implementation for your student—or use them as a starting point to create your own system of documentation. Other tools such as Google Docs and Google Sheets may also be helpful for organizing and sharing information team-wide.

Whatever system you choose to organize your follow-up work, know that this work is the final, critical step of your commitment. You, your student and their family, and the rest of the IEP team have worked hard to create an equitable, inclusive IEP. Now that IEP can serve as the basis for a rich and meaningful education that will impact your student's membership in communities, relationships with others, and opportunities to learn important, lifelong skills.

Resources for Implementing the IEP

1. After the Meeting Task and Responsibility List 187
2. IEP Matrix 188

After the Meeting Task and Responsibility List

Task or Action Item	Implemented		Team Member(s) Responsible	Other Notes
	Before IEP	During IEP		

IEP Matrix

CLASS/PERIOD	Daily Activities					
GOALS	Period 1	Period 2	Period 3	Period 4	Period 5	Period 6
Goal 1						
Goal 2						
Goal 3						

FORM 11B **IEP Matrix** (continued)

Goal 4					
Supplementary aids and services					
Data collection procedures (Who will collect data? What data will be collected?)					

References

Allor, J. H., Gifford, D. B., Jones, F. G., Otaiba, S. A., Yovanoff, P., Ortiz, M. B., & Cheatham, J. P. (2018). The effects of a text-centered literacy curriculum for students with intellectual disability. *American Journal on Intellectual and Developmental Disabilities, 123*(5), 474–494. https://doi.org/10.1352/1944-7558-123.5.474

American Occupational Therapy Association (2016). Fact sheet: Occupational therapy's role in school settings. https://www.aota.org/~/media/Corporate/Files/AboutOT/Professionals/WhatIsOT/CY/Fact-Sheets/School%20Settings%20fact%20sheet.pdf

Assistive Technology Act Amendments of 2004, PL 108-364, 29 U.S.C. §§ 3001 *et seq.*

Assistance to States for the Education of Children With Disabilities and Preschool Grants for Children With Disabilities; Final Rule, *71 Fed. Reg. 46676* (August 14, 2006).

Bacon, J., Rood, C. E., & Ferri, B. A. (2016). Promoting access through segregation: The emergence of the "prioritized curriculum" class. *Teachers College Record, 118*, 1–22.

Baglieri, S., & Shapiro, A. (2017). *Disability studies and the inclusive classroom: Critical practices for embracing diversity in education* (2nd ed.). Routledge.

Bambara, L., & Kern, L. (2021). *Individualized supports for students with problem behaviors: Designing positive behavior plans* (2nd ed.). Guilford Press.

Barnard-Brak, L., Stevens, T., & Valenzuela, E. (2018). Barriers to providing extended school year services to students with disabilities: An exploratory study of special education directors. *Rural Special Education Quarterly, 37*, 245–250. https://doi.org/10.1177/8756870518772308

Belfiore, P., & Browder, D. (1992). The effects of self-monitoring on teacher's data-based decisions and on the progress of adults with severe mental retardation. *Education and Training in Mental Retardation, 27*, 60–67.

Beukelman, D. R., & Light, J. C. (2020). *Augmentative and alternative communication: Supporting children and adults with complex communication needs* (5th ed.). Paul H. Brookes Publishing Co.

Billingsley, F., Gallucci, C., Peck, C., Schwartz, I., & Staub, D. (1996). "But those kids can't even do math": An alternative conceptualization of outcomes for inclusive education. *Special Education Leadership Review, 3*, 43–55.

Brock, M. E. (2018). Trends in the educational placement of students with intellectual disability in the United States over the past 40 years. *American Journal of Intellectual and Developmental Disabilities, 123*(4), 305–314. https://doi.org/10.1352/1944-7558-123.4.305

Brock, M. E., Cannella-Malone, H. I., Seaman, R. L., Andzik, N. R., Schaefer, J. M., Page, E. J., Barczak, M. A., & Dueker, S. A. (2017). Findings across practitioner training studies in special education: A comprehensive review and meta-analysis. *Exceptional Children, 84*(1), 7–26. https://doi.org/10.1177/0014402917698008

Browder, D., Demchak, M., Keller, M., & King, D. (1989). An in vivo evaluation of the use of data-based rules to guide instructional decisions. *Journal of Agriculture Safety and Health, 14*, 234–240.

Browder, D., Karvonen, M., Davis, S., Fallin, K., & Courtade-Little, C. (2005). The impact of teacher training on state alternate assessment scores. *Exceptional Children, 71*, 267–282.

Browder, D., Liberty, K., Heller, K., & D'Huyvetters, K. K. (1986). Self-management by teachers: Improving instructional decision making. *Professional School Counseling, 1*, 165–175.

Browder, D., Spooner, F., & Meier, I. (2011). In D. Browder & F. Spooner (Eds.), *Teaching students with moderate and severe disabilities.* Guilford Press.

Brown, L., Hamre-Nietupski, S., Pumpian, I., Certo, N., & Gruenewald, L. (1979). A strategy for developing chronologically-age-appropriate and functional curricular content for severely handicapped adolescents and young adults. *Journal of Special Education, 13*(1), 81–90. doi:10.1177/002246697901300113

Brown, L., Nietupski, J., & Hamre-Nietupski, S. (1976). The criterion of ultimate functioning and public school services for severely handicapped students. In T. M. Angele (Ed.), *Hey! Don't forget about me! Education's investment in the severely, profoundly, and multiply handicapped* (pp. 2–15). Council for Exceptional Children.

Burke, M. M., & Decker, J. R. (2017). Extended school year: Legal and practical considerations for educators. *TEACHING Exceptional Children, 49*(5), 339–346. https://doi.org/10.1177/0040059917692113

Carter, E. W., & Hughes, C. (2005). Increasing social interaction among adolescents with intellectual disabilities and their general education peers: Effective interventions. *Research and Practice for Persons with Severe Disabilities, 30*(4), 179–193.

Carter, E. W., Swedeen, B., & Trainor, A. A. (2009). The other three months. *TEACHING Exceptional Children, 41*, 18–26.

Carlin, C. H., Boarman, K., & Brady, E. E. (2016). Guiding student clinicians as they develop AAC goals and monitor progress during school-based externship. *Perspectives of the ASHA Special Interest Groups, 1*(12), 32-40.

Casey Family Programs. (2012). *Casey Life Skills Toolkit.* Author.

CAST. (2022). *The UDL Guidelines.* https://udlguidelines.cast.org/

Causton-Theoharis, J. N., Theoharis, G. T., Orsati, F., & Cosier, M. (2011). Does self-contained special education deliver on its promises? A critical inquiry into research and practice. *Journal of Special Education Leadership, 24*(2), 61–78.

Chamberlain, C., & Witmer, S. (2017). Students with intellectual disability: Predictors of accountability test participation. *Education and Training in Autism and Developmental Disabilities, 52*(1), 38–50.

Cheatham, G. A. (2011). Language interpretation, parent participation, and young children with disabilities. *Topics in Early Childhood Special Education, 31*(2), 78–88.

Cheatham, G. A., Hart, E., Malian, I., & McDonald, J. (2012). Six things to never say or hear during an IEP meeting: Educators as advocates for families. *TEACHING Exceptional Children, 44*, 50–57.

Chen, W. B., & Gregory, A. (2011). Parental involvement in the prereferral process: Implications for schools. *Remedial and Special Education, 33*, 447–457.

Claes, C., Van Hove, G., Vandevelde, S., van Loon, J., & Schalock, R. L. (2010). Person-centered planning: Analysis of research and effectiveness. *Intellectual and Developmental Disabilities, 48*(6), 432–453.

Collins, B. (2022). *Systematic instruction for students with moderate to severe disabilities* (2nd ed.). Paul H. Brookes Publishing Co.

Common Core State Standards Initiative. (2021a). *Standards in your state.* http://www.corestandards.org/standards-in-your-state/

Common Core State Standards Initiative. (2021b). *What are educational standards?* http://www.corestandards.org/faq/what-are-educational-standards/

Danneker, J. E., & Bottge, B. A. (2009). Benefits of and barriers to elementary student-led individualized education programs. *Remedial and Special Education, 30*(4), 225–233.

Dessemontet, R., & Bless, G. (2013). The impact of including children with intellectual disability in general education classrooms on the academic achievement of their low-, average-, and high-achieving peers. *Journal of Intellectual & Developmental Disability, 38*(1), 23–30. https://doi.org/10.3109/13668250.2012.757589

District of Columbia Department for Disability Services. (2017). *Person Centered Planning Survey.* https://dds.dc.gov/publication/person-centered-questionnaire

Donnellan, A. M. (1984). The criterion of the least dangerous assumption. *Behavioral Disorders, 9*(2), 141–150.

Downing, J. E. (2005). *Teaching communication skills to students with severe disabilities* (2nd ed.). Paul H. Brookes Publishing Co.

Downing, J. E. (2010). *Academic instruction for students with moderate and severe intellectual disabilities in inclusive classrooms.* Corwin.

Downing, J. E. (2015). *Teaching communication skills to students with severe disabilities* (3rd ed.). Paul H. Brookes Publishing Co.

Dynamic Learning Maps. (2013a). *Essential elements for English language arts..* https://dynamiclearningmaps.org/sites/default/files/documents/ELA_EEs/DLM_Essential_Elements_ELA_%282013%29_v4.pdf

Dynamic Learning Maps. (2013b). *Essential elements for mathematics.* https://dynamiclearningmaps.org/sites/default/files/documents/Math_EEs/DLM_Essential_Elements_Math_%282013%29_v4.pdf

Elder, B. C., Rood, C. E., & Damiani, M. L. (2018). Writing strengths-based IEPs for students with disabilities in inclusive classrooms. *International Journal of Whole Schooling, 14*(1), 116–153.

Enderle, J., & Stevenson, S. (2003). *Enderle-Severson Transition Rating Scale.* ESTR Publications.

Endrew F. v. Douglas County School District RE-1. 580 U.S. __ (2017). https://www.supremecourt.gov/opinions/16pdf/15-827_0pm1.pdf

Erwin, E. J., & Soodak, L. C. (1995). I never knew I could stand up to the system: Families' perspectives on pursuing inclusive education. *Journal of the Association for Persons with Severe Handicaps, 20*, 136–146.

Etscheidt, S. K. (2006). Progress monitoring: Legal issues and recommendations for IEP teams. *Teaching Exceptional Children, 38*(3), 56–60.

Etscheidt, S. K., & Bartlett, L. (1999). The IDEA amendments: A four-step approach for determining supplementary aids and services. *Exceptional Children, 65*(2), 163–174. http://doi.org/10.1177/001440299906500202

Every Student Succeeds Act (ESSA) of 2017, PL 114-95, 129 Stat. 1802.

Fish, W. (2006). Perceptions of parents of students with autism towards the IEP meeting: A case study of one family support group chapter. *Education, 127*(1), 56–68.

Flowers, C., Wakeman, S., Browder, D., & Karvonen, M. (2009). Links for academic learning (LAL): A conceptual model for investigating alignment of alternate assessments based on alternate achievement standards. *Educational Measurement: Issues and Practice, 28*, 25–37.

Forest, M., & Lusthaus, E. (1990). Everyone belongs with the MAPS action planning system. *TEACHING Exceptional Children, 22*, 32–35. https://doi.org/10.1177/004005999002200210

Garriott, P., Wandry, D., & Snyder, L. (2000). Teachers as parents, parents as children: What's wrong with this picture? *Preventing School Failure, 45*(1), 37–43.

Gee, K., Gonzalez, M., & Cooper, C. (2020). Outcomes of inclusive versus separate placements: A matched pairs comparison study. *Research and Practice for Persons with Severe Disabilities, 45*(4), 223–240. https://doi.org/10.1177/1540796920943469

Gholson, M. (2018, June). *What do we know about English learners with significant cognitive disabilities?* Presentation at the National Conference on Student Assessment, San Diego, CA. http://altella.wceruw.org/pubs/WhatDoWeKnow_NCSA2018.pdf

Giangreco, M. F. (2011). *Choosing outcomes and accommodations for children* (3rd ed.). Paul H. Brookes Publishing, Co.

Giangreco, M. F. (2013). Teacher assistant supports in inclusive schools: Research, practices, and alternatives. *Australasian Journal of Special Education, 37,* 93–106.

Giangreco, M. F., & Boer, S. M. (2007). School-based screening to determine overreliance on paraprofessionals. *Focus on Autism and Other Developmental Disabilities, 22,* 149–158.

Giangreco, M. F., Dennis, R. E., Edelman, S. W., & Cloninger, C. J. (1994). Dressing your IEPs for the general education climate analysis of IEP goals and objectives for students with multiple disabilities. *Remedial and Special Education, 15*(5), 288–296. https://doi.org/10.1177/074193259401500504

Giangreco, M. F., Suter, J. C., & Graf, V. (2011). Roles of team members supporting students with disabilities in inclusive classrooms. In M. F. Giangreco, C. J. Cloninger, & V. S. Iverson, *Choosing outcomes and accommodations for children: A guide to educational planning for students with disabilities* (3rd ed., pp. 197–204). Paul H. Brookes Publishing Co.

Glatthorn, A., Boschee, F., Whitehead, B. M., & Boschee, B. F. (2016). *Curriculum leadership: Strategies for development and implementation.* SAGE.

Grigg, N. C., Snell, M., & Loyd, B. (1989). Visual analysis of student evaluation data: A qualitative analysis of teacher decision making. *Journal of Agriculture Safety and Health, 14,* 23–32.

Golden, C. (2018). *The data collection toolkit: Everything you need to organize, manage, and monitor classroom data.* Paul H. Brookes Publishing Co.

Hammond, Z. L. (2014). *Culturally responsive teaching and the brain.* Corwin Press.

Hanreddy, A. (2021). Distance learning and students with extensive support needs: (Re)defining access to education from a distance. *Inclusive Practices, 1*(1). https://doi.org/10.1177/27324745211014154

Harry, B. (2008). Collaboration with culturally and linguistically diverse families: Ideal versus reality. *Exceptional Children, 74*(3), 372–388. https://doi.org/10.1177/001440290807400306

Harry, B., & Ocasio-Stoutenburg, L. (2020). *Meeting parents where they are: Building equity through advocacy with diverse schools and communities.* Teachers College Press.

Hauser, M. D. (2017). The essential and interrelated components of evidenced-based IEPs: A user's guide. *Teaching Exceptional Children, 49*(6), 420–428. https://doi.org/10.1177/0040059916688327

Hernandez, S. J. (2012). Evaluation of push-in/integrated therapy in a collaborative preschool for children with special needs. *Journal of the American Academy of Special Education Professionals, 47,* 77.

Hoffman, A., Field, S., & Sawilowsky, S. (2014). *Self-Determination Assessment.* Early Education Group.

Hunt, P., McDonnell, J., & Crockett, M. A. (2012). Reconciling an ecological curricular framework focusing on quality of life outcomes with the development and instruction of standards-based academic goals. *Research and Practice for Persons with Severe Disabilities, 37*(3), 139–152. https://doi.org/10.2511/027494812804153471

Individuals with Disabilities Education Improvement Act (IDEA) of 2004, PL 108-446, 20 U.S.C. §§ 1400 *et seq.*

Jackson, L. B., Ryndak, D. L., & Wehmeyer, M. L. (2008). The dynamic relationship between context, curriculum, and student learning: A case for inclusive education as a research-based practice. *Research and Practice for Persons with Severe Disabilities, 34*(1), 175–195. https://doi.org/10.2511/rpsd.33.4.175

Janney, R. E., & Snell, M. E. (2013). *Teachers' guides to inclusive practices: Modifying schoolwork* (3rd ed.). Paul H. Brookes Publishing Co.

Jegatheesan, B. (2009). Cross-cultural issues in parent-professional interactions: A qualitative student of perceptions of Asian American mothers of children with developmental disabilities. *Research and Practice for Persons with Severe Disabilities, 34*(1), 123–136.

Jimenez, B. A., & Kamei, A. (2015). Embedded instruction: An evaluation of evidence to inform inclusive practice. *Inclusion, 3*(3), 132–144. https://doi.org/10.1352/2326-6988-3.3.132

Jimenez, B. A., Mims, P. J., & Browder, D. (2012). Data-based decisions guidelines for teachers of students with severe intellectual and developmental disabilities. *Education and Training in Autism and Developmental Disabilities, 47*(4), 407–413.

Johnson, J. W., McDonnell, J., Holzwarth, V. N., & Hunter, K. (2004). The efficacy of embedded instruction for students with developmental disabilities enrolled in general education classes. *Journal of Positive Behavior Interventions, 6*(4), 214–227.

Jones, B. A., & Gansle, K. A. (2010). The effects of a mini-conference, socioeconomic status, and parent education on perceived and actual parent participation in individual education program meetings. *Research in the Schools, 17*(2), 23–28.

Jones, J. K. (2014). *Career Key.* Career Key

Jung, L. (2007). Writing smart objectives and strategies that fit the routine. *TEACHING Exceptional Children, 39*(4), 54–58.

Kalambouka, A., Farrell, A. F., Dyson, A., & Kaplan, I. (2007). The impact of placing pupils with special educational needs in mainstream schools on the achievement of their peers. *Educational Research, 49*(4), 365–382.

Kalyanpur, M., Harry, B., & Skrtic, T. (2000). Equity and advocacy expectations of culturally diverse families' participation in special education. *International Journal of Disability, Development & Education, 47*(2), 119–136.

Karvonen, M., & Clark, A. K. (2019). Students with the most significant cognitive disabilities who are also English learners. *Research and Practice for Persons with Severe Disabilities, 44*(2), 71–86. https://doi.org/10.1177/1540796919835169

Kaufman, A. S., & Kaufman, N. L. (2014). *Kaufman Test of Education Achievement Third Edition* (KTRA-3). Pearson Assessment.

Keilty, B. (2008). Early intervention home visiting principles in practice: A reflective approach. *Young Exceptional Children, 11*(2), 29–40. https://doi.org/10.1177/1096250607311933

Kleinert, H., Towles-Reeves, E., Quenemoen, R., Thurlow, M., Fluegge, L., Weseman, L., & Kerbel, A. (2015). Where students with the most significant cognitive disabilities are taught. *Exceptional Children, 81*(3), 312–328. https://doi.org/10.1177/0014402914563697

Kurth, J. A., Born, K., & Love, H. (2016). Ecobehavioral characteristics of self-contained high school classrooms for students with severe cognitive disability. *Research and Practice for Persons with Severe Disabilities, 41*(4), 227–243. https://doi.org/10.1177/1540796916661492

Kurth, J. A., & Gross, M. (2014). *The inclusion toolbox: Strategies and techniques for all teachers.* Corwin.

Kurth, J. A., Gross, M., Lovinger, S., & Catalano, T. (2012). Grading students with significant disabilities in inclusive settings: Teacher perspectives. *The Journal of the International Association of Special Education, 12*, 39–55.

Kurth, J. A., Lockmann-Turner, E., & Bubash, S. (2021). A framework for preparing educators to teach students with significant support needs in the 21st century. *Teacher Education and Special Education.* [Online before print.]

Kurth, J. A., Lockman Turner, E., Burke, K. M., & Ruppar, A. L. (2021). Curricular philosophies reflected in individualized education program goals for students with complex support needs. *Intellectual and Developmental Disabilities, 59*(4), 283–294. https://doi.org/10.1352/1934-9556-59.4.283

Kurth, J. A., & Mastergeorge, A. M. (2010). Individual education plan goals and services for adolescents with autism: Impact of grade and educational setting. *Journal of Special Education, 44*(3), 146–160. https://doi.org/10.1177/0022466908329825

Kurth, J. A., McQueston, J. A., Ruppar, A. L., Toews, S. G., Johnston, R., & McCabe, K. M. (2019). A description of parent input in IEP development through analysis of IEP documents. *American Journal on Intellectual and Developmental Disabilities, 57*, 485–498. https://doi.org/10.1352/1934-9556-57.6.485

Kurth, J. A., Morningstar, M. E., & Kozleski, E. B. (2014). The persistence of highly restrictive special education placements for students with low-incidence disabilities. *Research and Practice for Persons with Severe Disabilities, 39*, 227–239. http://doi.org/10.1177/1540796914555580

Kurth, J. A., Ruppar, A. L., McQueston, J. A., McCabe, K. M., Johnston, R., & Toews, S. M. (2018). Types of supplementary aids and services for students with significant support needs. *The Journal of Special Education.* [Online before print.]

Kurth, J. A., Ruppar, A. L., Toews, S. G., McCabe, K. M., McQueston, J. A., & Johnston, R. (2019). Considerations in placement decisions for students with complex support needs: An analysis of LRE statements. *Research and Practice for Persons with Severe Disabilities, 44*(1), 3–19. https://doi.org/10.1177/1540796918825479

Lalvani, P. (2012). Parents' participation in special education in the context of implicit educational ideologies and socioeconomic status. *Education and Training in Autism and Developmental Disabilities, 47*, 474–486.

Lesh, J. J. (2020). IEP 101: Practical tips for writing and implementing individual education programs. *TEACHING Exceptional Children, 52*, 278–280. https://doi.org/10.1177/0040059920917904

L. H. et al. v. Hamilton City Department of Education (United States Court of Appeals for the 6th Circuit 2018).

Lipscomb, S., Haimson, J., Liu, A., Burghardt, J., Johnson, D., & Thurlow, M. (2017). *Preparing for life after high school: The characteristics and experiences of youth in special education. Findings from the National Longitudinal Transition Study 2012. Volume 1: Comparisons with other youth: Full report* (NCEE 2017-4017). National Center for Education Evaluation and Regional Assistance.

Love, H. R., Zagona, A., Kurth, J. A., & Miller, A. L. (2017). Families' experiences in education decision-making for children and youth with disabilities. *Inclusion, 5*, 158–172. doi:10.1352/2326-6988-5.3.158

Lowrey, K. A., Hollingshead, A., Howery, K., & Bishop, J. B. (2017). More than one way: Stories of UDL and inclusive classrooms. *Research and Practice for Persons with Severe Disabilities, 42*(4), 225–242. https://doi.org/10.1177/1540796917711668

Macfarlane, C. A. (1998). Assessment: The key to appropriate curriculum and instruction. In A. Hilton & R. Ringlaben (Eds.), *Best and promising practices in developmental disabilities.* PRO-ED.

Martin, N. R. M. (2005). *A guide to collaboration for IEP teams.* Paul H. Brookes Publishing Co.

Mason-Williams, L., Bettini, E., & Gagnon, J. C. (2017). Access to qualified special educators across elementary neighborhood and exclusionary schools. *Remedial and Special Education, 38*(5), 297–307. https://doi.org/10.1177/0741932517713311

Mazzotti, V. L., Rowe, D. A., Sinclair, J., Poppen, M., Woods, W. E., & Shearer, M. L. (2016). Predictors of post-school success: A systematic review of NLTS2 secondary analyses. *Career Development and Transition for Exceptional Individuals, 39*(4), 196–215. https://doi.org/10.1177/2165143415588047

McCabe, K. M., Ruppar, A. L., Kurth, J.A., McQueston, J. A., Gross, S. M., & Johnston, R. (2020). Cracks in the continuum: A critical analysis of least restrictive environment for students with significant support needs. *Teachers College Record, 122*(5).

McWilliam, R. A., Casey, A. M., & Sims, J. (2009). The routines-based interview: A method for gathering information and assessing needs. *Infants & Young Children, 22*(3), 224–233.

Morningstar, M. E., Kurth, J. A., & Johnson, P. J. (2017). Examining national trends in educational placements for students with significant disabilities. *Remedial and Special Education, 38*(1), 3–12. https://doi.org/ https://doi.org/10.1177/0741932516678327

Movahedazarhouligh, S. (2021). Parent-implemented interventions and family-centered service delivery approaches in early intervention and early childhood special education. *Early Child Development and Care, 191*(1), 1–12. https://doi.org/10.1080/03004430.2019.1603148

Munger, G. F., Snell, M. E., & Loyd, B. H. (1989). A study of the effects of frequency of probe data collection and graph characteristics on teachers' visual analysis. *Research in Developmental Disabilities, 10*(2), 109–127. https://doi.org/10.1016/0891-4222(89)90001-2

Munk, D. D. & Bursuck, W. D. (2001). Preliminary findings on personalized grading plans for middle school students with learning disabilities. *Exceptional Children, 67*, 211–234.

Murawski, W., & Dieker, L. (2008). 50 ways to keep your co-teacher: Strategies for before, during, and after co-teaching. *TEACHING Exceptional Children, 40*, 40–48.

Murawski, W. W., & Lochner, W. W. (2011). Observing co-teaching: What to ask for, look for, and listen for. *Intervention in School and Clinic, 46*(3), 174–183.

National Center for Education Statistics. (2017). Number and percentage distribution of teachers in public and private elementary and secondary schools, by selected teacher characteristics: Selected years, 1987–88 through 2015–16. https://nces.ed.gov/programs/digest/d17/tables/dt17_209.10.asp

National Governors Association Center for Best Practices & Council of Chief State School Officers. (2010a). *Common Core State Standards: English/Language Arts.* Authors.

National Governors Association Center for Best Practices & Council of Chief State School Officers. (2010b). *Common Core State Standards: Mathematics.* Authors.

Newman, L., Wagner, M., Knokey, A.-M., Marder, C., Nagle, K., Shaver, D., Wei, X., with Cameto, R., Contreras, E., Ferguson, K., Greene, S., & Schwarting, M. (2011). *The post-high school outcomes of young adults with disabilities up to 8 years after high school. A report from the National Longitudinal Transition Study-2 (NLTS2)* (NCSER 2011-3005). SRI International.

No Child Left Behind Act of 2001, PL 107-110, 115 Stat. 1425, 20 U.S.C. §§ 6301 *et seq.*

O'Brien, C., & O'Brien, J. (2002). The origins of person-centered planning: A community of practice perspective. In S. Holburn & P. Vietze (Eds.), *Person-centered planning: Research, practice, and future directions* (pp. 3–27). Paul H. Brookes Publishing Co.

Pearpoint, J., O'Brien, J., & Forest, M. (1993). *PATH: A workbook for planning alternative futures.* Inclusion Press.

Pennington, R. C., & Courtade, G. R. (2015). An examination of teacher and student behaviors in classrooms for students with moderate and severe intellectual disability. *Preventing School Failure: Alternative Education for Children and Youth, 59*(1), 40–47. https://doi.org/10.1080/1045988x.2014.919141

Perkins School for the Blind. (n.d.). *What is CVI?* https://www.perkins.org/what-is-cvi/

Perske, R., & Perske, M. (1988). *Circles of friends: People with disabilities and their friends enrich the lives of one another.* Inclusion Press.

Piepzna-Samarasinha, L. L. (2018). *Care work: Dreaming disability justice.* Arsenal Pump.

Polychronis, S. C., McDonnell, J., Johnson, J. W., Riesen, T., & Jameson, M. (2004). A comparison of two trial distribution schedules in embedded instruction. *Focus on Autism and Other Developmental Disabilities, 19*(3), 140–151. https://doi.org/10.1177/10883576040190030201

Pugach, M. C., Blanton, L. P., & Boveda, M. (2014). Working together: Research on the preparation of general education and special education teachers for inclusion and collaboration. In P.T. Sindelar, E.D. McCray, M.T. Brownell, & B. Lignugaris/Kraft (Eds.), *Handbook of research on special education teacher preparation.* Routledge.

Reusch v. Fountain, 872 F. Supp. 1421 (N.D. Maryland 1994). https://law.justia.com/cases/federal/district-courts/FSupp/872/1421/1441979/

Richman, T. (2019, May 2). "Why would we even try?" Parents of disabled students almost never win in fights against Maryland districts. *The Baltimore Sun.* https://www.baltimoresun.com/news/investigations/bs-md-due-process-hearings-20190502-story.html

Roncker v. Walter (1983). 700 F. 2d 1058 (6th Cir.).

Rossetti, Z., Burke, M. M., Hughes, O., Schraml-Block, K., Rivera, J. I., Rios, K., Aleman Tovar, J., & Lee, J. D. (2021). Parent perceptions of the advocacy expectation in special education. *Exceptional Children, 87*, 438–457. https://doi.org/10.1177/0014402921994095

Rossetti, Z., Sauer, J. S., Bui, O., & Ou, S. (2017). Developing collaborative partnerships with culturally and linguistically diverse families during the IEP process. *TEACHING Exceptional Children, 49*(5), 328–338.

Rowe, D. A., Mazzotti, V. L., Hirano, K., & Alverson, C. Y. (2015). Assessing transition skills in the 21st century. *TEACHING Exceptional Children, 47*(6), 301–309.

Ruijs, N. M., & Peetsma, T. T. (2009). Effects of inclusion on students with and without special educational needs reviewed. *Educational Research Review, 4*(2), 67–79.

Ruppar, A. L., Allcock, H., & Gonsier-Gerdin, J. (2016). Ecological factors affecting access to general education content and contexts for students with significant disabilities. *Remedial and Special Education.* https://doi.org/10.1177/0741932516646856

Ruppar, A. L., & Gaffney, J. S. (2011). Individualized education program team decisions: A preliminary study of conversations, negotiations, and power. *Research and Practice for Persons with Severe Disabilities, 36*(1–2), 11–22. https://doi.org/10.2511/rpsd.36.1-2.11

Ruppar, A. L., Kurth, J.A., Lockmann-Turner, E., & Bubash, S. (2022). A framework for preparing educators to teach students with significant support needs in the 21st century. *Teacher Education and Special Education.* [Online before print]

Ruppar, A. L., Kurth, J. A., McCabe, K. M., Toews, S. G., McQueston, J. A., & Johnston, R. (in press). Present levels of academic achievement and functional performance: Unravelling the narratives. *Journal of Disability Studies in Education.*

Ruppar, A. L., Kurth, J. A., Toews, S. G., McCabe, K. M., & McQueston, J. A. (2019, December). *Reporting present levels of performance: Narratives and their consequences for students with significant support needs.* Presentation at the TASH Annual Conference, Phoenix, AZ.

Ruppar, A. L., Roberts, C. A., & Olson, A. J. (2017). Perceptions about expert teaching for students with severe disabilities among teachers identified as experts. *Research and Practice for Persons with Severe Disabilities, 42,* 121–135.

Salas, L. (2004). Individualized educational plan (IEP) meetings and Mexican American parents: Let's talk about it. *Journal of Latinos and Education, 3*(3), 181–192, doi:10.1207/s1532771xjle0303_4

Shapiro, E. S., Edwards, L., & Zigmond, N. (2016). Progress monitoring of mathematics among students with learning disabilities. *Assessment for Effective Intervention, 30*(2), 15–32. https://doi.org/10.1177/073724770503000203

Shogren, K., Wehmeyer, M., Schalock, R. L., & Thompson, J. R. (2017). Reframing educational supports for students with intellectual disability through strengths-based approaches. In M. Wehmeyer & K. Shogren (Eds.), *Handbook of research-based practices for educating students with intellectual disability.* Routledge.

Skrtic, T. M. (1991). The special education paradox: Equity as the way to excellence. *Harvard Educational Review, 61,* 148–206.

Smart, J. F. (2009). The power of models of disability. *Journal of Rehabilitation, 74,* 3–11.

Snell, M. E., & Brown, F. (2011). *Instruction of students with severe disabilities* (7th ed.). Pearson.

Soukup, J. H., Wehmeyer, M. L., Bashinski, S. M., & Bovaird, J. A. (2007). Classroom variables and access to the general curriculum for students with disabilities. *Exceptional Children, 74*(1), 101–120. https://doi.org/10.1177/001440290707400106

SWIFT Center. (2017). *Research support for inclusive education and SWIFT.* Author.

Taub, D. A., McCord, J. A., & Ryndak, D. L. (2017). Opportunities to learn for students with extensive support needs: A context of research-supported practices for all in general education classes. *The Journal of Special Education, 51,* 127–137. https://doi.org/10.1177/0022466917696263

Thoma, C., & Wehman, P. (2010). *Getting the most out of IEPs.* Paul H. Brookes Publishing Co.

Thompson, J. R., Bradley, V. J., Buntinx, W. H., Schalock, R. L., Shogren, K. A., Snell, M. E., Wehmeyer, M. L., Borthwick-Duffy, S., Coulter, D. L., Craig, E. P., Gomez, S. C., Lachapelle, Y., Luckasson, R. A., Reeve, A., Spreat, S., Tasse, M. J., Verdugo, M. A., & Yeager, M. H. (2009). Conceptualizing supports and the support needs of people with intellectual disability. *Intellectual and Developmental Disabilities, 47*(2), 135–146. https://doi.org/10.1352/1934-9556-47.2.135

TLS Books. (n.d.). Caterpillar alphabetizing worksheet. https://www.tlsbooks.com/pdf/alphabetical-dolch-gr1.pdf

Toews, S. G., Kurth, J. A., Turner, E. L., & Lyon, K. J. (2020). Ecobehavioral analysis of inclusive classrooms and instruction that support students with extensive support needs. *Inclusion, 8*(4), 259–274.

Trela, K., & Jimenez, B. (2013). From different to differentiated: Using "ecological framework" to support personally relevant access to general curriculum for students with significant intellectual disabilities. *Research and Practice for Persons with Severe Disabilities, 38*(2), 117–119. https://doi.org/10.2511/02749481380771453

Turnbull, A., Turnbull, H. R., Wehmeyer, M., & Shogren, K. (2016). *Exceptional lives: Special education in today's schools* (8th ed.). Pearson.

United Nations. (n.d.). *Universal declaration of human rights.* https://www.un.org/en/about-us/universal-declaration-of-human-rights

U.S. Department of Education, Office of Special Education and Rehabilitative Services, Office of Special Education Programs. (2003, February 4). *Letter to given on extended school year services.* Author.

U.S. Department of Education, Office of Special Education and Rehabilitative Services, Office of Special Education Programs (2020a). *IDEA Part B Child Count and Educational Environments for School Year 2019-2020 OSEP Data Documentation.* https://www2.ed.gov/programs/osepidea/618-data/collection-documentation/data-documentation-files/part-b/child-count-and-educational-environment/idea-partb-childcountand-edenvironment-2019-20.pdf

U.S. Department of Education, Office of Special Education and Rehabilitative Services, Office of Special Education Programs. (2020b). *42nd Annual Report to Congress on the Implementation of the Individuals with Disabilities Education Act, 2020.* http://www.ed.gov/about/reports/annual/osep

U.S. Department of Education, Office of Special Education and Rehabilitative Services, Office of Special Education Programs. (2021). *43rd Annual Report to Congress on the Implementation of the Individuals with Disabilities Education Act.* Author.

U.S. Department of Labor. (2002). *O*NET Career Interest Inventory.* Author.

Van Dycke, J., Martin, J., & Lovett, D. (2006). Why is this cake on fire? Inviting students into the IEP process. *TEACHING Exceptional Children, 38*(3), 42–47.

Vaughn, S., Bos, C. S., Harrell, J. E., & Lasky, B. A. (1988). Parent participation in the initial placement/IEP conference ten years after mandated involvement. *Journal of Learning Disabilities, 21*(2), 82–89.

Voss, K. S. (2000). Home-to-school communication. *Disability Solutions, 4*(2), 1–16.

Wakeman, S. (2010). Data-based decisions. *Modules addressing special education and teacher education (MAST).* https://mast.ecu.edu/Data%20Collection/Data-based%20Decisions/index.html

Watson, S. M. R., Gable, R., & Greenwood, C. R. (2011). Combining ecobehavioral assessment, functional assessment, and response to intervention to promote more effective classroom instruction. *Remedial and Special Education, 32*(4), 334–344.

Wehmeyer, M., & Kelcher, K. (1995). *The Arc's Self-Determination Scale Adolescent Version.* The Arc of the United States.

Weick, A., Rapp, C., Sullivan, W. P., & Kisthardt, W. (1989). A strengths perspective for social work practice. *Social Work, 34*(4), 350–354.

Weishaar, P. M. (2010). Twelve ways to incorporate strengths-based planning into the IEP process. *The Clearing House: A Journal of Educational Strategies, Issues, and Ideas, 83*(6), 207–210. https://doi.org/10.1080/00098650903505381

Westing, D. L. (2015). *Evidence-based practices for improving challenging behaviors of students with severe disabilities.* CEEDAR. https://ceedar.education.ufl.edu/wp-content/uploads/2015/11/EBPs-for-improving-challenging-behavior-of-SWD.pdf

Westling, D. L., Carter, E. W., Da Fonte, A., & Kurth, J. A. (2021). *Teaching students with severe disabilities* (6th ed.). Pearson.

White, O. R. (1986). Precision teaching—precision learning. *Exceptional Children, 52*(6), 522–534.

White, S. W., Scahill, L., Klin, A., Koenig, K., & Volkmar, F. (2007). Educational placements and service use patterns of individuals with autism spectrum disorders. *Journal of Autism and Developmental Disorders, 37*(8), 1403–1412.

Wolman, D., K., Campeau, P., Du Bois, Mithaug, D. E., & Stolarski, V. (1994). *AIR Self-Determination Assessment.* The University of Oklahoma.

Yell, M., Katsiyannis, A., Ennis, R. P., Losinski, M., & Christle, C. A. (2016). Avoiding substantive errors in individualized education program development. *TEACHING Exceptional Children, 49*(1), 31–40. https://doi.org/10.1177/0040059916662204

Zeitlin, V. M., & Curcic, S. (2014). Parental voices on individualized education programs: "Oh, IEP meeting tomorrow? Rum tonight!" *Disability & Society, 29*(3), 373–387. https://doi.org/10.1080/09687599.2013.776493

Index

Tables and figures are indicated by *t* and *f*, respectively

AAC, *see* Augmentative and alternative communication
ABC, *see* Antecedent-behavior-consequence charts
AbleData, 140
Ableism, 5
Academic curricula, 111
Academic Standards for Students with Significant Cognitive Disabilities in Inclusive Classrooms, 104
Access, 5
Accommodations, 5
   curricular, 140*t*, 141
   testing, 141
   timing, pacing, length, frequency, 141
Accuracy recording, 62
Active listening, 175–176
Adaptive physical education teachers, 8–9
After the Meeting Task and Responsibility List, 180, 180*f*, 187
Agenda, individualized education program (IEP) meeting, 167–168
   co-construction of, 169–170
   educators' identities and, 168–169
   kept available throughout meetings, 170
   practices for before, 169–170
   see also Meeting, individualized education program (IEP)
Alternate assessment, 103–104, 123
Alternate English Language Learning Assessment, 99
American Sign Language (ASL), 97
American Speech-Language-Hearing Association (ASHA), 7, 124, 143
Anecdotal data, 102*f*
Antecedent-behavior-consequence (ABC) charts, 98
Anxiety supports, 142
ASHA, *see* American Speech-Language-Hearing Association
ASL, *see* American Sign Language
Assessment, alternate, 103–104, 123
Assistive technology (AT), 100, 139, 140
Assistive Technology Act Amendments of 2004 (PL 108-364), 100
Association for Positive Behavior Supports, 142
AT, *see* Assistive technology
AT3 Center, 100
Augmentative and alternative communication (AAC), 7

Behavior dimension of supplementary aids and services (SAS), 142
Behavior interventions, 97–98

Behavior specialists, 9
Behavior supports, 142
Blindness or visual impairment, 99–100

CASEL, *see* Collaborative for Academic, Social, and Emotional Learning
CAST Online Tools, 100
Caterpillar alphabetizing worksheet, 112, 114*f*, 115*f*–116*f*
CCSS, *see* Common Core States Standards
Center for Parent Information and Resources, 98, 100
Center on Disability and Technology, 140
Center on Secondary Education for Students with Autism Spectrum Disorders, 98
Choosing Outcomes and Accommodations for Children (COACH), 5
Circle of Friends, 5
Closing the Gap, 140
COACH, *see* Choosing Outcomes and Accommodations for Children
Cognitive/memory supports, 142
Collaborative dimension of supplementary aids and services (SAS), 143
Collaborative for Academic, Social, and Emotional Learning (CASEL), 124
Common Core States Standards (CCSS), 123
Communication, 13–14, 21–22
   culture and cross-cultural, 40–43, 43*f*
   data collection plan form, 23–27
   effectively involving general education teachers in, 18
   elementary level home-school communication notebook, 47
   individualized education program (IEP) meeting and effective, 175–176
   involving paraprofessionals in, 19–20
   involving students in, 20–21, 20*f*, 21*t*
   managing good, 14–15, 22
   planning meeting, 15–16, 16*f*, 17*t*–18*t*
   and preparing for individualized education program (IEP) meeting, 16–18
   secondary level home-school communication notebook, 48
   setting timelines for, 15–18, 15*f*, 36*f*
   special factors, 97
   strengths-based, 18–19
   working with outside service providers on, 20
Communication supports, 143
Conditions in individualized education program (IEP) goals, 114

Considerations in individualized education program
(IEP) goals, 118–119
Cortical visual impairment (CVI), 99
Counselors, school, 9
Criterion in individualized education program (IEP)
goals, 117–118, 118f, 119f
Culture and cross-cultural communication, 40–43, 43f
Curricula, 109–110, 125–126
    academic, 111
    accommodations in, 141
    ecological assessment, 112–113, 113t
    ecological frameworks of, 112–113, 113t
    general education, 84, 86, 90–92, 110–111
    making sense of areas of, 111–112
    modifications to, 140–141, 140t
    nonacademic, 111, 123–124
    types of, 110–111, 111t
CVI, see Cortical visual impairment

Data
    anecdotal, 102f
    avoiding pseudo-, 57
    baseline, 83
    connected to outcomes, 75
    dealing with conflicting, 66
    deciding on type of, 63
    decision-making based on, 55–56, 75–76
    extended school year (ESY), 102f
    graphing, 67–75, 67f, 69f–74f
    in Present Levels of Academic Achievement
        and Functional Performance (PLAAFP)
        statements, 86–88
    predictive, 102f
    qualitative, 57–61, 58t, 102f
    quantitative, 57–58, 58t, 62, 102f
    retrospective, 102f
    types of, 56–57
Data collection
    comprehensive and interdisciplinary, 89–90
    creating and sharing a plan for, 64, 65f–66f
    deciding who is involved in, 63–64
    form, 23–27, 77–78
    frequency of, 63
    planning for, 183–184
    resources on, 63
    strengths-based, 57
Data Collection Toolkit, The, 63
Dead Man's Test, 120
Deafness, 97
Deficit model of disabilities, 169
Disabilities, Opportunities, Internetworking, and
    Technology (Do-IT), 140
DLM, see Dynamic Learning Maps
Duration recording, 62
Dynamic Learning Maps (DLM), 123

Early Childhood Technical Assistance Center, 140
Ecological assessment, 58, 59t, 128–129
    caterpillar alphabetizing worksheet, 112, 114f, 115f–116f
        of curricula, 112–113, 113t
    supplementary aids and services (SAS), 135,
        136f, 145–146

Ecological frameworks of curricula, 112–113, 113t
Elementary level home-school communication
    notebook, 47
Emotional supports, 142
Endrew v. Douglas County, 155
English language proficiency, 98–99
Environmental supports, 139
ESSA, see Every Student Succeeds Act
ESY, see Extended school year
Every Student Succeeds Act (ESSA) of 2017
    (PL 114-95), 55, 103
"Evidence-Based Practices for Improving
    Challenging Behaviors of Students With
    Severe Disabilities," 142
Explicit curricula, 110, 111t
Extended school year (ESY), 95, 104–105
    data used to make decisions about, 102f
    defined, 101
    planning for, 102–103, 103f
    reasons for, 101–102
    summer activities planning tool, 106–107
Extracurricular activities, 111

Family members
    co-developing goal activity matrix after
        individualized education program (IEP)
        meeting with, 39–40, 40f, 53–54
    co-drafting the agenda and individualized
        education program (IEP) with, 37–39, 38f, 39f
    communications with, 31–32, 36f
    conducting pre-individualized education program
        (IEP) surveys, interviews, and data reviews with,
        35f, 36–37, 37f, 49–51
    culture and cross-cultural communication with,
        40–43, 43f
    handling differing opinions of, 173–174
    home visits with, 42–43, 43f
    on individualized education program (IEP) teams,
        7, 34–40
    improving partnerships with, 33–34
    input before individualized education program
        (IEP) meeting, 169
    learning to advocate, 29–30
    listening actively to, 175–176
    removing barriers to participation by, 32–33, 33f–34f
    scheduling individualized education program (IEP)
        meetings with, 34–36, 36f
    supporting, advocating for, and empowering,
        29–31, 43–45
    understanding feelings of, 174–175
FBA, see Functional behavioral assessment
Follow-up meeting, 182–183, 182f
Frequency recording, 62
Functional behavioral assessment (FBA), 97–98
Functional goals, 124–125
Functional skills, 111–112
Funds of knowledge, 41–42

General education
    least restrictive environment (LRE) and
        percentage of time removed from, 159
    standards and curriculum in, 84, 86, 90–92

General education teachers, 6, 18
Goal, service, and support development Google
    document, 52
Goal activity matrix, 39–40, 40f, 53–54
Goals, individualized education program (IEP),
    113–114, 125–126
    aligned with Present Levels of Academic
        Achievement and Functional Performance
        (PLAAFP), 122
    aligned with standards, 122–124, 123f
    alternate assessment and, 123
    blueprint for, 117f, 121f, 130
    conditions, 114
    considerations in, 118–119
    content of, 121–125
    criterion in, 117–118, 118f, 119f
    date in, 119
    defined, 114
    final tests for, 119–120
    functional, 124–125
    inclusion and, 123
    least restrictive environment (LRE) and, 156
    logistical issues in aligning, 124, 124t
    nonacademic needs requiring, 123–124
    objectives of, 120
    put all together, 120, 121f
    reflecting student priorities, 122
    specific skill in, 117
    student in, 117
    supplementary aids and services (SAS) and, 137
Grading criteria, 141

Hard of hearing students, 97
Health and safety supports, 139
Hearing specialists, 9
Hearing supports, 139
Hearing-impaired students, 97
Hidden curricula, 111, 111t
Home visits, 42–43, 43f
Home-school communication notebook
    elementary level, 47
    secondary level, 48
Home-school communication supports, 143

IDEA, see Individuals with Disabilities Education
    Improvement Act of 2004 (PL 108-446)
Inclusion
    individualized education program (IEP)
        goals and, 123
    placement and, 150–152, 151f
Individualized Supports for Students with Problem
    Behaviors: Designing Positive Behavior Plans, 98
Individuals with Disabilities Education Improvement
    Act (IDEA) of 2004 (PL 108-446), 4, 55
    definition of least restrictive environment
        (LRE), 149
Instructional dimension of supplementary aids and
    services (SAS), 139–142, 140t
Interest inventories, 61
International Association for Augmentative and
    Alternative Communication (ISAAC), 143
Interpreters, 42

Interval recording, 62
Interviews, 60–61
ISAAC, see International Association for
    Augmentative and Alternative Communication

Latency recording, 62
Laurent Clerc National Deaf Education Center, 97
LEA, see Local education agency
Least Dangerous Assumption, 35
Least restrictive environment (LRE), 133–134,
    147–148, 161–162, 163
    decision making on, 155–159
    defined, 148–150, 150f
    effect on peers of, 154
    factors to consider and not consider in, 152–155,
        152t, 153f, 154f
    individual abilities and needs and, 152
    Individuals with Disabilities Education Improvement
        Act (IDEA) of 2004 (PL 108-446) definition of, 149
    initial decisions before placement in, 156
    making the placement decision for, 156–159, 158f
    patterns in, 150–152, 151f
    percentage of time removed from general education
        and, 159
    Planning Matrix for, 156, 157t
    potential benefits in, 152–153, 153f
    potential harms in, 153–154, 154f
    rationale for removal from, 157, 159
    relationship between placement and, 150, 150f
    supports the student will receive in, 154–155
    who decides, 149
    written statement on, 159–160t, 159–161
Limited English proficiency, 98–99
Listening, active, 175–176
Local education agency (LEA), 6

Making Action Plans (MAPS), 5
Matrix, individualized education program (IEP),
    181–183, 183f, 188–189
Medical supports, 139
Meeting, individualized education program (IEP), 165
    After the Meeting Task and Responsibility List,
        180, 180f, 187
    agenda for, 37–39, 38f, 39f, 167–177
    avoiding "monologues" and structured turn taking
        in, 172–173
    beginning with introductions, 171
    communication after, 179–185
    conducting pre-individualized education program
        (IEP) surveys, interviews, and data reviews prior
        to, 36–37, 37f
    ensuring student participation and preferences in,
        171–172
    family input before, 169
    first steps after, 180–181, 180f
    focusing on effective communication in, 175–176
    goal activity matrix after, 39–40, 40f
    handling difficult situations in, 173–174
    individualized education program (IEP) matrix
        and, 181–183, 183f, 188–189
    individualized education program (IEP) team
        follow-up meeting after, 182–183, 182f

Meeting—*continued*
   making a plan to collect data after, 183–184
   myths and misunderstandings about, 41*t*
   planning individualized education program (IEP)
      implementation after, 181–183, 182*f*
   planning transdisciplinary interventions after, 183
   planning when and where to teach after, 183
   strategies to use during, 170–171
   time management during, 176
   understanding family feelings at, 174–175
   welcoming everyone to, 170–171
Memory supports, 142
Modifications, 5
   curricular, 140–141, 140*t*
   grading, 141
   testing, 141
   timing, pacing, length, frequency, 141

National Center for Pyramid Model Innovations, 142
National Center on Accessible Educational
   Materials, 100, 140
National Center on Educational Outcomes, 104
National Technical Assistance Consortium for
   Children and Young Adults Who Are
   Deaf-Blind, 97
No Child Left Behind Act (NCLB) of 2001
   (PL 107-110), 55
Nonacademic curricula, 111
   requiring individualized education program (IEP)
      goals, 123–124
Null curricula, 111, 111*t*
Nurses, school, 8

Observations, 58, 59*t*
Occupational therapists (OTs), 8
Ohio Center for Autism and Low Incidence (OCALI)
   autism, 98, 140
OTs, *see* Occupational therapists
Outside service providers
   communication with, 20
   on individualized education program (IEP)
      teams, 7–9
Overt curricula, 110, 111*t*

Paraprofessionals, 8, 19–20
   support for, 143
Parents, *see* Family members
PATH, *see* Planning Alternative Tomorrows
   with Hope
PBIS, *see* Positive Behavior Intervention and
   Supports
Perkins School for the Blind, 100
Person-centered approach, 5
Person-centered planning, 60
Person-centered planning survey, 50–51
Personnel supports, 143
Physical education teachers, 8–9
Physical therapists (PTs), 7–8

Physical/accessibility dimension of supplementary
   aids and services (SAS), 138–139
PL 107-110, *see* No Child Left Behind Act (NCLB) of
   2001
PL 108-364, *see* Assistive Technology Act
   Amendments of 2004
PL 108-446, *see* Individuals with Disabilities
   Education Improvement Act of 2004
PL 114-95, *see* Every Student Succeeds Act (ESSA)
   of 2017
PLAAFP, *see* Present Levels of Academic Achievement
   and Functional Performance
Placement and least restrictive environment (LRE),
   150–152, 150*f*
Planning Alternative Tomorrows with Hope
   (PATH), 5
Planning meetings, individualized education program
   (IEP), 15–16, 16*f*, 17*t*–18*t*
Positive Action, 124
Positive Behavior Intervention and Supports (PBIS),
   97–98, 142
PrAACtical AAC, 97, 143
Predictive data, 102*f*
Present Levels of Academic Achievement and
   Functional Performance (PLAAFP), 57, 81–82
   baseline data in, 83
   collecting data that are comprehensive and
      interdisciplinary for, 89–90
   components of, 83–84, 92, 92*f*
   defined, 83
   goals aligned with, 121
   incorporating quality, interdisciplinary data in,
      86–88
   individual student needs described in, 83
   involvement and progress in general education
      curriculum, 84, 86
   least restrictive environment (LRE) and, 156
   questions to consider regarding student ability and, 86*t*
   referencing general education settings and
      standards in, 90–92
   strengths-based approaches to, 85–86
   writing, 84–92, 93–94
Project CORE, 97
Pseudo-data, 57
PTs, *see* Physical therapists

Qualitative data, 57–61, 58*t*, 102*f*
   interviews, 60–61
   observations, 58, 59*t*
   person-centered planning, 60
   student interest inventories, 61
Quality Indicators for Assistive Technology
   Services, 140
Quantitative data, 57–58, 58*t*, 62, 102*f*

RBI, *see* Routine-based assessment interview
Regression and recoupment, 101
Rehabilitation Engineering Research Center
   on AAC, 143

Retrospective data, 102*f*
Reusch v. Fountain, 101
Roncker portability test, 155
Routine-based assessment interview (RBI), 60–61

SAS, *see* Supplementary aids and services
SDI, *see* Specially designed instruction
Secondary level home-school communication
    notebook, 48
Sensory needs of autistic people, 8
Sensory supports, 139
Shallow culture, 41
SLPs, *see* Speech-language pathologists
SMART goals, *see* Goals, individualized education
    program (IEP)
Social model of disability, 168–169
Social supports, 142–143
Social workers, school, 9
Social-communication dimension of supplementary
    aids and services (SAS), 142–143
Special education teachers, 6
Special factors, 95–96, 104–105
    assistive technology, 100
    behavior, 97–98
    blindness or visual impairment, 99–100
    communication needs/deafness, 97
    limited English proficiency, 98–99
Specially designed instruction (SDI), 137, 147
Specific skill in individualized education program
    (IEP) goals, 117
Speech-language pathologists (SLPs), 7, 88
Staff training and support, 143
Standards, 84, 86, 90–92
    goals aligned with, 122–124, 123*f*
"Start with the End in Mind: Decisions about Student
    Participation in the Alternate Assessment," 104
Stranger Test, 119–120
Strengths-based approaches to Present Levels
    of Academic Achievement and Functional
    Performance (PLAAFP), 85–86
Strengths-based communication, 18–19
Strengths-based data collection, 57
Student interest inventories, 61
Students
    blind, deaf, or hard of hearing, 9
    goals reflecting priorities of, 122
    in individualized education program (IEP)
        goals, 117
    included in individualized education program (IEP)
        teams, 7
    individual needs of, in Present Levels of Academic
        Achievement and Functional Performance
        (PLAAFP), 83
    involved in their own individualized education
        program (IEP), 20–21, 20*f*, 21*t*
    not making progress, 184
    participation and preferences in individualized
        education program (IEP) meetings, 171–172
    professionals with expertise about, 7–9
Summer activities planning tool, 106–107

Supplementary aids and services (SAS), 131–132, 144
    accessibility of, 134–135
    behavior dimension of, 142
    collaborative dimension of, 143
    defined, 133
    ecological assessment, 135, 136*f*, 145–146
    in generalized contexts, 137
    guiding questions for making decisions about,
        134–137, 136*f*
    individualized education program (IEP) goals
        and, 137
    instructional dimension of, 139–142, 140*t*
    language and phrasing of, 135
    least restrictive environment (LRE) and, 133–134,
        154–155, 156
    physical/accessibility dimension of, 138–139
    social-communication dimension of, 142–143
    specially designed instruction versus, 137
    support domains framework for, 137–138, 138*f*
    types of, 137–143
Surface-level culture, 41
Surveys, family, 35*f*, 36–37, 37*f*, 49–51
*Systematic Instruction for Students with Moderate
    and Severe Disabilities,* 112
Systems-centered approach, 5

*Taking the Alternate Assessment Does NOT Mean
    Education in a Separate Setting,* 104
Task-analytic recording, 62
Teams, individualized education program (IEP)
    adaptive physical education teachers on, 8–9
    addressing considerations for access, 5
    assembling, 3–12
    behavior specialists on, 9
    data collection by, 63–64
    determining who should be involved in, 5–9
    effective leadership of, 4, 9–10
    ensuring accommodations and modifications are
        in place on Day 1, 5
    family members on, 7, 31–34, 33*f*, 34–40, 34*f*
    follow-up meeting with, 182–183, 182*f*
    general education teachers on, 6, 18
    handling differing opinions of, 173–174
    identifying and communicating with
        members of, 4–5
    individuals to interpret evaluation results on, 7
    local education agency representative on, 6
    occupational therapists on, 8
    paraprofessionals on, 8
    physical therapists on, 7–8
    planning before the first meeting, 1
    planning worksheet for, 11–12
    school nurses on, 8
    school social workers or counselors on, 9
    special education teachers on, 6
    speech-language pathologists on, 7, 88
    student involvement with, 7
    taking a person-centered approach, 5
    vision and hearing specialists on, 9
Testing modifications, 141

TIES Center, 104
Time management during individualized education
        program (IEP) meetings, 176
Timelines, communication, 15–18, 15*f*, 36*f*
Training, staff, 143
Transition supports, 142
Translators, 42

UDL, *see* Universal design for learning
Unique Learning Systems, 104
Universal design for learning (UDL), 138

VIA Survey, 85–86
Vision specialists, 9
Vision supports, 139
Visual impairment, 99–100
Visual supports, 141

Wide Range Achievement Test (WRAT),
        87–88